A Voice in Time

BY THE SAME AUTHOR

Elgar: A Life in Photographs
Elgar on Record: the composer and the gramophone

JERROLD NORTHROP MOORE

A Voice in Time

THE GRAMOPHONE OF FRED GAISBERG

1873–1951

HAMISH HAMILTON

LONDON

First published in Great Britain 1976
by Hamish Hamilton Ltd.
90 Great Russell Street London WC1B 3PT

SBN 241 89374 7

Printed in Great Britain by
Western Printing Services Ltd, Bristol

Acknowledgements

This book owes a great part of its existence to the constant encouragement of Fred Gaisberg's niece, Isabella Valli Wallich. Her deep affection for her uncle's memory provided the firmest foundation upon which to build the research and the writing. Her recollections and those of her mother, the late Louise Gaisberg Valli, have provided information about Fred Gaisberg's family life late and early. The manuscripts and private papers in her possession have enriched the book throughout its length.

David Bicknell, Gwen Mathias, and Bernard Wratten have generously contributed their reminiscences of Gaisberg's Gramophone work. Leonard Petts, D. J. M. Abdey, and I. J. Milliner have given guidance through E.M.I. archives. Peter Andry, Humphrey Tilling, and John Whittle have testified once again to Fred's true immortality in their Company by that responsive understanding which means so much more than mere official sanction. Mrs. Arthur Gibbs has helped with information about the careers of her father and cousin, Trevor Williams and Trevor Osmond Williams, as has Mrs. Clark over the career of her husband, Alfred Clark.

Much of the material herein is quoted from unpublished sources, and an attempt has been made to identify these. Quotations without footnoted source references have been taken from Gaisberg's MS. diaries or from *Music on Record* (which more or less reproduces considerable portions of the diaries). Grateful thanks are due to Warren R. Forster and V. F. Valli for permission to quote from the writings of Fred Gaisberg, and to General Gramophone Publications Ltd. for quotations from articles published in *The Gramophone*; to Messrs. EMI Ltd. for permission to quote from material in the Company files; to Sir Adrian Boult for his letter to Fred Gaisberg, and to the administrators of the Elgar Will Trust for quotation from letters written by Sir Edward Elgar; to Messrs. V. Gollancz for quotation from W. H. Reed's *Elgar as I Knew Him*, Hodder & Stoughton for quotation from Sir Landon Ronald's *Variations on a Personal Theme*, Hutchinson & Co. for quotation from Peter Dawson's *Fifty Years of Song*.

And at the end of the chapter have come many kind friends to read drafts as a whole or in parts. Their comments, together with the editorial skill of Helen Thomson, have given the book a final benefit.

JERROLD NORTHROP MOORE

Hampstead,
20 August 1975.

Illustrations

Many of the photographs have been lent by Michael Wyler, to whom the author and publishers wish to express grateful thanks.

Chapter One

THE EARLY gramophone developed under two special influences. First, its immediate origins were all in the somewhat rarefied atmosphere of Washington D.C.—a city devised and built for the sole purpose of providing a setting for the government of the United States. And second, most of the men closely associated with the gramophone in its earliest days were immigrants to the United States or the sons of immigrants. Thus the combination of nostalgia and opportunity which inspires every time-machine suffused the atmosphere in which the gramophone was born.

Emile Berliner, the machine's inventor, left his native Germany in 1870—just before his nineteenth birthday—to pursue opportunity as yet undefined in the new land across the ocean. Sixteen years before him an entire German family, who were to contribute so much to the success of Berliner's great invention, had come to the same decision. The Gaisbergs looked back upon a family tradition of membership in the minor Bavarian nobility, but by 1848 the social and political upheavals of Europe had reduced their status and their hopes to a vanishing point. When they arrived in the New York harbour in 1854, their expectations were no better or worse than those that would await the young Berliner on his later arrival.

The youngest Gaisberg to grow up in the United States was Wilhelm, who followed his father's trade as a book-binder and in 1869 went to work in the Government Printing Office in Washington. From Washington in March 1870 he sent a letter of news to his cousins in the old country:

. . . You will be surprized to hear that I intend to gett married to the girl I spoke of in my previous letter in the course of the present year. That enstead of studying medicine as I told you I am now preparing to study household economy and meekness in order that I may be able to stand the curtain lectures, which I expect I shall have to listen to in the state of matrimony. I like Oncle Sam's government well enough; but I doubt wether I shall like a pettecoat government. What do you think of it? things are coming to a crisis with me. I have employed all strategem imaginary to win the girls affection and now that she has concented to be mine, I feel mor like retreating . . .

Her name was Emma Klenk, and she dressed her little figure to such perfection as her pocketbook allowed. But what Wilhelm seems not to have realised at the time he wrote his letter was that she was also musical. One of the few evidences of 'petticoat government' after her marriage to Wilhelm Gaisberg was the prompt appearance of a piano in the household of that upright and cautious servant of the Federal Printing Office.

In 1871, the year after their marriage, they commenced their family with a daughter Carrie. She was followed on New Year's Day 1873 by the first son, whom they proudly christened Frederick William.

And so on [as Fred was later to recall] with a variation of 16 months came Charlie, Emma, Will, Isabel, John (who died at 13 months of age), then the last, Louise . . .

It was in '82 (about) that my father bought our first home, 1217 New York Avenue. I don't believe any edifice existing represents a better-deserved reward than that little, two-storeyed red brick house. I believe that day was the happiest in my father's life. . . . He would have liked to see us better educated could he have afforded it. As it was we were all able to go through the Grammar Schools and most of us through the High School.

Emma entertained high hopes of musical ability for all her children. One by one, as soon as they were able to understand anything, she began to acquaint them with the piano. Carrie proved a disappointment in this respect, but Fred more than made up for it. He was clearly one of those children with a natural talent for the keyboard, and his mother made the most of this opportunity from the moment she began to teach him when he was four.

From the time Fred was eight until his voice broke he was a chorister at St. John's Episcopal Church. Then the boy was able to meet one of the most celebrated musicians of Washington—the young master of the United States Marine Band, John Philip Sousa.

> ... I also sang in Sousa's choir, which was organised for Sunday evening concerts, and I attended rehearsals in his then modest home in the Navy Yard in South Washington. He patted me on the head and made quite a pet of me. ... I can still see the small room that one entered direct from the street, and a very old 'tin-panny' square piano from which he conducted rehearsals. In hot weather the front door used to be left open and a circle of negro children would surround the entrance, silently enjoying the music we made ...
>
> ... On Saturday afternoons in the spring and summer the Marine Band formerly gave concerts on the lawn in the grounds of the White House ... I was one of the music-mad youngsters who hovered by his podium and never missed a concert. On windy days his music used to become unmanageable, and he would turn round and beckon to me. It was my pride then to stand beside him to turn over and hold down the music.

But the piano remained his first love. During his school years Fred's precocity was given official recognition in a scholarship awarded by the City of Washington for several years of lessons with a brilliant young teacher there called Henry Xander. Soon his skill at accompanying and playing solos was in demand with a variety of amateur and charitable organisations throughout the city.

In the summer of 1889, while he was still at school, Fred Gaisberg heard of a novel way to earn pocket-money. A firm called the Columbia Phonograph Company had been organised to manufacture Edison's invention for preserving the sounds of a dictating voice so that they could be reproduced later for a stenographer to take down at leisure. Now this company had decided to expand their activities in a musical direction: they would try to reproduce the sounds of songs and so encourage the use of their equipment for home entertainment. They needed someone to play the piano loudly and clearly enough for its sounds to be captured by the apparatus as the accompaniment to whatever musician might be chosen to 'record'. That was the portentous word used to describe the whole activity.

One of the first musicians they selected was John York Atlee, a whistler. Fred remembered especially

> . . . his pompous announcements which introduced each performance in tones that made the listener visualise a giant. In reality he was a mere shrimp of a man, about five feet in his socks, that little Government clerk with the deep, powerful voice. Of this and his fine flowing moustache he was mighty proud. After his office hours, from nine to four, as a wage-slave of the U.S. Government, he would return to his modest home where I would join him. In the parlour stood an old upright piano and a row of three phonographs lent to him by the Columbia Phonograph Company. Together we would turn out, in threes, countless records of performances of 'Whistling Coon', 'Mocking Bird', and the 'Laughing Song'. I can still hear that reverberating announcement:
>
> > 'THE MOCKING BIRD', BY JOHN YORK ATLEE, ARTISTIC WHISTLER, ACCOMPANIED BY PROFESSOR GAISBERG.
>
> I was then only sixteen. *Some* professor . . .
>
> Atlee's unaccompanied repertoire included Mark Antony's speech in *Julius Caesar* commencing 'Friends, Romans, Countrymen', the Lord's Prayer, and 'The Ravings of John McCullough, the Mad Actor'. What a nuisance we must have been on those long summer nights to our suffering neighbours seeking rest and fresh air on their front porches! From our open window, evening after evening that beastly little man, with myself as sole accessory, would keep up this infernal racket till all hours.

The recordings were made on small, hollow cylinders of wax, each mounted on a revolving drum. Above each cylinder was a needle, attached to the small end of the horn into which the sounds were to be directed. To make the recording, the cylinder drum was rotated by a hand crank as the needle was lowered onto the wax. The needle itself was then moved gradually in a lateral way while the cylinder rotated, so that a close spiral of grooves containing the patterns of the sound responses was etched round the outside of the wax cylinder. In this way its entire surface would be covered in about two minutes, and the recording would then end.

By a judicious arrangement of equipment, it was possible to get as many as three sets of recording horns and cylinders close enough to the performers to make a record on each from a single rendition—if it was loud enough. When Sousa's Band came to record, Fred saw this technology temporarily advance. The Band created such a volume of sound that no fewer than ten cylinders could be made from every performance. This made a great saving of everyone's nervous resources. If twenty copies of a given selection were wanted, the Band could accomplish that by going through the piece only twice; for more ordinary artists it would mean seven performances one after the other.

As he spent more and more time making recordings during the holidays of his final school years, Fred Gaisberg began to find out something about the tiny industry he had stumbled into. The Columbia Phonograph Company was the subsidiary of an organisation called the North American Phonograph Company, which had been put together in the autumn of 1888 to combine Edison's phonograph interests with the later improvements of two Washington scientists, Bell and Tainter. 'Columbia' was the division of the larger company charged with conducting the business in the States of Maryland and Delaware and in the District of Columbia, the government city of Washington. The 'Columbia' Company had been founded in January 1889—just six months before Fred Gaisberg began to work for them. The principals were two former stenographers of the United States Supreme Court, and they quite naturally had established the main lines of the business to cater for the dictation needs of the many government offices throughout the city. Machines were rented from the Company, not purchased outright.

At the year's end Columbia was the only one of the North American Phonograph Company's subsidiaries to have turned sufficient profit to pay its shareholders a dividend. But by the beginning of 1890, the government stenographers whose jobs were threatened with redundancy had begun to take real alarm. The Columbia machines rented to the Congressional offices began mysteriously to develop all sorts of troubles. Before long

Fred was to witness the return of the whole lot—'some hundreds of the instruments . . . all being returned as unpractical'.

By the start of 1891 the entire North American Phonograph Company was in serious trouble. Thomas Edison, the phonograph's inventor, remained the Company's principal creditor, and when he assumed control the first thing he did was to make it possible to purchase the machine. But as the price was $150, very few people thought of acquiring a phonograph for home entertainment. Fred Gaisberg was later to remember:

> The Columbia Company seemed headed for liquidation . . . but it was saved by a new field of activity which was created, almost without their knowledge, by showmen at fairs and resorts demanding records of songs and instrumental music.
>
> Phonographs, each equipped with ten sets of ear-tubes through which the sound passed, had been rented to these exhibitors. It was ludicrous in the extreme to see ten people grouped about a phonograph, each with a listening tube leading from his ears, grinning and laughing at what he heard. It was a fine advertisement for the onlookers waiting their turn. Five cents was collected from each listener, so the showman could afford to pay two or three dollars for a cylinder to exhibit.

This seemed a promising development, as it would naturally increase demand for the musical recordings that Fred Gaisberg was making. But when the young man asked for a full-time job after his graduation from High School in June 1891, the directors wondered whether their business would ever warrant the exclusive services of a musician. Eventually a compromise was reached. Fred could have a job, but it must involve the technical as well as the performing side. He spent the next several months at the North American Phonograph Company's factory at Bridgeport, Connecticut. There he received a thorough grounding in the building and working of phonographic machinery from Thomas Hood Macdonald, a Scotsman as brilliant as anyone in the business.

Macdonald showed Fred some fascinating experiments for rotating the cylinder-drum by means of a clock-work motor. Successfully applied, this would make possible both the recording and the reproducing of music at a constant pitch—something that could never be achieved while either operation depended on hand-cranking. Edison agreed that there should be a motor, but he favoured an electrical affair with complicated storage batteries and cells. So far Macdonald had not been able to convince Edison that a clock-mechanism was the answer.

Meanwhile the coin-in-slot business was thriving in shops and saloons, and within a year Fred found himself back in Washington making records again. By now the Columbia Company had produced a printed catalogue of their recordings, and the phonograph performers were being kept busy duplicating popular titles to satisfy the demands of the coin-in-slot operators for their customers' favourites. In addition to John York Atlee, Fred now began to accompany other performers whose abilities were suited to the machine. One of the most formidable of these natural talents was Dan Donovan, 'a big, fat Irishman who announced the train departures at the Potomac railway station: "Richmond, Atlanta, Savannah, and all points south." He had a mighty bass voice and I was particularly proud to accompany him at our local "smokers" in songs like *Rocked in the Cradle of the Deep* and *Anchored*.'

Donovan brought Fred into contact with a man who had been responsible for many of the recent improvements in phonograph recording—notably the cylinder of wax. This was Charles Sumner Tainter, who had been associated with the Bell brothers in founding the Volta Laboratory in Washington with the money that had been awarded to Alexander Graham Bell for his work on the telephone.

> Charles Sumner Tainter was a scientist as well as a mechanical genius. I can see him now working at a watch-maker's lathe with a glass to his eye; he had a touch as delicate as a woman's. I never knew anyone who lived so abstemiously . . .
>
> Tainter was an Englishman and a confirmed tea-drinker. Indeed, he taught me how to brew and enjoy it. The perfume of that special China blend of his haunts me still. Between the cups he would mount the diaphragm and adjust the angle of the cutting stylus. In his clear Yorkshire voice he would test them with:
>
> 'Caesar, Caesar, can you hear what I say—this, which; s-ss-sss.'
>
> The stress was always laid on the sibilants, these being the

most difficult sounds to record. In playing back the test, at the slightest indication of the 's' sound, he would smile with joy and treat himself to another cup.

Tainter was just then experimenting with a new type of cylinder, whose greater sensitivity would permit the cutting of far more recordings from a single performance:

> His cylinders took the form of a roll of paper eight inches long and about one and a half inches in diameter, coated with ozokerite, on which a sapphire point cut the sound. In his studio he had installed a battery of twenty recording heads that worked as a unit. From each head hung a trumpet directed towards the piano behind which stood the singer. One performance produced twenty records, but from the singer plenty of volume was required.

Soon Fred was working for Tainter. At the beginning it was menial enough: 'I worked at making the paper cylinders & coating them with ozokerite, a natural mineral wax.' Then he was given more responsibility. The Volta Laboratory was about to become the scene of record-making on a larger scale: 'Tainter had just obtained a concession for coin-operated machines at the Chicago World's Fair and was engaged in recording music on the cylinders for use with these machines.' What he needed was someone who could bring in talented performers, and that was Fred Gaisberg:

> To earn my $10 a week I had to find the artists, load up each of the twenty units with the paper cylinders, set the recording horns, and play the accompaniments. Our entire repertoire consisted of 'Daisy Bell' and 'After the Ball was Over', and sometimes we would perform the latter as many as seventy times a day.

By the time the World's Fair opened on 1 May 1893 an impressive array of coin-in-slot phonographs had been installed in Chicago, together with sufficient cylinders to satisfy the anticipated demand. But Tainter's machines were not a success there:

> His slot-controlled automatic phonograph ... proved too delicate to stand the rough handling at the Chicago Fair Grounds. It was withdrawn and shipped to Washington where, acting on Tainter's instructions, I installed some

dozens in the local saloons, restaurants, and beer-gardens. They were not infallible and sometimes would accept a coin without giving out a tune. In carrying out my job of collecting the coins in the morning and reloading the machines with cylinders, I would at times be badly handled by an irate bartender who accused me of taking money under false pretences.

This was not at all the sort of life Fred wanted, and soon he went back to the Columbia Company. There the commercial wisdom of making musical records on a really large scale had finally been seen. 'They had just moved into an imposing five-storeyed building on Pennsylvania Avenue, Washington's principal shopping street. The entire ground floor was fitted up as a nickel-in-the-slot Audition Saloon. They installed about a hundred automatic coin-operated phonographs. There were no seats; the patrons had to stand with rubber listening tubes in their ears. . . . The top floor of this building was fitted up as a recording studio. . . .'[1]

Fred's months with Tainter had not been a total loss, because his experience of artist-recruitment enabled him to offer himself now as 'pianist and talent scout' to the Columbia director, a young New Englander called Calvin Child. Fred was hired, and so became

> . . . accompanist to such famous cylinder artists as Daniel Quinn, Johnny Meyers, George Gaskin, Len Spencer, and Billy Golden. . . . Favourite records of those days were made by the U.S. Marine Band playing Sousa's Marches, the Boston Cadet Band, Eisler's Band, the minstrel-comedian Billy Golden whistling 'The Mocking Bird' and giving his negro shout 'Turkey in de Straw', and the tragic negro George W. Johnson in 'The Whistling Coon' and 'The Laughing Song'. George achieved fame and riches with just these two titles. . . .
>
> Perhaps because of his unsavoury reputation, my particular pet and hero of this time was the handsome Len Spencer. His father, the originator of the florid Spencerian handwriting, was the chief bugbear of thousands of schoolboys, myself included. The son had many and varied gifts. As a popular baritone, I accompanied him at concerts and for record-making. I first saw him seated at a small table in Pennsylvania

[1] Typescript article, 'Charlie Gregory's fifty years of talking machines'.

> Avenue, surrounded by admiring darkies, writing out visiting-cards at six for a dime. His beautiful, ornate Spencerian writing, ending up with two doves, looked like engraving. Later I was always to remember his handsome face disfigured by a scar, the result of a razor-slash in an up-river gambling brawl. He was said to have been an adroit poker-player. His records of 'Anchored', 'Sailing', 'The Palms', and 'Nancy Lee' were important items of our meagre record repertoire.

But Fred's work for Columbia gave a hint of what might be accomplished if a recording programme could be planned with a balance of artists and repertoire.

Chapter Two

THE APPARENT prosperity of Columbia toward the end of 1893 did not reflect the state of affairs in the complex parent–company, North American Phonograph. For months Edison had been trying vainly to bring the entire organisation under his direct control. When no real progress was made, he decided that the various subsidiaries must be competing with one another. So he took the extreme measure of throwing the entire North American Phonograph Company into bankruptcy to make possible total re-organisation.

When this news emerged early in 1894, there was general consternation amongst the employees. Columbia itself was said to be exempt, but everyone wondered how long such an exemption would continue. Many of those connected with the Company were beginning to look about them. Fred Gaisberg talked to his friends on the performing side.

> It was Billy Golden who asked me one day . . . if I would go with him to see a funny German who had started experimenting with a flat-disc talking-machine record and wanted to make some trials. I was only too eager to see him at work.
>
> We found Emile Berliner in his small laboratory on New York Avenue and received a warm welcome from the inventor. Billy was right, Berliner certainly did make me smile. Dressed in a monkish frock he paced up and down the small studio buzzing on a diaphragm.
>
> 'Hello, hello!' he recited in guttural, broken English. 'Tvinkle, tvinkle, little star, how I vonder vot you are.'

Introductions accomplished, the three of them settled to the business at hand:

Berliner placed a muzzle over Golden's mouth and connected this up by a rubber hose to a diaphragm. I was at the piano, the sounding-board of which was also boxed up and connected to the diaphragm by a hose resembling an elephant's trunk. Berliner said, 'Are you ready?' and upon our answering 'Yes', he began to crank like a barrel-organ, and said 'Go'.

The song finished, Berliner stopped cranking. He took from the machine a bright zinc disc and plunged it into an acid bath for a few minutes. Then, taking it out of the acid, he washed and cleaned the disc. Placing it on a reproducing machine, also operated by hand like a coffee-grinder, he played back the resulting record from the etched groove.

To our astonished ears came Billy Golden's voice. Berliner proudly explained to us just how his method was superior to the phonograph. He said that in his process the recording stylus was vibrated laterally on a flat surface, thus always encountering an even resistance, and this accounted for the more natural tone.

Acquainted as I was with the tinny, unnatural reproduction of the old cylinder-playing phonographs, I was spell-bound by the beautiful round tone of the flat gramophone disc. Before I departed that day, I exacted a promise from Berliner that he would let me work for him when his machine was ready for development.

Here was a man who had upset two of the cardinal principles of recording. First, he recorded on a flat disc surface, with grooves spiralling inward. And second, his groove was of the same depth everywhere: the needle moved laterally rather than up and down to etch the sound-pattern. And the sound was incomparably better. Furthermore, the use of a flat disc gave Berliner a way of multiplying copies from a negative image, just as a photographer or an artist-etcher could do.

A few months later, I received a postcard asking me to come and see him. In great anticipation I called at his house. He informed me that in recent months his laboratory experiments had culminated in the production of a recording and reproducing apparatus and also a recording process sufficiently advanced to place on the market. He also confided to me that three of his relatives and friends had formed a small syndicate to exploit his gramophone. With the limited funds available he wanted to make a small programme of songs and music for demonstration purposes in order to raise capital for promoting a company. [He] told me I was just the person he was looking for. . . . My value to Berliner rested in the fact that I could collect quickly a variety of effective talent to make these demonstration records.[1]

Yet furthermore this eccentric inventor presented a figure very different from the businessmen and shop-keepers with whom Fred had had largely to deal since he left Tainter: 'For many years Berliner was the only one of the many people I knew connected with the gramophone who was genuinely musical and possessed a cultured taste.'

So Fred Gaisberg's professional life moved over to 1410 Pennsylvania Avenue, Berliner's laboratory and the office address for his infant company.

In our small laboratory on Pennyslvania Avenue, Berliner did the recording, I scouted for artists, played the accompaniments, and washed up the acid tanks. Berliner's nephew, Joe Sanders, made the matrices and pressed the samples.

. . . Billy Golden . . . recorded . . . his famous negro song 'Turkey in de Straw' . . . Next was O'Farrell, an Irish comedian from Ford's Burlesque Show, who contributed 'Drill ye Terriers, Drill' and 'Down went McGinty to the Bottom of the Sea' . . . Then there was George W. Graham . . . a member of an Indian Medicine Troupe doing one-night stands in the spring and summer and in winter selling quack medicines at the street corners. His tall, lanky figure, draped in a threadbare Prince Albert coat and adorned with a flowing tie, his wide-brimmed Stetson hat and his ready stream of wit combined to extract the dimes and nickels from his simple audience in exchange for a bottle of coloured water.

[1] In *Music on Record* (pp. 15–17) the meeting with Berliner is dated 1891. But Gaisberg says that when he started to work for Berliner 'a few months later . . . I was then twenty-one.' That places the beginning of his employment with Berliner in 1894. Berliner's small syndicate had been formed in 1893 (see Gelatt, *The Fabulous Phonograph*, p. 64). Gaisberg had worked for Tainter in the year of the Chicago World's Fair, 1893, and in his Charles Gregory article specifies November 1893 as the date when Gregory joined him at Columbia, where Fred was working again after leaving Tainter. And there is no suggestion anywhere that Fred Gaisberg ever returned to the phonograph industry once he had commenced to work for Berliner.

I discovered him one day on the corner of Seventh and Pennsylvania Avenue selling a liver cure to a crowd of spellbound negroes. He was assisted by John O'Terrell, who strummed the banjo and sang songs to draw the crowd. I brought this pair to Emile Berliner. Always a student of humanity, he was delighted. . . . George recorded . . . his famous talk on 'Liver Cure', in which he cited the instance of a sick man taking one bottle of his liver cure, and when he died the liver was so strong they had to take it out and kill it with a club.

I took Donovan, the train-announcer, to record for Berliner, and also a boy I discovered on the train selling sweets and magazines between Baltimore and Washington. Above the noise of the locomotive you could hear his powerful voice calling 'Magazines, peanuts, bananas, apples, *Harper's*, *Youth's Companion*, *Saturday Evening Post*.' . . . He had phenomenal lung power that would move a brick wall. We taught him to recite nursery rhymes . . .

To complete this repertoire, Emile Berliner himself recited 'The Lord's Prayer' and 'Twinkle, Twinkle, Little Star' in very guttural, broken English. He explained that everyone knew these two selections by memory, so that they could easily understand every word when the records were played back.

About this time a lucky thing happened. The much-advertised burlesque show entitled *Faust Up-to-Date* visited the Albaugh Theatre next door to our lab. The stage manager was Russell Hunting. He also played the part of Mephistopheles and, dressed in red tights, he was shot up from the bowels of the theatre into the midst of a bevy of dancers.

I knew him as the originator of the 'Michael Casey' series of phonograph records. They consisted of rapid-fire cross-talk between two Irish characters, with Hunting taking both parts. His fine voice had an infinite capacity for mimicry. In his spare time he made these cylinder records in his hotel room, and they had become famous among exhibitors.

I argued with Berliner that by an investment of $25 for five titles, we would have a dazzling attraction in our campaign for capital. It was, for us, a huge investment, but we took the plunge. . . .

One day when things were slack Berliner and I improvised a record called 'Auction Sale of a Piano'. He did the auctioneering and called out to me: 'Professor, show dem vat a peautiful tone dis instrument has.' When no bids were forthcoming, with anguish in his voice he would complain: 'Why, ladies and gentlemen, on *dis* piano Wagner composed *Die Götterdämmerung*. Still no bids? I see you know nothing about music. Johnny, hand me down dat perambulator!'

The magnetism of Berliner's studio seemed to grow almost from day to day, especially in the imagination of the youngest Gaisberg brother, sixteen-year-old Will, who later recalled:

> My brother [Fred] who was always something of a dreamer, was extremely happy in having just the sort of position he longed for, and that was as an assistant in Mr. Berliner's laboratory. Many happy hours of my school holidays were spent in the old laboratory watching Mr. Berliner and my brother experimenting and testing, very delighted if they called upon me to hold a tube or hand them a tool from the bench. I can recall the intense excitement when I formed one of the small audience to hear those first records: crude as they were in those first early days, we all thought them wonderful.[1]

On the financial front, things were moving a good deal less smartly. The records seemed to succeed in every purpose save the most important—that of attracting investors. Fred recalled:

> A stream of punters and speculators, rich and poor, visited Berliner's small laboratory. They were all interested and amused but sceptical. They would not part with their money and Berliner's funds and courage were getting lower and lower. Even his friends began to doubt and avoid him. He often confided to me that something would have to be done or he would be forced to close down. I had been weeks without my modest salary, but as I was earning money with my piano-playing in the evenings this was no great hardship for me. Still my heart warmed towards Berliner and I was sorry to see him discouraged. I searched my young brain as to what could be done to raise the wind.
>
> Among my friends were the apparently flourishing Karns family living on Capitol Hill. B. F. Karns was a retired Methodist minister, at that time engaged in lobbying a bill

[1] William C. Gaisberg, 'Romance of Recording: Early Days in Washington', typescript article.

through Congress to secure a right of way for his Eastern Shore Railroad scheme. This imposing gentleman, by frequent references to Rockefeller, J. Pierpont Morgan, Harriman, and the rest, impressed my youthful imagination and I was hopeful that he would be the very man to rescue Berliner. That Karns was a persuasive talker and magnetic personality was proved by the fact that within twenty-four hours after I had brought them together the nearly bankrupt Berliner advanced him $100. Then we waited for the miracle to happen.

At each appointment for a demonstration to Rockefeller or Morgan the most devilish forces seemed to intervene to obstruct their appearance. Rockefeller's wife had measles or Morgan's wife was going to have a baby. At the end of six months we were no further along, except that I personally had lent Karns $40 and Berliner $200, and Karns's family was reduced to living on liver at ten cents a pound. . . .

Eventually Berliner got Karns and myself on the train for Boston, equipped with a first-class gramophone exhibit and letters to the directors of the Bell Telephone Company. At the close of a directors' meeting we were shown into the board-room. The directors, oozing opulence and exhaling fragrant Havana cigars, signalled us to demonstrate our gramophone. When I played Berliner's record of the Lord's Prayer they wept with joy; they thought his recitation of 'Twinkle, twinkle, little star' especially touching, but in the gramophone as a musical instrument they took no interest. . . .

. . . In New York City we demonstrated to Mr. Schwarz, the greatest toy dealer in America, and to many others, all of whom asked for a talking doll.[1]

Through that winter of 1894–5 their failures were so consistent that Fred began to wonder whether the fault lay in himself: 'The reproducing apparatus . . . was a simple hand-driven turntable, and upon the uniformity of the hand movement depended the steadiness of the musical pitch. In playing this machine to possible investors, my anxiety to make a good impression was so great that often my hand would waver, causing the pitch to

[1] In *Music on Record* (pp. 19–20) the sums lent are cited in sterling. They are given as dollar-figures in Fred's untitled typescript article beginning 'When I crossed the ocean'. In view of Berliner's and Gaisberg's economic circumstances, the dollar-amounts are much more likely.

falter and taking with it my hopes of securing money for our company.'[1]

By March all the money that Berliner had advanced for the trip was gone, and there was nothing to show for it. Gaisberg and Karns were on the point of returning to Washington when they were overtaken by a savage winter's-end blizzard that immobilised the entire life of New York: 'We were snowed up in a dollar-a-day hotel for one whole week without funds and with all communications cut off. For food we patronised the free-lunch counters when the bartender's face was turned away. Altogether we spent a week of great discomfort.'

On the way back to Washington, they decided to make one more attempt in Philadelphia.

> . . . Our records, to say nothing of our patience, had by this time nearly worn out. . . . I knew every record by heart, but had to maintain an amused smile in sympathy with my audience. . . .
>
> My No. 1 record was 'The Lord's Prayer' recited by Emile Berliner himself in clear but guttural pronunciation of strong German accent. Every word was understood.
>
> No. 2 was 'The Mocking Bird', whistled by John York Atlee, accompanied by Professor Gaisberg.
>
> No. 3 was a star turn, 'Drill ye Terriers, Drill', sung by George J. Gaskin, one of the half-dozen male singers with a voice clear and powerful enough to record.
>
> No. 4 was 'The Auction Sale of a Grand Piano'. . . .
>
> No. 5 was an imitation of a Cat and Dog Fight, by George Graham, [the] street entertainer in Washington's Pennsylvania Avenue.
>
> Two choice morsels, 'Twinkle, Twinkle, Little Star' and 'Johnny Reciting "Mary Had a Little Lamb" before Company' I held in reserve.[2]

The Philadelphians were non-committal, but they didn't say no.

While they were in Philadelphia, Fred found an opportunity to improve the gramophone's repertory: 'On a visit to Atlantic City one day I discovered the handsome tenor Ferruccio Giannini in a provincial Italian opera company. The next day he

[1] 'When I crossed the ocean'.

[2] 'Emile Berliner Picks a Winner', in *The Gramophone*, Dec. 1943, p. 97.

came and made records of 'La Donna è mobile' and 'Questa o quella' [from Verdi's *Rigoletto*]. These were most successful and were the first opera excerpts we ever brought out. They filled us with pride and for many months represented our only concessions to highbrow taste.'[1]

In the small laboratory in Pennsylvania Avenue, meanwhile, the experiments continued.

> Berliner had been using 'ebonite' or vulcanised rubber for pressing records. 'Ebonite' required a great deal of pressure and would not retain the impression permanently. Pondering over this, he remembered that the Bell Telephone Company had abandoned vulcanised rubber and had adopted a plastic material for their telephone receivers.
>
> The Durinoid Company of Newark, N.J. were button manufacturers who undertook to furnish pressings of a similar substance from matrices supplied by Berliner. The new substance was a mixture of powdered shellac and byritis, bound with cotton flock and coloured with lamp-black. It was rolled under hot calenders into 'biscuits'. When heated, these 'biscuits' were easily moulded under pressure and when cooled they retained the impression.
>
> I was present when Berliner received the first package of gramophone records from the Durinoid Company. With trembling hands he placed the new disc on the reproducer, and sounds of undreamed quality issued from the record. It was evident that the new plastic material . . . had under pressure poured into every crevice of the sound-track, bringing out tones hitherto mute to us. Berliner shouted with excitement, and all of us, including the venerable Werner Suess . . . our eighty-five-year-old mechanical genius . . . danced with joy around the machine.

Perhaps it was this news that finally tipped the balance in Philadelphia. At all events, before the summer's end the Philadelphians announced that they were ready to form a syndicate for investment in Berliner's gramophone. It was a motley group of business men—a couple of steel jobbers, a clothing manufacturer, and two building contractors. But they had $25,000 to offer, and that established their interest. The United States

[1] Dated to 1895 from surviving copies of the Giannini discs.

Gramophone Company, which they incorporated on 8 October 1895, would control and administer Berliner's gramophone patents. The new company was to have its office in Philadelphia. Under licence from this firm, the Berliner Gramophone Company of Washington would manufacture equipment and discs. It was Berliner's first opportunity to proceed on a sound commercial footing.

The inventor's first thought was that he might now increase his research staff. Fred's mind flew to his brother Will, now in his last year of High School and therefore soon to be in need of employment. When Will himself heard of it he was just as excited:

> I will never forget the one night when my brother came home and told my father that another assistant was needed in the laboratory, and how hard I pleaded with my father to allow me to join the staff. But it was not to be, as my father informed my brother that he did not think that he should let two of his sons start their careers in such an uncertain business as the talking machine. His friends with whom he had discussed it agreed with him. I was put to selling coal, and a school chum of mine, William Sinkler Darby, was given the position.[1]

It was a happy coincidence that the United States Gramophone Company had found its home in Philadelphia, for there was the seat of the Franklin Institute, where Berliner had given the gramophone its first public showing in 1888. In the spring of 1896 he asked Fred Gaisberg to represent him at the meeting.

> ... Berliner gathered all the successful results of his gramophone experiments under one exhibit, which he delegated me to take to Philadelphia and demonstrate before the Franklin Institute. Every year or so Berliner was in the habit of showing off before this venerable body his achievements of a scientific order and his experiments in sound as embodied in the gramophone. To receive their blessing was flattering to his vanity, and the demonstrations served to register his claim to priority of invention. . .

[1] W. C. Gaisberg, 'Romance of Recording: Early Days in Washington' typescript.

> I had several zinc-etched disc records and six black pressings of [the] new plastic material just received from the Durinoid Company. . . . These constituted the most outstanding advance Berliner had to show. . . .
>
> The members turned up to full capacity to hear my modest programme. The programme was similar to what you would expect in a small town church concert, but it amused the bearded and dignified professors, who eagerly examined my equipment and asked endless questions. . . . The demonstration was a huge success. . . .[1]

Except for the new pressings, the equipment was in fact precisely that shown to the potential investors a year earlier. The now widely advertised clockwork-driven phonograph, which Edison had at last been persuaded to manufacture, was protected by patents. In contrast, it was humiliating for Fred to realise that 'My equipment was the simple hand-driven 7-inch turntable. As it was without a governor I had to rotate it with cool nerves and a steady motion, or the music would play out of tune.'[2]

During his stay in Philadelphia, however, Fred happened to see an advertisement in a local paper:

> WHY WEAR YOURSELF OUT TREADING A SEWING-MACHINE? FIT ONE OF OUR CLOCKWORK MOTORS.

> I sped hot-foot to the address given. In a back street I found a dingy workshop and a venerable old gentleman with a flowing beard who announced that he was the inventor. When I saw that his motor was a vast, unwieldy contraption like a beer-barrel my heart sank. For an incredibly long time the old man wound it up with a crank, like a man hauling a bucket of water from a deep well. Then for an incredibly short time the sewing-machine buzzed away. I asked the inventor how many clockwork sewing-machines he had sold, and he answered:
>
> 'As yet, none at all.'
>
> He assured me, however, that he could easily design a clock mechanism for my gramophone, as it was a much simpler problem.

[1] 'Emile Berliner Picks a Winner'.
[2] *Ibid.*

I left him my gramophone, and commissioned him to go ahead. A week later he appeared before our directors with the results.[1]

The old man's motor was still impractical, and the Company were forced to reject it. It had been built, however, not in the shed of the inventor himself, but in the machine shop of a young mechanic called Eldridge Johnson across the river from Philadelphia in Camden, New Jersey. Johnson later recalled: 'Not a small part of my early business was the manufacture of experimental models for new inventions. Such models now are generally made in the laboratories of large factories, but in those days independent, poverty-stricken inventors were numerous and their haunts were invariably the small machine shops. . . . During the model-making days of the business one of the very early types of talking machines was brought to the shop for alterations. The little instrument was badly designed. It sounded like a partially-educated parrot with a sore throat and a cold in the head, but the little wheezy instrument caught my attention and held it fast and hard. I became interested in it as I had never been interested in anything before.'[2]

Fred Gaisberg was to remember Johnson as the very type of American success from humble origins.

I can see him now as he was when I went to that little shop across the river . . . tall, lanky, stooping and taciturn, deliberate in his movements and always assuming a low voice with a Down-East Yankee drawl. . . .

His quick, inventive brain saw what the old man was trying to do. On his own account he built and submitted to our directors a clockwork gramophone motor which was simple, practical, and cheap. It was the answer to our prayers and brought Johnson an order for two hundred motors. . . .

As a commercial beginning it was small enough. But even then the Gramophone directors wondered whether they had

[1] In *Music on Record* (p. 21) the date is given as Spring 1895. Fred Gaisberg was in Philadelphia then for the demonstrations with Karns before potential investors. But the rest of the events leading to the gramophone clockwork motor are all firmly datable to the summer and autumn of 1896, and Fred's Franklin Institute demonstration in the spring of 1896 had been given with a hand-driven machine.

[2] *Eldridge Reeves Johnson (1867–1945) Industrial Pioneer*, passim.

sufficient experience to direct a marketing and sales campaign. So they hired a New York business man called Frank Seaman to handle the promotion. Seaman set up still another company for this purpose—the National Gramophone Company. This meant that the gramophone interests were now split into three parts: the original Berliner Company of Washington to make discs and equipment; the National Gramophone Company of New York to advertise and market them; and the United States Gramophone Company of Philadelphia to administer the patents. But of course it allowed Berliner and his men to concentrate still more on improving the gramophone and making its recordings.

As if to vindicate that way of thinking, Berliner announced that he had received a letter from a young man then working for the great Edison. The writer said that he was then engaged in making motion-picture films for Edison, but that he also had experience with the inventor's talking machines, and would like to see what Berliner's gramophone could do. Fred Gaisberg remembered:

> Berliner was patently flattered by the magic name of Edison and appointed a Sunday morning to receive Alfred Clark, then twenty-two years old. I was also curious to meet the caller and assisted in the demonstration which was given. I took particular note of this youth whom I knew to be a candidate as colleague in recording and other gramophone processes.
>
> He was, I remember, a youth big and well-proportioned, perfectly dressed in a tailor-made suit which, in those days of 'off the peg' clothes (which I and even Berliner wore) struck a note of distinction. Further, his dark eyes and curly brown hair set off by a boyish blush whenever he spoke, made him irresistible, quite apart from his wisdom and the fact that he had emerged from the shadow of the great Edison.
>
> That Berliner was greatly impressed I knew by the many references he made to him. Six months afterwards Clark came down to Washington to be initiated in the process of making zinc records. . . .[1]

Meanwhile the New York promoter Frank Seaman had organised a vigorous advertising campaign for the autumn of 1896.

[1] 'Emile Berliner Picks a Winner'.

He then demanded a permanent recording installation and a retail shop for gramophone goods. The investors decided that these should be in Philadelphia. So Berliner set about persuading Fred Gaisberg to leave home and become the Philadelphia recording expert. It would be a real test of his whole professional and personal experience, for Fred was to have considerable autonomy in the selection of artists and repertoire—provided the results proved saleable. And Berliner would be sending Alfred Clark to open and manage the Gramophone retail shop.

Thus it came about that Fred Gaisberg established the first gramophone recording studio early in 1897, over a shoe shop in Twelfth Street, Philadelphia.

> Clark and I had living rooms adjoining this studio and so were frequently in each other's company and exchanged views on the artist's life, the gramophone industry and its future. That it had a future neither of us doubted. We were both in on the ground floor and had all the enthusiasm of youth.
>
> It was an exciting year for both of us. That year was election year; I cast my first vote and that for McKinley. Around the corner was the opera house with *El Capitan*, *Belle of New York*, *Erminie*, *Robin Hood*—with Francis Wilson, De Wolf Hopper and those devastating soubrettes, Alice Nielsen, Edna Wallace and Fritzie Scheff. These formed endless topics of conversation and of a summer evening we would occasionally have supper in Willow Grove while listening to . . . Victor Herbert's . . . band. . . .
>
> There were evenings when we stopped at home and enjoyed the leather-perfumed atmosphere of the studio over the shoeshop. There was a piano, as usual mounted on a two-foot high platform, and the recording machine invited exciting experiments in sound recording. Clark had a violin he was very fond of and occasionally tucked under his chin. . . .
>
> We met plenty of hospitality and kindness in the Quaker City and often found ourselves as guests in the homes of our directors. I remember one dinner party in the home of the Sommerfeldts, when we were taught to say greetings in Hebrew. Our pronunciation caused great merriment to our orthodox host. Another dinner was at the Parvins's, who were Quakers. Their home in Walnut Street was shiny with heavy

polished furniture, but their hospitality to two young bachelors in a strange town was sincere.

These were the well-to-do homes of the capitalists who financed the early Gramophone Company. In sharp contrast we were also guests in the more modest homes of Eldridge R. Johnson and B. G. Royal, then small mechanics who ran the small tool shop across the river in Camden. At that time they were making the first two hundred spring-motor gramophones for the Company. Their little shop was destined to expand into the great Victor Talking Machine Company before the decade was over.[1]

Could Fred Gaisberg himself have foreseen any such possibility in 1897? Though he might sometimes dream, Fred was always forced back to realising that 'Its novelty alone accounted for the gramophone's great popularity, since the repertoire recorded at this time covered only popular and comic songs, valses, and marches in their simplest settings. The records were single-sided, 5 inches and 7 inches in diameter, with a playing time of 1½ to 2 minutes. A fee of two to three dollars per song was paid to singers, and sales-royalties to artists and music publishers were undreamed of. We pirated right and left without remorse.'

Fred Gaisberg tried to use his new responsibility to foster better things in the recording room when he could. He invited the operatic tenor Giannini to make some records in the Philadelphia studio. Giannini obliged again with very much the same fare as before. And one other notable artist entered the Philadelphia studio:

> I had a Syrian friend, a cigarette manufacturer, who for months had boasted of a fellow-countryman from Smyrna called Maurice Farkoa who was the greatest singer of chansonettes in the world. Now Farkoa was to visit Philadelphia with the American tour of the *Artist's Model* company . . . and my friend undertook to bring him to our studio.
>
> True to his word, one bright afternoon the greatest exquisite of his day, Farkoa, arrived with his friend and accompanist, Frank Lambert. . . . My friend did not exaggerate. As an artist Farkoa more than justified his extravagant praise. A most successful record of the famous laughing song 'Le fou

[1] 'Emile Berliner Picks a Winner'.

rire' was made. It was the first time he had heard his own voice reproduced and Farkoa was amazed and delighted.

In fact, this record served as one of our great stunt-records for climaxing a recital.

Fred's recording policy was working well. Frank Seaman persuaded Berliner to open a second studio in New York. And the man hired to run the Gramophone's affairs in New York was none other than Fred's former chief at Columbia, Calvin Child. Child proved to be more of a visionary than Fred Gaisberg himself. Before the end of 1897 Child had begun a series of discs by famous speakers. One of his first prizes was the free-thinking philosopher Robert Ingersoll. He was followed by Dwight Moody, the evangelist. Chauncey Depew, the celebrated after-dinner orator, repeated for the Gramophone the peroration of the speech he had delivered at the dedication ceremony for the Statue of Liberty. America's greatest living actor, Joseph Jefferson, was persuaded to record some extracts from his inimitable stage version of *Rip Van Winkle*. And an equally celebrated actress, Ada Rehan, recited several scenes from classic English drama, including Shakespeare. Meanwhile, however, the Gramophone's interests were being pursued on broader horizons still.

Chapter Three

WITH THE establishment of recording studios in Philadelphia and New York in addition to the Washington headquarters, the time seemed ripe to develop the Berliner Gramophone Company farther afield. Europe was the obvious choice. The success of the talking machine there was clearly shown in the growth of the three-year-old Pathé Company in Paris, and it had been hinted that Columbia might soon set up an international office there. Someone should be sent to stimulate European financial interest in the Gramophone.

The man finally selected for this task was William Barry Owen, a legal assistant to Frank Seaman. In Fred Gaisberg's opinion, 'Berliner could have selected no finer agent than Owen to exploit his invention. He was an opportunist of quick decision and a bold gambler. . . . You would always find him sitting at the stiffest game of poker in the smoking room . . . and his eyes would bulge as he laid a full house on the table. . . . He brought to London an infectious enthusiasm and energetic leadership which I believe was quite new to the conservative English city man of that day.'

Owen arrived in London in July 1897 and took rooms at the Hotel Cecil in the Strand. Within a month he had succeeded in bringing together a tiny syndicate of potential investors. It soon became clear, however, that considerably more money would be required if anything serious was to be accomplished. Then Owen met Trevor Williams, a Lincoln's Inn solicitor. Williams, though he had no background in talking machines or musical instruments, was enthusiastic enough to seek the interest of two of his brothers-in-law and a close friend.

By December 1897 Williams was able to offer $5,000 for the European rights to Berliner's Gramophone on condition that the existing syndicate be reformed. Owen was delighted. He assured them that the present American facilities were capable of producing sufficient machines and records to answer any English or Continental demand. All that was necessary was to import the Berliner products ready-made. The Williams syndicate cautiously agreed to importation of the machines provided that a clause could be inserted permitting their European manufacture 'if service from America not maintained to standard required'.[1]

On the matter of recording, the English investors dissented. If the gramophone was to make a lasting success in Europe, it must be able to reproduce recordings made in Europe by European performers. Such a notion went against all of William Barry Owen's instincts for quick exploitation of a novelty, but he protested in vain. Trevor Williams was in a position to insist, and insist he did. It was the Berliner interests' first full encounter with the character of the man who was to guide the fortunes of the Gramophone Company in Europe over the next three decades.

The new company held its first meeting at the Hotel Cecil in April 1898. Trevor Williams was elected Chairman and William Barry Owen became Managing Director. It was decided to order 3,000 machines and 150,000 of the American records as a beginning stock, until a recording expert could be sent over from the States to begin his operations in London. The nomination of the expert to be sent fell to Berliner. He consulted with Alfred Clark. Whatever the sacrifice in Philadelphia and Washington, their choice fell unhesitatingly upon Fred Gaisberg.

The Gaisberg family may have had mixed feelings about the prospective departure of their eldest son, but Fred himself saw the opportunity of a lifetime. It meant being first in the European field with the recording process which now at last seemed ready to fulfil all their persistent hopes. It meant the chance to negotiate repertoire with a range and variety of performers hitherto inaccessible to the gramophone. Most of all it meant undertaking a programme of recording in a society where long-term artistic goals might be taken very seriously indeed. Illuminated by these enthusiasms, the question of whether to go answered itself.

With Fred Gaisberg would go Berliner's nephew Joseph

[1] [E.M.I. Ltd.] 'Chronological list of interesting events in the history of The Gramophone Company Limited'. typescript.

Sanders. He was to have the task of setting up a factory to press all the discs that were to be recorded in Europe, as supply lines from America would have been impossibly long. The Berliners' fear of British trade unionism had discouraged the idea of building the factory in England. Then Emile Berliner's brother Joseph, in Hanover, offered to finance the pressing plant if it could be situated there. So it was decided that Joe Sanders would join his uncle in Germany.

Fred's personal preparations for life across the sea were simple: 'My baggage consisted of a complete recording outfit plus a twenty-five dollar bicycle with pneumatic tyres, and a notebook stuffed with receipts, addresses, and advice. . . .' Into this notebook had gone all the information about the Berliner recording process that might be required at a remote distance from the source of the ideas. Then Fred wrote in it a long list of the American records currently available from stock. At the back he began noting expenses. In odd spaces he jotted down fugitive ideas for possible recordings.

As the notebook habit grew, he found himself putting in brief descriptions of some experiences as well—usually to document expenses or ideas, but just occasionally as if to commemorate the very pressure of living. In those last days of preparation and the journey from Washington to New York for the boat, everything seemed momentous:

> July 21. Took Carrie with me. 12.45 train for N.Y. via Pa.R.R. Arrived at Uncle Fred's 8 o'c.—Met Aunt Pauline and her son Christian. Had supper and spent night at Aunt Sophie Horn's.
>
> July 22. . . . Met Joe Sanders. Three of us go downtown, fix up Steamer ticket. Visited top of World Building—had magnificent view of city. Ate a Chinese dinner on Mott St. Took photo. Visited Atlantic Garden, heard $45,000 World's Fair orchestrion. Visited Uncle John Mills in Brooklyn . . . from there to Aunt Anna's.

Suddenly it was all over and the two young men were boarding the Cunard Liner *Umbria*. After the whirl of visits with all the northern cousins there was only Carrie, waving her handkerchief from the pier, to represent the family of Fred Gaisberg's childhood as the ship pulled slowly away.

The voyage yielded an interesting acquaintance in the person of the music hall comedian Bert Shepard: 'As an old minstrel man he was very versatile. His repertoire comprised negro airs, Irish and English ballads, comic and patter songs, parodies and yodels. The spontaneous and boisterous laugh he could conjure up was most infectious. . . .' Fred revelled in Shepard's company when he could get the great man to himself, and extracted a promise that he would visit the future recording studio in London for a demonstration.

On the ship's arrival in Liverpool, the notebook was consulted. A page toward the back yielded the following:

> The Gramophone Co.
> 31 Maiden Lane
> London
>
> Telegraph from Liverpool when starting. If nobody at Station take hack, have all bgge put on top of hack & drive to Hotel Cecil evenings or to 31 Maiden Lane daytime.

First experiences remained sharp in recollection.

> I remember arriving in London at the tail end of a strawberry glut of which I took the fullest advantage. The first evening, which was a Sunday, [William Barry] Owen gave a supper to myself, Joe Sanders . . . and B. G. Royal [who had come over to supervise the assembly of Johnson's gramophones from parts shipped from Camden]. We were all 'small town' boys, and Owen was in the Seventh Heaven of delight at our astonishment at the luxury of the Trocadero Grill and the 'wickedness' all round us on that sabbath night.

Typically, Fred was able to see gramophonic potential even in the midst of this lavish moment: 'I actually found my first artists here in the person of Leopold Jacobs. He and his band made many a successful record.'

Before anyone could make records, however, it was necessary to procure a long list of chemicals, vessels, and tools. During the first days a welter of purchases was entered in the notebook: a gallon of coal oil, jars and pitchers of earthenware and glass, a soldering iron, acid, gasoline, an etching tank, scissors, oil cloth, linoleum, cotton cloth, a bucket. There was also the problem of a lodging. Three days of life in the Owen style at the Hotel Cecil had cost $4.50—Fred was still learning to convert dollars into sterling—so something more humble was clearly in order.

Somehow by the beginning of August most of the immediate difficulties had been solved. Recording could henceforth be carried out in a basement room of the dingy old hotel where the Gramophone Company office and studio had been set up. The epithet that attached itself to this place in Fred Gaisberg's recollection was 'grimy'.

> Yes, grimy was the word for it. The smoking-room of the old Coburn Hotel was our improvised studio. There stood the recording machine on a high stand; from this projected a long, thin trumpet into which the artist sang. Close by, on a high movable platform, was an upright piano.

As a recording site, however, 31, Maiden Lane had its advantages. It was close to the theatres and music halls of London's West End, and it stood almost next door to Rule's—then as now a notable gathering place for theatrical folk. Indeed who should turn up amongst the regulars there but Bert Shepard. Before long he had been enticed down the steps and into the recording room. 'Our diaphragm was not very sensitive and we still required robust, even voices to make good records. Fat, jolly Bert Shepard, with his powerful tenor voice and clear diction, gave us our most successful results.'

Fred soon found a way to return the favour. Within a short time he was increasing Shepard's repertoire by teaching the professional some of the negro songs learned during his youth in Washington. It was a question of playing over and singing the song to Shepard from memory, and if he liked it writing out a transcription for him to study and perfect. Two of the songs Fred taught him, a 'Laughing Song' and 'The Whistling Coon', became enduring Shepard specialities, and through the means of the gramophone both went round the world. In after years Fred Gaisberg was to meet with these records in strange parts of the globe.

> In the bazaars of India I have seen dozens of natives seated on their haunches round a gramophone, rocking with laughter, whilst playing Shepard's laughing record; in fact this is the only time I ever heard Indians laugh heartily. The record is still available there [1940] and I believe that to this day it sells in China, Africa, and Japan.

Soon Shepard was introducing his poker cronies from Rule's—among them two famous music hall performers of the day, Eugene Stratton and R. G. Knowles. 'Shepard brought his companions to us to be amused and this served to give us contact with the greatest artists of the then flourishing music-hall world. Their names proved lodestones that brought to our catalogue other stars—Ada Reeve, Vesta Victoria, Gus Elen, Albert Chevalier, Herbert Darnley, George Mozart, Marie Lloyd, Vesta Tilley, Connie Ediss.'

But these provided only highlights in a busy but often thankless recording programme. Day in and day out came the endless procession—trombonists, bagpipe players, people who whistled, people who sang, or tried to. Usually it wasn't worthwhile attaching the performer's name to his records. And when they did name the artist, as often as not it led to confusion:

> Some of our staff knew little about music in those days, and I remember one bright young man receiving a request for music by 'men called . . . Mozart and Haydn'. He labelled the writer as 'crackers', and offered him 'Steamboat comin' round the bend' with real steamboat effect, by the '*Hayden* Male Quartet', or 'Imitation of Railway Trains on the Side Drum' by George Mozart. . . . That was as near as we could get in those days![1]

If it sometimes seemed that those in the Gramophone Company were missing important points, even its performers sometimes betrayed ludicrous misconceptions:

> I remember George Mozart . . . arriving in a four-wheeler and unloading a heavy theatrical wicker trunk. This was dragged into the studio and I asked George to rehearse while I continued my preparations. After what I thought was a rather long lapse of time, I looked into the studio to find him standing before the trumpet in full make-up, complete with red nose, whiskers and costume. Dear, simple George had anticipated television by thirty-five years. With difficulty I explained to him that to record his songs he need not have troubled to put on his make-up.

The environs of Maiden Lane also boasted a full complement

[1] 'The First Christmas with "His Master's Voice",' in *The Voice*.

of pubs, and they too contributed richly to the flavour of life in the new recording studio.

> Stout was the great standby of our artists in those days. It amazed me to see the number of empties that accumulated at the end of a session. Harry Fay's capacity was six bottles, but Ernest Pike and some of the ladies ran him a close second.
>
> In Maiden Lane we kept open house and our good friend Mr. Hyde, himself a publican, acted as runner. I had my recording machine ready to receive at any time the interesting visitors Mr. Hyde would bring in from Rule's. I remember Dan Leno arriving without an accompanist, so that I had to start the recording machine and then quickly run to the piano and accompany 'Mrs. Kelly'. . . .
>
> After that we always kept Airlie Dix, composer of 'The Trumpeter', standing by to act as accompanist. Even this did not always work, as he would often disappear to a nearby tavern. This gifted pianist could not keep off the bottle, but those were hard drinking days and Scotch was only 3s. 6d. a bottle, full proof.

About the time recording had commenced in London, the record presses from America arrived in Hanover—well before Joseph Berliner's factory to house them was finished. The first of Fred Gaisberg's London recordings soon followed, and it became crucial to get them into the market quickly so that some return might begin to offset the formidable columns of red figures that showed inevitably in the new Company's books. Joe Sanders had done all he could do: he set up the presses under a large tent, and during the next few months the entire supply of European Gramophone discs was produced from this improvised plant. Once started, however, the supplying of discs went forward with reasonable regularity, finished pressings being received in London four to six weeks after their 'masters' had been despatched to Hanover. By December there were no fewer than six hundred shopkeepers and agents who dealt in Gramophone products.

Trans-Atlantic communication was less reliable. Just at the critical moment the supply of Eldridge Johnson's gramophone parts failed.

We looked upon that first Christmas as our last opportunity

to turn a debit balance into credit [but] our stock of machines was cleared out early in December. Shipments of parts from America were held up, and dealers were 'sitting on our door-step' demanding goods. When eventually the cases did arrive, a few days before Christmas, everybody from the manager down to the office boy worked into the early hours assembling the parts. With faces and hands smeared with black-lead from the spring-cages, we must have been a comical sight.

Nevertheless, early on Christmas Eve our stock rooms in Maiden Lane were cleared of machines and records, so we 'trooped' into Rule's to celebrate our achievement with drinks all round.[1]

[1] 'The First Christmas with "His Master's Voice" .'

Chapter Four

AT THE beginning of 1899 Alfred Clark arrived in Europe. He had left Berliner to go to Paris as Edison's representative there. Clark had obtained the great inventor's permission not only to market Edison machines and cylinders in Paris, but to make new recordings there for the Edison catalogue. As soon as Clark established his talking machine agency in Paris, he set about persuading Trevor Williams that a French Gramophone Company would advantageously combine under his own energetic direction with the Edison facilities already in existence there.

Now Clark was demanding the same kind of on-the-spot recording from the Gramophone Company that he had been given by Edison. So William Barry Owen decided to send Fred Gaisberg to the Continent to do some recording with 'portable' equipment. With Fred would go Sinkler Darby, who had now come over from Berliner's laboratory in Washington to act as second recording expert in Europe. Fred began jotting down continental addresses that might be useful in the weeks ahead. To these he appended some of the most distinguished names of the French musical and dramatic stage:

Mlle. Ackté—soprano—Opéra
M. Delmas—basso
M. Affre—tenor
Rose Caron—soprano
Mlle. Bernhardt.

But those aspirations were to prove too high for the Gramophone of 1899.

At last the preparations were complete. The 'portable' recording equipment filled six large packing cases weighing anything up to 260 lb. each. The two recorders left London in the middle of May, going first to Hanover for a sight of the new factory.

It was decided to begin recording in Leipzig, a city not too far from Hanover and possessing an energetic musical life. There Gaisberg and Darby made two hundred records in the latter half of May, including a number of operatic arias by well-known singers. Next on the list of cities was Budapest. For the recruiting of artists there they relied on a local man, who brought them many performers who specialised in the traditional music of eastern Europe. It was in Budapest that Fred found a way to record the cymbalom.

In Vienna they recorded a wide variety of artists, ranging from yodlers and folk musicians to the Viennese band of Carl Ziehrer—or as much of it as could be crowded round the recording horn. But one special coup excited them all: the famous virtuoso Alfred Grünfeld consented to make some records on the old upright piano they had hired to equip the temporary recording studio during the three-week stay in Vienna.

It was only when they arrived in Italy early in July, however, that Fred Gaisberg's responses to the life of the Continent seemed fully to waken.

> My first visit to Milan in . . . 1899 was rich in experiences that stamped it unforgettably in my mind. La Scala Theatre seemed to occupy the focal point socially and intellectually [and] exciting things could happen in this romantic town. For instance, after a particularly fine performance of *Il Trovatore* the enthusiastic mob carried Tamagno to his hotel close by and there demonstrated until he appeared on the balcony and sang 'Di quella pira'. . . .
>
> I often saw the venerable Verdi, who would regularly take an afternoon drive in an open landau drawn by two horses. People would stand on the curb and raise their hats in salute as the carriage proceeded down Via Manzoni to the Park. A frail, transparent wisp of a man, but the trim of his pure white beard so corresponded with the popular picture of him that one could not fail to identify him. . . .
>
> One could sit at the Café Biffi in the Galleria and have pointed out to him Puccini, Leoncavallo, Mascagni, Franchetti, Giordano, Tamagno . . . as they sauntered through the throng of chattering citizens on their way to have their mid-

day aperitif. Mid-day was the great moment . . . when the whole city converged on the Galleria. There were throngs of singers from many lands to make contact with impresarios. Students of singing and *maestri di canto* who battened on them, *comprimarii* (small part artists) and *choristi* went to make up this clearing house of the opera world.[1]

By the time Fred Gaisberg and Sinkler Darby arrived in Italy, Gramophone Company agents were already established there in the persons of the two Michelis brothers—William in Naples and Alfred in Milan. They were men of 'restless' imagination. Alfred talked about the possibility of recording complete operas at La Scala. But the only singers he could persuade to come into their recording studio that summer were nonentities. In view of what Milan might have offered the Gramophone, it seemed almost a mockery.

Finally in the middle of July they arrived in Paris. Here was another city that offered great possibilities for the gramophone. But Alfred Clark dominated the situation in Paris in a way the Michelis brothers had not begun to equal in Italy. Fred Gaisberg was to remember especially this first foreign meeting with his colleague of Washington and Philadelphia days.

Alfred Clark had all the vision of youthful enthusiasm, and it was not long before he had enticed to his recording studio the great stars of the opera and concert halls. . . . I recorded the first discs in Paris in 1899 under Alfred Clark's direction. Cleve Walcott, his assistant, would record simultaneously the same artists on cylinders, as he was then building up both a cylinder and a disc catalogue. But before long the . . . cylinder was abandoned and he concentrated only on disc records.[2]

Clark had done a remarkable job of preparation for the recording experts' visit. He had recruited some of the most notable performers from the world of the *Café concert*, in addition to distinguished singers from the *Opéra* and *Opéra Comique*. And somehow he had secured the services of a veritable *doyen* of French singing, the fifty-six-year-old Melchissedec, whose orotund and plummy baritone was there and then recorded for the instruction and edification of students and amateurs alike.

[1] Typescript article, 'All Roads Lead to La Scala'.

[2] From an untitled typescript article devoted to the beginnings of the Gramophone in France.

Paris might well have made a triumphant conclusion to the recording expedition, but Alfred Clark thought that his friends ought to venture across the Pyrenees to Spain. He also had money with which to finance the journey. Early in August, therefore, Gaisberg and Darby went to Madrid, where some dozens of records were made. A few days later they went on to Valencia, thinking perhaps even to see what Lisbon might hold. But all this was anti-climax after Paris. Fred Gaisberg, finding himself master of an uncertain situation, rather self-consciously began a formal diary:

> Thursday Aug. 17th 99. Plaza de Montesino, Valencia. . . . Here again the terrible uncertainty of whether to proceed to Lisbon or return to Madrid seized us, and for two hours we sat discussing the pros and cons. Our fate was decided when we discovered our luggage was already placed on the relief train and we sprang aboard . . . [then] the station-master informed us no connections for Lisbon would be made that day, but if we waited for *Manãna* ('tomorrow') connections would surely be made.
>
> Already knowing that a Spaniard's 'tomorrow' means 'never', we quickly had our luggage transferred to the Madrid train and at 7 o'c p.m. we re-journeyed over the same ground travelled last night—sad, tired, and provoked. However, before starting we invested 9p. in a sausage, three rolls, and a bottle of wine. This we tackled with great relish, as we were nearly famished.
>
> The night was awfully close, and as these European railroad carriages give no draft (as there is no vestibule) we suffered awfully from the heat and thirst caused by the salty sausage.
>
> Friday Aug. 18th 99. We entered Madrid at 8 in the morning. . . . Arriving at the station we finally accomplished the difficult task of registering trunks, and tried to find a place in the coach—but they were all full. At last, finding an empty seat, I jumped in and sat down just as a fat matron with a bitter tongue claimed it. I refused to move, and she plumped down in my lap and there remained, while Darby on the outside frantically ran about looking for me. At last I gave her a push and slipped out from beneath her, and she fell back into the seat with a jar. Then Darby got in, and as the fat woman got out of the car to give the seat to her daughter for whom

she was preserving it, Darby slapped himself into it, and immediately two men and the old woman yelled and pulled and tugged and punched at him. Finally he had to give it up, and with a long face squeezed himself in a place opposite, and then it was my turn to laugh.

Well, the ride was the worst I ever endured. This was our third successive night on a train—and that in a car so crowded that one had to sleep as in a straight-jacket.

Saturday Aug. 19th 99. . . . Just before reaching the frontier a lady and gentleman entered our coach. The gentleman was deaf and dumb, and the lady surprised me by addressing me in English. I had a nice chat with her. She is a Spanish–American, her husband is an American artist. Later on I brought out the gramophone, and the old fellow was highly delighted because he was able to hear it. . . .

Reaching Bordeaux about 6 o'c, we drove to the quay and engaged our passage to London on the S.S. *Albatross*. The vessel is a trading steamer—carries mostly freight, wine, and canned fruit. She makes an average of 12 miles an hour. . . .

On their arrival back at Maiden Lane, William Barry Owen was pleased with the success of the recording expedition—so pleased that he arranged for Fred Gaisberg and Sinkler Darby to attempt a similar circuit of cities in the British Isles to commence almost immediately. By 3 September they were off to Glasgow:

4th, Monday. Arrived early in fine condition. Put up at Cockburn Hotel. Darby set up machine while I went with Buchanan (who met us in the morning) to see our agents and artists. . . .

5th, Tuesday. Started record-taking with Miss Jessie MacLoughlan, the first singer of Scotch songs in Scotland. Mr. Buchanan (her husband) will act as our regular accompanist.

6th, Wednesday. More record making. . . .

Then comes a comment that measures the young recording expert's distance, even at this stage of his career, from the ordinary loyal employee carrying out his assigned task:

Very poor artists. They would be run out of town in Italy. Scotch songs and music are good, characteristic and original, but its singers are poor, lacking quality and evenness of tone.

Since these records were intended largely for local sale, such international comparison was commercially beside the point. But as this tour went on, its results emerged clearly in Fred Gaisberg's opinion as a virtual insult to the gramophone, on a ground that would have occurred to very few in 1899—the machine's artistic potential. Thus in Belfast on 14 September: 'There are very few good singers at all in this city.' And the artists they found in Dublin a few days later were 'a poor, conceited lot'.

But in Dublin they met two chorus members from a local production of *The Greek Slave* that starred the popular Maud Boyd. Fred saw at least one opportunity: 'They happened to mention that Miss Boyd was to take dinner with them tomorrow, and I made them promise to bring Miss Boyd over to make a record.' All day Thursday they waited.

> A very disappointing day from a record-making standpoint. Miss Boyd did not appear during the day, but upon going to dinner that evening I discovered the whole crowd of them and reminded them of their promise, and after a good lot of coaxing they followed me over. Miss Boyd proved a charming lady with a grand, big voice. She sang 'The Golden Isle' from *The Greek Slave*, and a sweet girl, Mrs. Medlicott, played her accompaniment.

This was the only moment of the entire British tour circuit that was to give anything like real success. Cardiff was the final city on their list:

> 30th [September], Saturday was a very busy day, between taking the Rhondda Male Choir and a few other artists, and getting packed up at both hotels. The members of the Rhondda Glee Choir are hardy colliers from the coal districts. All are swarthy and of a small frame, but they take an absorbing interest in their music. They sing with great precision and show good drilling.
>
> In Wales there is at present a vocal prodigy craze among all classes. Every dairy maid or collier's child is watched and studied in hopes that in him or her might exist a future Patti or DeReszke.

When Fred and Sinkler Darby arrived back in London at the beginning of October, William Barry Owen was not dissatisfied.

A fortnight later Fred dined at Owen's home. During the evening the Managing Director presented the young recording expert with one thousand shares of Gramophone Company stock.

For the remainder of autumn 1899, Fred Gaisberg stayed in London. It was during these months that the military crisis in South Africa began to occupy everyone's attention. 'Raw recruits facing a Gatling gun', Fred scribbled at the back of his notebook as an idea for a miniature drama that could be mounted in the recording studio. But then his actor friend Russell Hunting, who had recently arrived in London, offered a better suggestion:

> .... a descriptive record entitled 'The Departure of the Troopship', with crowds at the quayside, bands playing the troops up the gang-plank, bugles sounding 'All ashore', farewell cries of 'Don't forget to write', troops singing 'Home, sweet home', which gradually receded in the distance, and the far-away mournful hoot of the steamer whistle.
>
> The record became enormously popular and eventually historic. It brought tears to the eyes of thousands, among them those of Melba, who declared in my presence that this record influenced her to make gramophone records more than anything else. I was directly and solely responsible for acquiring 'The Departure of the Troopship' for my company, and, together with my good colleague Russell Hunting, its author, staged the recording.

The acquisition of such artists as Melba still lay some distance in the gramophone's future, but 1899 had brought a great expansion of horizons. In comparison, private frustrations counted less. Near the year's end, Fred discovered that nearly two months had slipped away since his diary had been opened: 'The lapse of time between my last entry and that of Dec. 9th was hardly worth recording as no occurrence of importance transpired, excepting probably my becoming a stockholder in the English Gramophone Co., and the breaking off of the engagement between Miss Hall and myself due to Mrs. Hall attempting to force a speedy marriage. . . . I spent many pleasant evenings at the home of Mr. Owen, and for the rest led a typical life of a London bachelor.'

There were always to be women in the background of Fred

Ia Emile Berliner (*lower left*) with the laboratory staff at 1410 Pennsylvania Avenue, Washington, D.C., ca. 1897: Werner Suess (*lower right*); (*upper left to right*) Fred Gaisberg, William Sinkler Darby, Gloetzner, Joe and Zip Sanders

Ib Fred's first holiday home from Europe, Christmas 1899: (*lower left to right*) Mr. and Mrs. Gaisberg, Carrie, Isabel; (*upper left to right*) Emma and her husband Rudolf Forster, Will, Charles, Fred, Louise

II The first Gramophone studio in London, 31 Maiden Lane, 1898. The Recording Department secretary and accompanist, Amy Williams, is seated at the studio piano, which is raised so that its sound can be captured by a recording horn adjusted to the height of a singer's mouth

Thinking about Christmas!!

Why not a . . . . .

Gramophone

This style . . .

Price complete, with Brass Horn,

£5 10 0 Nett Cash.

RECORDS, extra, 2s. 6d. each, nett cash.

Other styles, £2 2s., £3 3s., £4 4s., £5 10s., £6 10s., £7 10s., £10

A **GRAMOPHONE** makes a capital present. Welcome everywhere and by everybody. Endless amusement for the festive season. Pleases your family and friends. It more than takes the place of a piano, banjo, mandolin, or cornet, for you hear not only one, but all these instruments, and many more, as they are played, not by amateurs, but by the most celebrated artists. No matter how remote your habitation, it brings within the family circle the actual voices of orators, singers, comedians, and story-tellers, who perhaps at that very moment are delighting Metropolitan audiences with the same eloquence, melody, humour, and dialect that is coming from the Gramophone in the quiet of a country home hundreds of miles away.

NO LIMIT TO SELECTIONS.

There is practically no limit, either in number, quality, variety, or freshness. For instance, no sooner does an artist become a popular favourite than he or she is invited to sing or play for us, into a Gramophone. As many reproductions are possible from one such performance, we can secure the very highest talent, and what costs us originally £20 to £100 can be sold for 2s. 6d.

GRAMOPHONES can be seen, heard, and purchased at all music shops, fancy dealers, stores, &c., all over the country.

Manufactured and Guaranteed by the . .

GRAMOPHONE Co., Ltd., Maiden Lane, Strand, London, W.C.

CATALOGUES FREE, WITH NAME OF OUR NEAREST AGENT.

Do not forget it amongst your Xmas Gifts.

II An advertisement of 1900

IV The first recording trip to the Continent, 1899.
a. Recording in Budapest: Fred Gaisberg at the piano, Theodore Birnbaum, Marcella Lindh, Sinkler Darby
b. A letter home from Vienna: Sinkler Darby and Fred writing in their hotel room, which doubled as a temporary recording laboratory

Gaisberg's bachelor existence, but private life was for him a thing apart. In February 1900, for instance, several names appear in the diary as if they had been taken for granted all along:

> 25th, Sunday. . . . I went to take Miss Waite's package to Miss Edell's, and there spent a delightful afternoon, at the same time taking tea with them. Returning to town, I dropped in at the Horse Show, and to my great surprise who should I see sitting there but Henrietta. I hardly recognised her at first. She looked entirely prosperous, and decked out in fine dresses and jewels. She tried to urge on me to enter old associations with her, but I stoutly resisted the magnetism of her beautiful brown eyes. She waxed most furious. What an uncontrollable passion this spoilt beauty has!
>
> 26th, Monday. After work Henrietta met me at the office, where we had a short dance and singing. Then after supper we went to the gallery of the Savoy Theatre to see *The Rose of Persia* on Newton's invitation. She followed me all the way to my Kensington lodgings, where I abruptly left her.

The same system of water-tight compartments had emerged when Fred went home to share the Christmas holidays at the end of 1899 with his family in Washington. He spent just over a week with them. On 26 December:

> I gave a concert at the Mission, and from there Carrie, Charlie, Louise, and I drove in a cab to Emma's, where we finished out the evening.

But after that, attention was turned to the Gramophone:

> 27th, Wednesday. I took the train for Phila. to report in Johnson's shop for work on new process. . . .'

For two years Eldridge Johnson had been secretly experimenting with the use of a wax engraving process for cutting 'master' disc recordings. Of course the wax process seemed to belong to the cylinder patents. And the atmosphere of competition between cylinder and disc had been growing more and more bitter with each new Gramophone success. Since Fred Gaisberg's departure eighteen months before, the cylinder manufacturers had begun to fear the Gramophone's competition so greatly that they had hired a lawyer to try to discover some way in which the gramophone had infringed older cylinder patents. The lawyer was a clever man, and at length he had been able to obtain a court order restraining the sale of the Gramophone and its products throughout the United States.

This of course directly affected Frank Seaman and his National Gramophone Company—the sales division of the Berliner interests. And Seaman had then decided that his own fortunes no longer lay with Berliner. So he had quietly set up businesses to manufacture and sell his own disc products, which he called 'Zonophone'. Thereupon Seaman's orders for both Berliner records and Johnson gramophones had suddenly come to a complete halt. Johnson told Fred Gaisberg that he now feared Seaman might further double-cross them by attempting to form an alliance with the cylinder interests.

It was clear that if the gramophones made at Johnson's factory were to be sold, Johnson himself had better sell them. And if Berliner's patent protection was really threatened, then Johnson would have to find a way of making the disc records as well. Thus Johnson's experiments with wax materials represented what he felt was the only possible precaution he could take. Regardless of who seemed to control which patents, the firm that made the best recordings might well win the day. The use of wax as a basic recording material must result in better sound Johnson felt, because the process of cutting in wax made a far smoother groove than etching in zinc could do. The difficulty had been to find a way of converting an original recording made in soft wax into a metal negative—a disc having ridges instead of grooves, which gave the means of pressing positive copies for the market. This wax-positive-to-metal-negative problem had now been solved.

Johnson then went on to describe another discovery that had come on the heels of the first. If records could be produced by a positive-negative-positive process without appreciable loss of quality, they could probably be manufactured in five phases as well—by adding a second negative and a third positive stage. The importance of this was obvious. When the whole process relied on just one negative, the entire supply of positive copies had to derive from that one negative. Fred knew that only five hundred to a thousand copies could be anticipated before a negative wore out, and even in 1899 this had begun to pose a problem. Some discs had already sold so well that the demand for copies had exhausted the plate: then there was no alternative but to ask the artist to record the same selection all over again. If Johnson had now found a way to produce secondary negatives at a later stage, this would permit such a multiplication of copies that the original negative matrix need never be exhausted. And this part of Johnson's thinking was immediately available to them, whatever the result of contentions over the wax recording process.

Fred Gaisberg spent most of January 1900 at the Johnson factory in Camden, leaving weekends for the family in Washington. On the 24 January he sailed eastward once again. The voyage was an interesting one.

> My second Atlantic crossing brought me into contact with the *Belle of New York* company, coming to London to launch that wonderful operetta. . . . This led to Frank Lawton recording his famous whistling solo. Even beautiful Edna May herself, the dazzling daughter of a Schenectady letter carrier, sang her 'Follow On' song. Were we thrilled when she entered our grimy studio?

What had begun as a family holiday was thus turned to account in still another way. If the Gramophone could begin to attract performers of this calibre, the tact of an agent might be as important a qualification for the successful recording expert as any technical skill.

Chapter Five

FRED GAISBERG had been back in London for less than a month when an opportunity came that was to test all his skills.

> 28th [Feb., 1900], Wed. Am informed I go to St. Petersburg on Friday to make records with Darby, whom I pick up at Berlin.

It meant that the very next evening, Thursday, would be his last in London for some time. Fred secured a pair of front stalls for Leslie Stuart's *Floradora* at the Lyric Theatre and asked William Barry Owen's daughter Jennie to go with him.

At the theatre their seats were immediately behind the conductor, a young man of about Fred's age called Landon Ronald:

> My attention was quickly concentrated on this dynamic person with his easy command of the orchestra and the stage. It seemed to throw me into a hypnotic state. . . . I made enquiries and found that this young man of 27 had unexpectedly valuable associations with Covent Garden and a broad experience among the very people that our Company was desirous of interesting in recording. . . .
>
> It is important to reflect what a primitive little affair the gramophone was in 1900. . . . Whenever we approached the great artists, they just laughed at us and replied that the gramophone was only a toy. In Landon Ronald [I] saw the agent who could bring us into contact with these unapproachables . . . and when, for two hours, I had watched the dynamic youngster conduct, I said to myself, 'That's the man our company needs.'
>
> . . . I immediately searched for him behind the stage, disclosed who I was and explained to him in what way he could

be of use to me and my Company. . . . Ronald recited his qualifications—associate conductor at Covent Garden, accompanist to Melba, Patti, Plançon, Renaud, and so on. For our young company it was like finding the Koh-i-Noor diamond.[1]

Before he left for Russia the following day, Fred told William Barry Owen about this interview, and Landon Ronald eventually agreed to becoming the Company's 'Musical Advisor' and talent scout. It was the beginning of an association that was to last until Ronald's death almost forty years later.

Meanwhile Fred Gaisberg had started on his long journey across Europe. After a few days in Hanover and Berlin, he and Sinkler Darby found themselves travelling eastward.

7th [March], Wednesday. We started our trip for Russia at 9.18 Friedrichsstrasse [Station]. The day was very beautiful, and we enjoyed the rest. 10 o c. that evening we reached the Russian frontier at Eidkunen, where our agent met us to assist us declaring our apparatus. This was indeed a tough job. Every one of our 7 cases was opened the contents taken out. Our duty bill amounted to £7. At 1 o c. a.m. we resumed our journey in a very good sleeper (except for the candles used for illuminating). After a sound night's rest, we had a breakfast of tea and bread.

8th, Thursday. The day is beautiful and the country is covered with a heavy fall of snow, and at the different stops en route the natives are interesting, wrapped up in their heavy sheep-skins and bear-robes. We would give a gramophone concert at these stops, and the amusement of the natives was great to see. I really think that the train tarried an extra long time so we could finish our concert. We took a number of interesting photographs of these motley mobs listening to our concert. The snow around here must be about 3 ft deep, covering the fences.

On arriving at the station at St. Petersburg we were met by Blumenfeld, Raphoff, and Lebel, our agents. They escorted us to a small hotel in Liteingry Prospect near Nevsky, and after a wash-up we went to a large café for supper. Over this we lingered until 11 o c, when we retired.

[1] Combined from 'Sir Landon Ronald', in *The Gramophone*, Sept. 1938, p. 147 and *Music on Record*, pp. 41–2.

9th, Friday. We set up our apparatus and made our different purchases. I rode in a sleigh to the station to bring up our luggage. All the vehicles are on runners. The ground is covered with ice from Nov. to April. The Neva is frozen five to six feet thick, and every winter an electric trolley-line is laid on the ice crossing the river. The effect of Petersburg on a stranger and southerner is very fascinating. I wanted to be out in a sleigh all the time, watching the dashing sleighs and their occupants so warmly clad in their heavy furs. . . .

The local dealers in Gramophone products had joined forces to introduce the two young Americans to their country. Behind the façade of co-operation, jealousy and corruption were rife. Almost immediately Fred began to find himself the recipient of unsought confidences. Raphoff, for example, 'would draw me apart and whisper in my ear: "Don't trust Lebel. He'd cheat his own father." Then Lebel would take me into a corner and advise me: "Look out for Raphoff: he seduced a girl-pupil and was transported to Siberia; he's only free because of the amnesty on the Romanoff Centenary." '[1]

11th, Sunday. . . . That evening we had tea at Lebel's home, and about 10 o'c we started for the most popular resort of Petersburg, *Christofski*—a sort of combination of a café and a music hall. Here we ordered dinner (starting with oysters at 4R. for ten) and with eating slowly and listening to the artists we managed to stretch our dinner out until 4 a.m. The programme consisted of chorus singing of folk-songs, solo singing of romances, balalaika-playing in solos and orchestras. . . . When we arrived at our hotel, morning was just beginning to break.

12th, Monday. We arose more dead than alive about 11 o'c. Today we made our first Russian plates—a comic singer. They were unsuccessful. We retired early that evening.

13th, Tuesday. We made records of Golitzner, a balalaika player, and harmonium.

14th, Wed. Made records of Blumen, a tenor. . . .

Gradually it became clear that the Russian agents had done very little recruiting of artists for the recording visit. If this

[1] In *Music on Record* (pp. 30–1) it was thought necessary to change Raphoff's name to 'Rappaport'.

expensive journey was to produce any sort of success, Fred and Sinkler Darby would have to draft themselves in effect to be their own agents:

> 21st, Wed. We became so desperate for talent that we set out together this evening in search. We first went to a song recital. . . . After the first part of the concert we went to the Opera House . . . and heard part of a production of *A Life for the Czar*. Soloists and chorus very good voices and strong; chorus badly trained, orchestra very much out of tune. The frequent and stubborn applause given the soloist by the audience was very annoying and interfered with the pleasure of an auditor. This is a great fault of a Russian audience. They spoil their artists—make pets of them. Indeed we found them for this reason hard to approach. They expect presents of diamonds and jewellery.

The star of the performance they had just seen was an enormous young bass called Chaliapin:

> We opened negotiations to record Chaliapin, but at that time he was still dizzy with success and would not respond to our humble offers. The same can be said of that marvellous lyric tenor Sobinov, who was even more spoilt and unattainable than Chaliapin.
>
> After the Opera we went to *Pompeii*, a brilliant *café chantant* of the *Christofski* order. Securing a chorus at this place, we returned home about 3 o'c cold and sleepy.

But this kind of donkey-work began to produce results.

> 22nd, Thursday. Made records of Nevsky. . . .

Peter Nevsky was a comedian and concertina-player of huge popularity. The records resulting from this session and that of the following day were to sell in thousands all over Russia.

> 23rd, Friday. Nevsky again; also Kamionsky, the baritone from the Opera, sang a few songs.

This was a singer of considerable eminence. Kamionsky's visit might well attract other operatic figures.

> 24th, Saturday evening, after letter writing, we attired in our frock coats and set out for *Pompeii*, where Lebel and

Raphoff had promised to join us. They did not show up, but we enjoyed our dinner and the entertainment—especially the dancing by our Russian chorus. I engaged a very popular and good [Gypsy] romance-singer also . . . returned about 3 a.m.

On 6 April several 'Opera celebrities' came to the little studio to make records, among them a beautiful young soprano called Radina.

April 8th, Sunday. We attended an afternoon performance of the opera *Demon* by Rubinstein. Radina was our *prima donna*—took the leading role and acquitted herself commendably. Between the acts, we would present ourselves at the dressing-room of our beautiful *prima donna* and congratulate her on her performance of the foregoing act. . . . I told her I wished I was the Devil in the last Act, when he was embracing her. . . .

The sojourn in St. Petersburg was drawing to a close. Raphoff, perhaps fearing the reports that would be made in Hanover and London, had begun at last to bestir himself. Several days earlier they had all gone in evening dress to the home of a princess to give a gramophone exhibition. Raphoff had promised that it would lead them all to great things. He hinted at an invitation to record the voice of the Czar himself.

When Gaisberg and Darby returned from *The Demon* that Sunday afternoon, there was a message from Raphoff. They were 'to prepare to give a recording exhibition before the Czar's secretary that evening'. The demonstration was to take place in the palace of the Grand Duke Michael.

We drove in a sleigh with our apparatus to the great palace, where we were directed to the servants' entrance. We passed the guards, who examined us suspiciously, and were shown by a major-domo, with his snub Russian nose in the air, to a corner in a vast salon, furnished with chandeliers, tapestries, and soft Persian carpets. With bated breath we set up our modest outfit near a Steinway grand piano.

Just after nine o'clock the company trooped out from the dining room and ranged themselves round our machine. There was His Excellency General Bobrikoff, Chancellor Lerche (Secretary to the Czarina), and Alexander Taneiev. Taneiev's two lovely young daughters and his two sons were also present with their mother. As they came up one by one and introduced themselves to me I was amazed and almost ashamed at having had to come the whole way to Russia to hear such flawless English. Each of them was ready with an impromptu message for the recording trumpet. To crown all Taneiev himself, a great musician, played one of his own compositions on [the] wonderful Steinway.

Then Fred, and Sinkler Darby amused the company by performing 'a negro ditty' while recording it at the same time. They had brought with them their etching tank and acid, so that within twenty minutes it was possible to play back all these records for the company. 'They served us with tea & fruit, and treated us fine.'

After that evening, they waited for several days, but there was no Royal Command to record the voice of the Czar. Still, recording in Russia had been in the end a success. Fred could summarise the results of his first journey as 'a rich programme performed by Russian choruses, by gypsy singers, among whom was the beloved Panina, and by such artists as the Romance-singer Tamara.'

On the return journey, Fred, and Sinkler Darby made a recording visit to Warsaw.

16th April, Monday. This evening I attended a performance of the Polish National Opera, *Halka*. . . . The Opera House was large and handsome, and the people were well-dressed. The orchestra was good, and on the whole a better performance than I saw in Petersburg . . . [I] was spellbound by the beautiful singing and acting. . . . The *prima donna* Krusceniski was excellent. . . . She is a great favourite.

Later in the week Krusceniski agreed to come to the studio they had set up in the hotel to make records. She was followed by other leading singers of the Opera, including the soprano Messal —'beautiful and equally fine in opera and operetta'—and a marvellous young bass called Didur. But they were not easy to deal with: 'In common with all Polish artists they were suspicious of us and made us pay in advance before they sang. The artists in Russia were more trusting.'

By the end of the week a considerable number of really good records had been made, and Gaisberg and Darby were exhausted. On Friday night they retired early to bed and slept soundly.

> ... About 2 a.m. we were awakened by terrible battering on our door. The porter and three or four others wanted to know what terrible happenings were going on, the room below was all dripping with what might be blood or something deadly, and was falling on the face of the sleeping occupant. We went into our 'lab' and to our dismay found a bucket filled with old acid had sprung a leak, and the floor was flooded. ... The bright red fluid dripped through the ceiling on to the sleeping guest; when his body began to smart he roused the hotel. We had the disagreeable task of sopping it up in our night-shirts, and expecting the manager up every moment to pitch us out bag and baggage.

In the event the management was placated, but when they came to depart on the Monday 'our hotel bill included 14R. charges for repairing the room under our lab.' On that note of East European serio-comic misadventure ended the most far-reaching and successful Gramophone recording tour yet carried out.

Fred had hardly arrived back in London before he was sent to Italy again in June. His companion this time was Eldridge Johnson's friend Belford Royal. Royal had been asked to go because, as Fred noted in his diary: 'We had with us both the new Johnson process and the old etching process.'[1] Johnson had decided to brave the American patent storm, found his own company, and begin recording in wax. The Gramophone Company in London had purchased the European rights to Johnson's process, and Fred Gaisberg was to make his attempts at wax recording under the supervision of Belford Royal.

Disc making began in Milan in the middle of June. The greater sensitivity of the wax process tempted them to try recording vocal solos with an orchestral accompaniment. It could be only a few instruments at best, but the verisimilitude and atmosphere of the operatic excerpts especially would be deci-

[1] Diary entry for 14 June, 1900. It is erroneously stated in *Music on Record* (p. 48) that the wax process was first used for the Milan recordings of March and April 1902. Gelatt's *The Fabulous Phonograph* (p. 111) gives the correct date.

sively enhanced. In the centre of each new disc Fred wrote under the singer's name the two significant words, 'with orchestra'.

Recording in wax also brought a new difficulty: there was no way to develop a playable positive on the spot, as could be done simply by etching the old zinc plates. Every finished wax had to be carefully packed unheard and shipped to the factory at Hanover for a negative plate to be developed. Only from this negative could a positive be developed in a material hard enough to permit its being played without damage.

In Rome they pursued the real quarry of this journey to Italy:

> 27th June. In the afternoon we had a conference with Sig. Federici, the party who is supposed to engineer us to obtain the Pope's voice.

But negotiations broke down somewhere in the extravagant web of intentions and understandings spun by the Michelis brothers, and the gramophone did not come as close to Leo XIII as it had to the Czar of Russia. In the end there was nothing for it but to turn homeward. On the way northward Fred made some more records in Milan: 'These include Grand Opera choruses with orchestral accompaniment, solos with orchestral accompaniment—so far the most pretentious yet attempted on a talking machine.'

In London during the autumn of 1900, the most notable visitors to the recording room in Maiden Lane came from the world of operetta. Leslie Stuart and Paul Rubens arrived to play and accompany selections from their own currently running West End successes. With them came Ada Reeve, Maud Marsden, and a young baritone who was already becoming a firm favourite in the Savoy operas of Gilbert and Sullivan, Henry Lytton.

> The tunes from the autumn productions at Daly's, the Gaiety and Shaftesbury Theatres were of vital importance to our Christmas sales . . . *Floradora* . . ., *The Geisha* . . ., *Belle of New York* with Edna May were hits that made a gramophone Christmas list of rich fare for our dealers in the year 1900. When we counted the profits on that Christmas Eve, our eyes were opened and, for the first time, we caught a glimpse of the rich possibilities of the gramophone.[1]

[1] 'The First Christmas with "His Master's Voice".'

It was announced that the Gramophone Company would expand its manufacturing interests. William Barry Owen had always felt that the popularity of the gramophone was a temporary phenomenon, and he had persuaded the directors to diversify. Henceforth they would also make and sell a new kind of typewriter. The firm would be known as 'The Gramophone and Typewriter Company Ltd.'. The capital had been enlarged to £600,000, and a dividend was to be paid. Fred Gaisberg's cheque, when it arrived, amounted to £126. All in all the end-of-year fortunes ought to be marked in a more social way.

To celebrate this success I gave a dance in the recording studio in our Maiden Lane premises. I remember that our guests of honour were George Power and his wife Kate Sargent. George Power (Tyrone Power's uncle) was a very fine comedian. He set the pace which carried us through the night and led us away from the offices, and we eventually finished up at the Covent Garden Ball.[1] [A notable figure at this celebration was Belford Royal.] Having spent many years at sea as an engineer, he had a sailor's taste for public-houses. He was normally shy and awkward in society, but nevertheless he so forgot himself that he did a sailor's reel and hornpipe. Sailor-like, he overdid the whoopee, and it was not long before he looked very untidy and became tired. He dropped into the background and we lost sight of him until about noon the next day, when, on going through the shop, our manager discovered him at work at the bench in his evening clothes and top hat.

[1] 'The First Christmas with "His Master's Voice".'

Chapter Six

EARLY IN 1901 the Russian agent Raphoff turned up in London. Fred found his impression of the previous spring more than confirmed: 'He is a brilliant man and a true artist, but a devil for intrigue and foxiness. He put some bad notions in my head concerning breaking away from the Company. He is said to have caused his partner Skuridin to commit suicide.'

Raphoff had made the journey to London to encourage the Company to send a further recording expedition to St. Petersburg. He considered an immediate venture indispensable to the burgeoning market there. William Barry Owen agreed, but demands for recording services were coming in from every quarter. Already there was more than Fred Gaisberg and Sinkler Darby could properly manage. And from America came news that Eldridge Johnson had perfected a new recording disc of ten inches' diameter, which offered a playing time of up to three full minutes. This was of incalculable importance to the cause of serious music recording: there were very few arias, songs, or piano pieces that could be fitted onto a seven-inch, two-minute disc without abridging, but a three-minute playing time offered a wider scope for classical repertoire. Both developments suggested an increase in the recording staff.

Fred, remembering his brother Will's disappointment over not joining Berliner four years earlier, saw his opportunity.

> 22nd March 1901. I am endeavouring to get my brother Will over here with me. Mr. Owen has sanctioned the idea, and has offered him £4 per week. [Meanwhile,] I had a huge task making preparations for my Russian trip.... Friday night I leave the Victoria Station, bound for Flushing.... This trip is to last 2 weeks, as I am to be in London by the

10th of April to meet Royal, who will initiate me in the making of big [10 inch] plates.

The morning of 25 March found Fred Gaisberg arriving in St. Petersburg for the second time: 'A heavy snow was falling and the weather very cold, so my hopes for a regular Russian winter were fulfilled.' At the station he was met by the Company's new Russian manager, Rodkinson.

> I am to stay with Mr. Rodkinson, who lives over his offices. My lab is nicely adapted for the work. I met Mrs. Rodkinson at dinner—a very sweet lady. The day occupied in making preparations. In the evening we had a game of cards. [Rodkinson was] the well-educated son of a Russian-American Rabbi. [He] was handsome and ruthless in business and love, his two absorbing pursuits. He pretended to speak Russian well, but he stuttered so badly that he was never able to convince me of this claim. The combination of Russian and American business methods, introduced by him, showed a versatility that amazed even the hardened Polish and Russian-Jewish dealers of the old Russian Empire.
>
> It is possible that Rodkinson was not so corrupt and that it could all be traced to his stuttering. He would begin by making it known that his wife's birthday was in April—or that his own birthday or wedding anniversary was in March—and that, of course, credit to a certain dealer would be reduced unless he d-d-d-. The dealer in question, without waiting for him to finish, would rush out to a jeweller's and return with a diamond brooch or a gold watch with a card saying 'Many Happy Returns of the Day'. The tap of credit would be given one or two more turns according to the purity of the diamond or the weight of the gold watch. . . .
>
> One day on coming home . . . he greeted me on the doorstep of his apartment, saying:
>
> 'C-c-come here, Fred. I want to show you s-s-something.' With that he threw open the door of his salon, in which an array of gifts was displayed, comprising silver samovars, cut-glass vases, gold cigarette cases, baskets of hot-house fruit and elaborate photograph frames.
>
> 'L-l-look, Fred', he said, 'at the response to my birthday. Don't they l-l-love me?'[1]

[1] In *Music on Record*, Rodkinson's name is disguised as 'Max Rubinsky'.

27th March, Wednesday. We went to the opera *Eugene Onegin* by Tchaikovsky. The performance was given by the Imperial Opera troupe at the Conservatory of Music. It was a very fine production. The tenor, Sobinov, and the baritone, Maxakov, were especially good actors. . . .

When approached this time, the 'unattainable' Sobinov actually agreed to record. And during Fred's fortnight in St. Petersburg quite a number of other opera singers visited his studio—Anna Kravetz, the tenor Labinski, Sharanov, Maxakov, and the wonderful bass Buchtoiarov. One day some of the Imperial Opera Chorus crowded round the horn to record a few discs. Only the great Chaliapin remained aloof from the Gramophone's most tempting offers.

Nevertheless the Russian agents had been right. Whatever shortcomings they had, these merchants took the gramophone seriously. Just how seriously, Fred was soon to discover:

April 5th, Friday. The last few days have been much warmer and the streets are sloppy. During the morning I completed my packing and in the afternoon Mrs. Rodkinson and I went out to do some shopping. . . .

While passing through the new Arcade I was surprised to see Mrs. Raphoff in a shop, and upon further inspection I noticed the shop was newly and elegantly fitted up and well stocked with gramophones and talking machines. I asked Mrs. Rodkinson to excuse me for a short while, and I stepped in the shop to say 'How do you do' to Mrs. Raphoff; and who should I find there but old Raphoff himself.

Raphoff explained he was just starting a new *magasin*, and showed me over the place. We then stepped out to have a bottle of wine together. Over our wine he explained to me his enmity towards Rodkinson, and we talked of other things.

One of the 'other things' was a cool proposal by which Raphoff and his friend Lebel, now established as the Company's agent in Moscow, might turn the tables on the Gramophone people and form a rival syndicate. Fred found himself being invited to join. The reply was too easy. One merely pointed to the long list of recording successes just completed, with Sobinov heading the list. The Gramophone was beginning to command the respect of many artists. And now there was the prospect of a large record that could play for three minutes.

Catching the wind from that quarter, Raphoff smoothly reversed. Naturally, 'to be a success in business one had to be *frech* (Yiddish or German slang for "fresh").' That was why he was congratulating his young friend on enticing all those eminent artists to record for him. And that was just why he himself had 'at once opened [his] *de luxe* Gramophone store on the Nevsky Prospect, with red-plush chairs and potted palms complete. He also advised affixing a red label to the . . . Sobinov records and selling them for £1 each. Needless to say, only the aristocracy and the wealthy merchants could afford to own a gramophone. . . .'

Now they *must* get Chaliapin, Raphoff was saying. And why not the fabulous Nikolai Figner, first tenor of the Imperial Opera—and then his wonderful Italian wife Medea Mei? The Figners had the highest distinction: had they not been the friends of Tchaikovsky and created the leading roles in his operas? If they could snare such birds as these, there would be some other records worthy of the red label. After all, as Raphoff pointed out to Fred, 'having fitted out the first *de luxe* Gramophone shop, he simply had to have something to sell.'[1]

> It was this rogue who, to secure goods of distinction for his emporium, always forced us to attempt the impossible in music and artists. Still, he lifted us out of our 'small town' mentality.

At the end of their interview, Raphoff walked out triumphantly with Fred: 'He asked me to take some presents, which he would purchase, to London for distribution among his various friends. This I did. He made frequent use of the words "Never mind! I make the grosse Akklam!" ' (When later Fred told this to Ed Footman, the Company's book-keeper in Maiden Lane, they both gleefully pounced on it as their by-word of the moment.) As they parted, Raphoff insisted that Gaisberg must return as soon as ever he had the ten-inch recording plates. He would find many artists now eager to record.

Early in April 1901 the 254 new records Fred had made in St. Petersburg were on their way to the pressing plant in Hanover, and Fred himself was back in London:

> Monday, 8th April. I drove to the office and there met

[1] 'When I crossed the ocean . . .'

Royal & Mr. Owen. That day we made a few big records, and in the evening we had dinner at Mr. Owen's.

Tuesday 9th. This evening we saw the first night of the Alice Nielsen Opera Co. in *The Fortune Teller*. We (Ed, Royal, & I) enjoyed the clever work and Americanism exceedingly. Royal came over on the same boat as the troupe, and pointed out to us the different characters. We had supper at the Trocadero, where we met two of the troupe, Miss Dolly Weston & Miss Ida Hamilton—both very pretty Americans. After the supper, we went to the 'lab', where we had some dancing & singing.

Wednesday, 10th. . . . Tonight we had supper at the Troc again. . . .

Saturday, 13th. Troc & Miss Weston.

Record-making seemed suddenly to take second place in Fred Gaisberg's life:

During the month of May I worked on the 10 inch records, making a set of rather indifferent plates. . . . Most of my spare time was occupied in showing Miss Dolly Weston the sights of London. In fact every Sunday I spent with her. Here are my Sundays in their order:

[28th April] Went to Taplow to visit the Hydes. Spent a delightful day.

[5th May] Went to Richmond Park; dined at the Star & Garter. Row on the river.

[12th May] Concert at Albert Hall. Walk through Hyde Park. Attended St. Peter's Church (Italian), we heard Rossini's *Stabat Mater*.

[19th May] A ride on the river boats as far as Woolwich; a visit to Westminster Abbey, and to Vesper Service at St. Paul's in the afternoon; also in the evening attended [Herbert] Darnley's birthday party, where we met Dan Leno and Louie Freear.

[26th May] Visit to Brighton.

In the same month Will Gaisberg had been hired and would shortly be arriving in London. Rodkinson and Raphoff had persuaded Owen to send Fred yet again to Russia, this time to make records in Moscow. Yet these plans did not interrupt the diary's lyrical record of springtime Sundays.

The last day of May brought Will himself: 'Looks absolutely unchanged. The same staunch and manly fellow. He brings me serious news of Papa's failing in strength and the necessity of his retiring from business.' After Will's arrival there had been one more wonderful Sunday, and they made a threesome.

> Sunday, June 2nd. Will, Miss Weston, & I took an early train for Kingston-on-Thames and rowed up to Hampton Court, where we dined at the Mitre. Afterwards we went through the grounds and Palace. Had a perfect day. . . .

Fred was to start for St. Petersburg on the Wednesday evening. It was Derby Day, and it began with the tiniest cloud.

> Dolly went to the Derby with a S.A. fellow. She threatened not to go if I so desired it. Real good of her. Will & I, Ed [Footman] and Miss Scott all dined together at Gatti's. I caught my train at 8.25. . . .

The journey to Petersburg, with its delays and baggage examinations, was becoming a familiar experience. This time it seemed 'awfully uninteresting'. And when he arrived at the hotel Rodkinson had booked for him, that struck him as 'rather a second-class affair'. On the other hand, there was progress of a sort on the Russian Gramophonic scene.

> The morning was occupied in unpacking and setting up. As I passed the office, whom should I see but Raphoff. He was overjoyed to see me, and gave me the customary kiss. He is a comical devil—only a few months ago he and Rodkinson were mortal enemies, and now they are bosom friends. He claims to be doing £2,000 Gramophone business a month. He went along with us to assist in purchasing a piano.

The Rodkinsons had arranged a whirl of sight-seeing during Fred's few days in St. Petersburg—drives through the beautiful parks in the late evening light, boat rides along the canals of the Neva finishing up at a place called *Arcadia*, and a wonderful excursion north to Imatra in Finland, where they saw a great inland sea reflecting the midnight sun.

They made a few records in Petersburg, but soon Rodkinson announced that the time had come to proceed to the real object of Fred Gaisberg's long journey:

Took 10 o'c train for Moscow, 'the Mother of Russia'. Rodkinson and Herr Gross (the pianist) formed the party. The railway journey was marked by an incident that will always live in my memory. Occupying the opposite berth in my sleeping compartment was a distinguished gentleman. The conductor called to collect tickets. I produced mine but the gentleman fumbled in his pockets, unable to find his. The conductor said he would call later. Again the passenger excitedly searched his pockets but without success. This time the conductor was impatient and said he would return in an hour and if the ticket was not produced he would have to stop the train and expel the traveller. As the railway between St. Petersburg and Moscow is a straight line drawn on the map by Czar Alexander III, it passes through no town of any size. This time, my fellow-traveller, protesting frantically that he had a ticket but could not find it, was deposited in the open fields as the train stopped.

In Moscow, a few days later, Lebel showed me a newspaper account of a body being discovered near the railway track. On enquiries being made this was found to be M—, a government official travelling on a pass, which was discovered in the ticket-pocket of his waistcoat, just where a ticket should be carried.

At the conclusion of the journey they were met by Lebel, the Moscow agent.

We took quarters at the Hotel Continental. Set up and made 10 records. In the afternoon visited Lebel's shop.

That evening brought an experience which seemed somehow admonitory—though Fred himself suffered no inhibitions.

. . . . We dined at the most popular garden in Russia, *The Aquarium*—a place very similar to Earl's Court. Lebel, Rodkinson, Gross, & I formed the party. I could see they were out for a 'Bummel'—all married men. It impresses me as criminally shocking, the lax manner in which most men observe their marriage vows. After supper we went to the theatre. About 12 o'c we decided to have dinner in a cabinette, and instructed the head waiter to send us in four artists to sing for us. These happened to be a quartette of Austrian dancers and singers—very swell girls and lively. They spoke

German and one spoke English. Well, for three hours we raised Old Ned. . . . You could bathe in the champagne. When we left the sun was shining bright, but still the garden was in full swing.
Wednesday, June 19th. Resting up. A few records.

Then Fred received 'a nasty letter' from Dolly Weston.

I hate to give utterance to my disappointment in Dolly. The affair was more trivial than I could at first get myself to believe. It was simply a case of the fellow who has the most cash and is the greatest fool wins. I had not the first and was not the latter, so 'there you are' . . .

Fred's next reaction, however, set the whole experience in a very different light. He had had Dolly Weston's letter less than twenty-four hours before deciding that the best way to drown his sorrows would be in an extra recording trip and an extended stay:

So I urged Rodkinson to telegraph Birnbaum [the Manager at Hanover] privilege to take a trip to Kazan to make records.

Saturday 22nd. Answer received today 'Yes Go.' So it was decided I should make the trip in company of Lebel.

Sunday 23rd. I arose early and finished my packing. . . . About six o'clock Lebel called for me, and after disposing of our luggage we drove to the *Aquarium* for dinner, then to the station, where we took the 9.30 train for Nizy Novgorod. The distance is about 300 miles. . . .

As he sat in the train, Fred ruminated over his five days in Moscow. 'Altogether about 67 records', he noted—most of them the new ten-inch plates. But record for record it had yielded the richest harvest of really important discs yet produced anywhere. They had taken advantage of the Moscow Season to secure more and better discs of some of the singers recorded in Petersburg during April, as well as records of other artists new to the gramophone.

We were recording in Moscow the tenors Sobinov and Davidov, the baritone Tartakov, the Gypsy singers Tamara and Vialtzeva. There was also an attempt to obtain Chaliapin, but we waited in vain.

It was still a glimpse of the kind of day-to-day recording programme that might some day be possible.

Next morning they arrived at Nizy Novgorod.

> At 12 o'c we boarded our ship, which looks more like a three-storey house-boat with paddle-wheels. . . . Interesting, if for no other reason, was the fish dinner on the open deck of the steamer, during which the ragged, half-naked stevedores sang while loading sacks of meal and cement. Shall I ever forget the rhythmical swing as the green watermelons were passed from deck to barge? On every hand one heard music. . . . The haulers moved in rhythm to their song; the loafers on the docks or the passengers on the decks below, with a small concertina, mouth-organ, or balalaika, joined in groups.

Seated comfortably on deck, Fred described for his diary the passing scene as they went slowly down the Volga.

> The banks on either side are rather low—sand-drifts cause the pilot to be on the look-out continually. There is great traffic up and down the river. We pass a great number of barges carrying oil and wood, cotton, etc. . . . The day is beautiful and cool, and I am enjoying the trip immensely.

As the late evening drew on, a strange repeating cry came through the air. Looking up, Fred saw a man standing in the very prow of the vessel:

> Navigation is very uncertain as the sand-bars shift so continually, and a man is always stationed in the bow of the boat. He has a long pole with which he sounds the depth, and all during the night you can hear him calling out 'vocim', 'davit', meaning '8 ft.', '9 ft.' . . .

They reached Kazan the following morning, 25th June.

> The Russian part especially contains handsome buildings and churches. Streets are orderly, and there are plenty of parks. But the Tartar section is beyond doubt the dirtiest, filthiest vile-smelling place I have ever come across. All the Tartars have that peculiar Oriental smell about them that seems to asphyxiate you. I always feel faint when near them. They are quite Oriental in appearance—small eyes; expressionless, immobile features. The women of the better class are never seen.

Strict seclusion is enforced, and should they go out, it is always closely veiled. (The custom is a laudable one if all women are as ugly as the commoner class we see. . . .)

Unfortunately it was the recording of Tartar music that was the object of the trip. Arrangements had been made for an agent in Kazan, a man called Malokov—who might help to find the musicians for recording:

He took us around to the Hotel de France . . . where I rigged my outfit, and old Malokov chased out to get Tartar artists.

The first he brought in was a petrified, yellow-skinned accordion player with a musty smell to him. Very likely he did his best, but his music haunts me still. We asked him would he stop if we paid him 5R., and bring in someone who could sing. He agreed.

But those he brought were if possible worse:

. . . two vile-smelling creatures with little, squeezed-up eyes and broad, fat faces. Their love for hair made them tack on their heads a variety of greasy, mildewed strands of false hair until it reached to their knees. Their singing would bring tears to your eyes. The song would be a rhythm of about 8 bars, repeated over & over again, to the accompaniment of a 5th in the bass (accordion), organ-point fashion.

We asked the accordion-player if that was the best he could do, and he said it was. He said Tartars have no artists or places of amusement, and he had to recruit these people from disreputable resorts. . . .

Wed., 26th [June]. Our first people [this morning] were some Tartar students & their master. They sang us some songs. Then two more women . . . I wanted to take a photo of the two girls and they refused, saying, 'God would be displeased'. A Ruble induced them to forget 'Allah'. These girls instinctively cover their faces when a man looks at them. We tried to get them to take off the mantle when singing into the machine, but without it they were as embarrassed as young school girls.

The different songs these people sang sounded every one like the other.

By evening they were thoroughly sick of it all, but Fred decided to put his own talent-scouting once more to the test:

I met Lebel at the hotel, & we started out in company of our accordion friend to a Tartar wine house, where I lost all of the little respect I ever had for them—filth and smell no name. . . . They would crowd about 8 men & 8 women in an unventilated box of a room—in the centre a table with a kerosine lamp. The harmonica would start up one of the merry monotone dirges; then the crowd would join in and continue for half an hour with the most solemn expressions on their stony faces. Well, we saw all we could and got out as quick as possible.

There was nothing for it but to return to St. Petersburg by the laborious route he had come out. He was back on the last day of June.

I found there awaiting me numerous and urgent telegrams from home office directing me to return to London. However, I was worn out by running about so much so decided to remain a few days in Petersburg.

As the train took Fred Gaisberg back over the countryside of western Russia and Germany in early July 1901, he tried to summarise for himself the three journeys of his Russian experience so far: 'I had put in six months, beginning in a zero winter of deep snow, fur coats, and troikas, and finishing in a blazing summer of buzzing bees and flies. . . . I had seen opera performances on a scale unbelievably lavish. Only the wealthiest family in the world, the Romanovs, could support them. I had heard and negotiated with a bevy of the greatest and perhaps the most spoiled artists of that epoch. Added to this were my first impressions of Russian music, ballet, and decorative art, then at the height of their freshness and vigour. Another and totally strange world of music and people was opened up to me. I was like a drug addict now, ever longing hungrily for newer and stranger fields of travel. Already I began to lay plans for a trip to the Far East.'

As soon as Fred was back in London, however, he moved in another direction.

I struck Mr. Owen for a raise in salary. We concluded these terms: my salary was to be £12 a week for a year, then for the 2nd year it was to be £13 per week, and 3rd year to be £14 per week.

It was all done so easily now after the advances won for the Gramophone in Russia—and after Dolly Weston: '. . . I have her to thank for putting the spurs on me, as I made a decided proposition to the Company saying I must have a salary of twelve pounds a week or leave. You see what love will do. At that, I needed money. Everything balances up even in the end.'

Chapter Seven

THE REMAINDER of 1901 was spent amongst more familiar scenes. A recording trip to Milan and Paris in the late summer yielded successful results but no striking advances. Otherwise Fred Gaisberg's life was spent between the recording studio in Maiden Lane and his bachelor flat: 'I remained quietly all the Fall living comfortably with my brother Will & Ed [Footman]. In fact we live so quietly that I find it uninteresting trying to keep a diary.'

For the second time Fred went home to Washington for Christmas, and as he re-opened his diary to describe the visit he found himself writing as one who feels his lot has finally been cast.

> I reached home about 6 o'c p.m. [on Christmas night] and rang the front door bell. It was answered by the black girl, who gave the alarm. There was a rush—a bustle. Louise was first upstairs and in my arms. It was worth the long trip to see the joy on their faces. . . . My dear mother and father fairly cried and devoured me with their eyes to notice any change that time had wrought. All were in excellent health; and except for Isabel and Louise (who had grown taller) & my father & mother (who had become whiter) there was little change to note. Carrie remains quite the same, and dear old Charlie has the same generous, open face as of yore. . . . That night they would hardly let me go to sleep—so eager to have me every moment of my stay. . . .
>
> I spent two weeks of thorough happiness in their midst. To even try to recall those blissful days gives me a smothered pang indescribable. Possibly in my next visit home some one of those sincere, honest faces will be missing. Who among my friends could compare to them? . . .

During my stay I visited a few of my old acquaintances—for I am sorry to say of the years I have spent in Washington I can count but one friend, and that is Emile Berliner.

Fred also spent a few days in Philadelphia and Camden, where affairs were in better order than two years ago. Eldridge Johnson had persuaded Berliner that the Johnson organisation offered the best means for manufacturing both gramophones and records. Berliner had agreed to throw in his lot with Johnson's new company, which had been named—in a crudely effective summary of past events—the Victor. Now it looked as if it might be possible to bury the hatchet with the phonograph interests: they had recently begun to manufacture flat discs as well, and everyone was beginning to realise that the pursuit of literal obligations over this patent or that idea was a course that would benefit only the lawyers.

The American visit drew to a close, and Fred sailed for England once more: 'Upon returning to London, I found Will has met my every expectation and acquitted himself with credit.' For Will had become a first-class recording expert in only a few months. But he also had the makings of a really brilliant manager. Fred watched his brother welcome Louise Kirkby Lunn, the latest in a growing list of singers that Landon Ronald was recruiting for the gramophone. For all his youth, Will had a natural flair for this side of the business which Fred recognised he himself could not match. When a request came toward the end of February 1902 for fresh recording in Italy, the two Gaisbergs were sent together.

The Michelis brothers had been working hard to try to reap at last some of the benefits that Italy seemed always to be promising the gramophone. First, the possibility of recording at the Vatican seemed to emerge again.

William Michelis, through his friend Capitano Pecci of the Swiss Bodyguard, the Pope's nephew, had involved himself in a tangle of complicated wire-pulling, the scope of which was the acquisition of the famous Capella Sistina (the private choir of the Pope dating back to the fourth century) and perhaps the voice of Pope Leo XIII himself.[1]

At the same time Alfred, in Milan, had decided that they might

[1] Typescript, 'Notes on Actual Performance Recording'.

after all do better to try recording there during the Scala season. The singers would be busier, but the important ones would all be on the spot.

> . . . Alfred especially was always hatching grandiose schemes which were years ahead of the technical possibilities of recording. He was anxious to record an opera during the actual performance in La Scala, and by dint of much bribery a recording outfit was secretly smuggled in and set up in a stage box behind a screen ready for the following night's performance.
>
> So far so good, but the packing cases were left in the corridor and during the evening the Managing Director of La Scala, passing through the dark passage, stumbled over these and severely hurt himself. In the hue and cry that followed we succeeded in hastily removing the equipment without being apprehended, but our dreams of recording a La Scala performance ended in failure.[1]

This experience made Alfred Michelis more anxious than ever to demonstrate his influence at the Opera House. He saw his opportunity when Mr. and Mrs. William Barry Owen came to Milan for a few days in company with Alfred Clark and his young wife. La Scala had just mounted Baron Franchetti's new opera *Germania*, whose premiere had caused a sensation—much of it owing to the young singers in the leading roles. Tickets were impossible to obtain. Very well, Alfred Michelis would secure a box to seat the whole party, and for the very next evening.

> . . . To obtain a box Michelis had to bribe certain powers. The Scala boxes were all owned in perpetuity by the wealthy and noble families of Milan, so it was hoped that the proprietor of the box Michelis had secured would not show up that evening.
>
> We arrived and filled every available seat. The overture had just started and we had settled ourselves for a grand treat, when we heard an insistent knock. Michelis, greatly annoyed, threw open the door—and there stood the proprietor, Baron de L—, and his guests.

[1] Typescript, 'Notes on Actual Performance Recording'.

In the real Italian fashion, a tempestuous scene immediately ensued. The altercation grew louder and louder as the vestibule quickly filled with attendants, urged on by the disturbed audience to stop the fracas. Michelis, most humiliated, pointed out that his guests were Americans who would carry back a very bad impression of Italian manners, but this was to no avail and we all filed mournfully out of the box. Michelis then challenged the Baron to a duel. Cards were passed, and my poor brother Will was asked to act as second to his friend.

All that night I remained in company of my very nervous brother, discussing the mode of procedure to be carried out by a second in a duel. However, the next morning calmer tempers prevailed and apologies for the misunderstanding were exchanged by both parties—much to the relief of my brother.

A few nights later, Michelis really did obtain some good stalls for *Germania*, and the Gramophone party were at last able to attend. In the opera's Prologue was a big aria for the leading tenor. This was a young man called Enrico Caruso.

I cannot describe my transports or the wild enthusiasm of the audience when Federico Loewe (Caruso) urged the students to revolt against the invader Napoleon—'Studenti! Udite!' . . . In the first act there was a wonderful love-duet with Ricke ([sung by Amelia] Pinto), rich in opportunities for both tenor and soprano, that held the audience spellbound.

I turned to Michelis and said, 'Find out what fee he will accept for ten songs' [the standard Gramophone contract in those days]. We had to run the gauntlet of all sorts of obstructions by those surrounding the good-natured and accessible singer. There were many hangers-on present, and each had a word to say or obstructions to raise just as we were on the point of coming to an agreement.[1]

At last Caruso promised to consider the matter. If a messenger was sent round the following day, they should have his answer. This task was given to the pianist Michelis had hired to play the accompaniments for their recording sessions.

[1] Typescript, 'I Recorded Caruso'. Michelis quotation from Gelatt, *The Fabulous Phonograph*, p. 114.

The next day Maestro Cottone . . . returned with a proposition. Caruso would sing ten songs for £100, all to be recorded in one afternoon. . . To us in those days these were staggering terms, but I transmitted them to London with a strong recommendation, feeling all the time how inadequate were words in telegraphic form to describe the merits of the case. A cabled reply came back quickly: FEE EXORBITANT FORBID YOU TO RECORD. This was humiliating and I felt it was hopeless to argue . . . as it was only by being on the spot that one could grasp the urgency of the opportunity. I therefore gave the word to Michelis to go ahead. . . . The die was cast.

Fred could so lightly disregard his cabled instructions only because he had decided to guarantee Caruso's fee out of his own pocket rather than lose the chance of recording him. It was the strongest possible declaration of faith in the artist, the moment, and above all the idea that had brought them together.

Caruso would have no time to visit their studio until near the end of *Germania*'s scheduled run. The same applied to Amelia Pinto, the soprano, who had signed a Gramophone contract for £40. The best plan was therefore to spend a week or so in Rome, pursuing what had been the central object of the trip. But there again the Gramophone found success.

Not total success, to be sure, for it had become evident that the idea of recording the Pope was hopeless. He was nearly ninety, and it had now been made explicitly clear that such a recording was impossible. But the Vatican had agreed to their making discs of the Sistine Chapel Choir. And thus the Gramophone would preserve the sound of the *castrato* voice, still represented in the Choir. The practice of obtaining male sopranos had been made illegal many years earlier, so the present exponents were the last representatives of this very rich vocal tradition.

For the recording, the authorities had granted the use of a richly decorated salon in the Palace of the Bishop of Rome for five days only.

The choir arrived and made record after record. I particularly remember their rosy-cheeked conductor and solo soprano, Professor Moreschi . . . who was amazingly fresh and youthful and boasted of a large family—which greatly interested me. . . . My brother Will and I worked fast and furiously packing the waxes as quickly as they were recorded.

During the last session an accident happened that might have proven serious. Suddenly a short circuit from the battery ignited the cotton wool used in packing. A flame shot up, and over and above the hysterical cries of the panic-stricken choristers one heard the laments of the male sopranos. They rushed for the door, where I saw them jam. My brother and I and the two brothers Michelis used our overcoats to beat down the flames, and we worked desperately. Will Michelis thoughtfully pulled the cases of completed and packed masters out of the way. We all received burns . . . but the records were saved and no very great damage was done to the salon or masterpieces.

The *pompieri* (Fire Department) appeared with hose and axe in hand, and seemed grieved that we had mastered the flames without their aid. . . . Reuter's cabled the incident over the world, featuring two Americans involved in the destruction of the Vatican by fire.[1]

Returning to Milan for the recording appointment with Caruso and Pinto, 'Alfred Michelis . . . engaged a private drawing-room on the third floor of the Grande Hotel. . . . A curtain divided the room, behind which we erected the recording apparatus and laid out the wax discs ready for receiving the sound. On the other side was an upright piano set up high on packing cases with its sounding board facing a bell-shaped, metal horn suspended five feet from the floor.'[2]

On the morning of 11 April Amelia Pinto, the soprano star of *Germania*, arrived and made her records, including an aria from the new opera. Early in the afternoon it was time for Caruso's appearance. As they all peered anxiously from the hotel windows, the young singer suddenly swung round the corner.

. . . Dressed like a dandy, twirling a cane, Caruso sauntered down Via Manzoni and—to the delight of those worshippers of tenors, the waiters—entered the Grande Hotel . . . where we were waiting for him.

We barred from the room his escort of *braves* with the exception of his accompanist Maestro Cottone. . . . Caruso

[1] 'Notes on Actual Performance Recording'.
[2] 'I recorded Caruso'.

> wanted to get the job over quickly as he was anxious to earn that £100 and to have his lunch, [but] he forgot all this when he started on the job.[1]

The first record was 'Studenti! Udite!' from *Germania.* Fred was so excited that he wrote the matrix number already used for the last Pinto disc all over again on this wax before realising his mistake. Then came 'Questa O quella' from *Rigoletto*, 'Celeste Aida', the Dream scene from *Manon*, and so on through the ten records.

> The items were all about two-and-a-half to three minutes long and one after the other, as fast as we could put the waxes on the machine, Caruso poured the fresh gold of that beautiful voice on to them. He was in the good humour of robust youth and success waited for him whichever way he chose to turn. As far as that goes, we were all in the same condition in those days—it seemed that we could not make mistakes no matter what risks we ran.[2]

As a souvenir of the occasion Caruso, already an accomplished caricaturist, made a sketch of Will standing by the recording machine. Suddenly it was all over: 'We paid Caruso his £100 on the spot. I was stunned at the ease with which such a vast sum was earned. . . .'

Of course it was a gamble. The Caruso records would have to sell no fewer than two thousand copies before Fred's £100 could be recouped. As Will was to recall fifteen years later: 'We were so afraid that something might happen to the delicate material on which Caruso's voice had been recorded that we did not dare trust it in transit except in our own arms, and we carried these originals all the way from Milan. . . .'[3] But the precious waxes were processed at Hanover without mishap, and the entire series reached the London market in time for Caruso's debut at Covent Garden on 14 May. They made an immense success. Long after-afterward Fred was to write: 'I heard the figure of £15,000 profit mentioned as a result of the venture.'

By the time the Gaisbergs arrived back in London, the influence of the Caruso coup had already begun to make itself felt.

[1] 'I Recorded Caruso'.
[2] Ibid.
[3] *The Voice*, Vol. I, January 1917, p. 16.

Even before they were available in the shops, the prospect of recordings by Caruso had a decisive effect on Landon Ronald's efforts to recruit great singers for the gramophone. Almost overnight, contracts had been signed with seven of the most distinguished artists shortly to appear with Caruso in the forthcoming International Season at Covent Garden.

The first to arrive at Maiden Lane, on 30 May, was the great French bass Pol Plançon. Fred saw him 'daintily booted and gloved like a Parisian dandy with that faint perfume of the salons about him.'[1] As Plançon cast an ironical eye over the Gramophone and Typewriter Company's dingy premises, his bearing struck Fred Gaisberg as carrying 'reserve and dignity' up to a very fine point: 'But all this was shattered by a few witty stories from Landon Ronald.'[2] Ronald was there not only as advisor but also as accompanist. By the time his ten discs were finished, Plançon had thawed sufficiently to sign a photograph of himself for his Gramophone friends.

Three famous baritones followed—Anton van Rooy, the American David Bispham, and Antonio Scotti—and all fared well. Then came another American, the soprano Suzanne Adams, followed by that celebrated exponent of French operatic heroines, Emma Calvé. Ronald had warned them that Calvé might prove difficult, despite the hundred-guinea fee she had been promised. And it turned out to be very far from the normal gramophone recording session, as Landon Ronald remembered it.

> She was staying at the Hyde Park Hotel, and I was to fetch her in a 'four-wheeler' and take her to Maiden Lane and accompany her on the pianoforte. After much running about after music she had forgotten, and picking up gloves she had dropped, I got her safely into the cab.
>
> I must admit that the offices in Maiden Lane at that time scarcely inspired confidence or gave the impression that they belonged to a large and prosperous company. Certainly they didn't impress *her*, because when I gaily said, 'Here we are; let me help you out,' a sharp rejoinder came:
>
> 'Mon Dieu, but never in my life will I enter such a place. It

[1] 'Sir Landon Ronald', in *The Gramophone*, Sept. 1938, p. 148.
[2] Ibid

is a tavern—not a manufactory! I shall be robbed there! I know it; I feel it in my bones! You have brought me to a thieves' den!'

. . . Nothing I could say would alter her decision, and there was everyone waiting and everything prepared. . . .

An inspiration! I would get a very good-looking young man who had just entered the business, named Sydney Dixon, to come down and hand her her cheque! I implored her to wait one minute, and I rushed up those stairs quicker than I have ever climbed stairs before or since. Dixon was there sure enough, and I shrieked at him, pushing him downstairs.

'Her cheque! Her cheque! Give it her! Look handsome! Be nice—she *won't come in*!'

He did it all. And the next thing I remembered was her saying in a cooing voice,

'Mais vous êtes gentil, Monsieur. Merci beaucoup. Oui, oui, oui; je vous suivrai avec plaisir. Venez, mon petit Ronald.'

[Down] stairs we went and we began to record. But our troubles weren't over! In the middle of the Habanera from *Carmen*, she turned and asked me if she was in good voice. Result—one record spoilt. Then, in another selection, she declared she could not proceed unless she was allowed to dance! Another record spoilt![1]

The dancing of course caused terrible worry to the Gaisbergs, who had the responsibility of producing successful discs. Then in coming up to the final high note of one of the *Carmen* arias, Calvé had a small but noticeable vocal disaster. Never mind, the record could be made yet again. Fred slipped a fresh wax onto the turntable and signalled Landon Ronald to begin the piano introduction once more. This time Calvé's performance was still more intense. There was more dancing, and then the final phrase leading up to the high note—which emerged precisely as it had done before. 'Ah, Mon Dieu!' exclaimed Calvé through her teeth, and these words were also recorded. After that they

[1] Sir Landon Ronald, *Variations on a Personal Theme*, pp. 100–1. Ronald writes of going upstairs to the recording room, but his memory has confused the Maiden Lane premises (where the recording room was in the basement) with the building in City Road which the Company occupied a few months later, and where the recording room was on the top floor.

gave up on *Carmen*. Sydney Dixon recalled the chaos left behind at the end of the session:

> Poor Landon Ronald, an artist to his finger tips, sat with blanched face recovering from the whirlwind excitement. . . . We prepared to close for the day. On the floor by the doorway was a crumpled ball of paper. Someone casually picked it up and smoothed it out. It was Madame Calvé's cheque.[1]

Following Calvé, Fred Gaisberg was relieved to welcome Maurice Renaud. He was the only one amongst all this group of singers who had any prior experience of disc-making. He recalled his first Gramophone session at Alfred Clark's studio in Paris during the previous summer. As Fred was to write after many years' experience: 'Those baritones were always wonderful fellows, intelligent and dependable; to me they always personified human sanity. Was it Hans von Bülow who said "A tenor is a disease"?'

The experience of making these records had shown that the Maiden Lane building was clearly obsolete for an organisation of the aspirations of The Gramophone and Typewriter Company Ltd. During the summer of 1902 they removed to new premises, where they would occupy the whole of a commodious and respectable building at No. 21, City Road, E.C. The new recording room was an enormous advance over the old basement room in Maiden Lane. A journalist described it:

> Here in the Gramophone laboratory practically every variety of sound-producing instrument is available—two pianos, a large Mustel organ, church chimes of all sizes, a variety of drums, horns, stringed instruments, and all manner of equipment for producing descriptive records, together with horns for receiving sound of every size and shape.
>
> . . . The recording room is at the top of the building, and it has been so situated in order to remove it as far as possible from the din and turmoil of the street traffic of the busy City Road. It is lighted by means of skylights. Stretching from one end of the room is a glass partition, behind which is placed the recording machine. . . . The recording horn projects through about the centre of this partition. . . . In the construction of this room every possible means has been

[1] *The Voice*, Vol. V, July 1921, p. 5.

utilised to secure its perfection from an acoustic point of view. . . .[1]

While all this was being completed, there was the excitement of a Coronation year. The Gaisbergs were amongst the thousands looking forward to watching the great procession, and when the new King's sudden illness forced the last-minute cancellation of everything, Fred wrote: 'The postponement of the King's Coronation disappointed us very much, as we had secured our seats and so forfeited the money. So when Edward VII really was crowned we thought we would escape the mob, and left on Aug. 8th for Paris.'

When he saw Alfred Clark, Fred heard news that made him forget all about the Coronation. A month earlier, the Paris office of The Gramophone and Typewriter Company had received a visit from the new manager-designate of the New York Metropolitan Opera, Heinrich Conried. Clark had demonstrated the Company's progress with some of its latest discs—the recently arrived pressings of Caruso's recordings. Conried had just heard Caruso at Covent Garden, and he was desperately keen to engage him for the Metropolitan. But his directors in New York had been sceptical. So Conried had taken a set of the Caruso records back to New York with him to play for the directors. On the evidence of those records alone, the Metropolitan Opera sent Caruso the contract which was to take him to North America for the first time. There could be no clearer proof of the gramophone's success as a 'recording' machine—or of Fred Gaisberg's ability to recognize a voice that would enhance the fortunes of the gramophone.

When Fred returned to London, he found the City Road office in a whirl of preparation for the issuing of a new *de luxe* catalogue that would contain nothing but the Company's Red-Label records. How Raphoff's suggestion had grown! Sinkler Darby had made the first discs destined for the Red Label in Russia during the previous winter: for these he had secured the great Figner and his wife Medea Mei. And they had finally netted the fabulous Chaliapin. Many of the discs which Fred and Will Gaisberg had made in Milan were also given Red-Label status—including of course the Caruso discs. The records made during the recent Covent Garden Season were also to have

[1] *The Sound Wave and Talking Machine News*, March 1907, p. 72.

Red Labels. From America came the news that the Victor Company was eager to publish many of these with their own Red Labels. It was difficult to realise that only five years had passed since the founding of the Company in 1898, when William Barry Owen had tried to persuade Trevor Williams that such recordings as could be supplied from the States could satisfy any European demand.

Chapter Eight

FRED GAISBERG's attention was mostly elsewhere in the late summer of 1902. For the biggest recording trip of his life was before him. 'My brother Will was now sharing my duties and this enabled me to volunteer as technical recorder and artistic advisor for an expedition to the Far East. The object was to open up new Markets, establish agencies, and acquire a catalogue of native records.'

The most considerable problem was how to use recording equipment in places where no power was available and where transportation was difficult. In the month before his departure Fred Gaisberg turned inventor. In consultation with B. G. Royal, 'I designed and built a successful weight-motor, enabling me to dispense with heavy storage batteries and fragile clock-springs.' By Monday 22 September everything was well in hand.

> The rest of the week was a busy one, finishing my preparations for sailing. I bid good-bye to my various friends, made a will & appointed my brother Will my sole attorney.

Most of the working hours of those days were spent at the docks, supervising the loading of equipment and baggage for a year's remote record making. Fred also packed samples of the Company's latest recordings, including the new Covent Garden discs just arrived in finished pressings from Hanover.

On board the *Coromandel* on 28 September, Fred quickly found his companions for the year.

> Tom Addiss, accompanied by his good-looking wife, was the business head, and I had as my helper young George Dilnutt.
>
> The *Coromandel* was of the vintage when shipbuilders could

not decide between sails and steam power, and so installed both. It was comfortable and carried only cabin and third-class passengers. In the long list of travellers there were no exalted names from the Civil Service, military or judicial. This did not mean that we thought less of ourselves. My fellow-travellers quickly divided into sharply defined social groups: tea planters, railroad and mining engineers and officials, departmental managers, a few young women going out to be married or seeking husbands. But only one thing reduced them all to a common denominator—returning from holidays in England, they were all broke! The Australians getting off at Colombo formed a clique apart. They gambled all day and seemed to resent the superiority of what were then called Anglo-Indians.

By the time we reached Gibraltar all the passengers were accounted for with the exception of a Mr. and Mrs. Norton. Curiosity ran high about this couple as soon as we had seen the very stylish baggage they brought on board. It was only as we passed by Stromboli, then in eruption, that they put in an appearance. They were a strikingly handsome American couple, well-dressed and exclusive. Mrs. Norton easily outdistanced in chic and elegance all our ladies, and we men hungrily admired her as the Nortons paced the deck, absorbed in each other.

At Suez we took on water & provisions, but did not go ashore. Weather very hot. Our passage through the Red Sea very, very hot. We slept on deck.

Wed., Oct. 15th at 6 o'c a.m. we arrived at Aden, Arabia. Supposed to be one of the hottest places in Creation and I believe it. . . . The weather was burning hot, and two hours on shore was enough to make us glad to return to the shade of our ship.

Then there was the stop at Colombo, and at last the *Coromandel* arrived at the river entrance to Calcutta:

Monday night [27th October]. We had a fancy-dress ball that was a great success. The quarter-deck was gaily trimmed with bunting. I went as a Japanese, George as a white-eyed Kaffir. The boat was perfectly still, so we were able to dance without any trouble. The reason for this was that we were anchored in the River Hooghly. As this river is dangerous navigation on account of the swiftness of the ebb and sand-banks, boats can only proceed by day.

Tuesday morning we proceeded at sunrise up the river. . . . After the quarantine the climax of our journey was reached when we were boarded by an inspector and a squad of policemen. They had warrants for the arrest and extradition of Mr. Norton, a banker from Philadelphia, on a charge of embezzlement. He had left his wife and children for the lady we knew as Mrs. Norton, a chorus girl!

It took three days to unload our thirty heavy cases and pass the customs officers. Our agent, Jack Hawd, had arranged a location and had assembled a collection of artists, who watched us curiously as we prepared our studio for recording. It was the first time that the talking machine had come into their lives and they regarded it with awe and wonderment.

I soon discovered that the English, whom we contacted and who were acting as our agents and factors, might be living on another planet for all the interest they took in Indian music. They dwelt in an Anglo-Saxon compound of their own creation, isolated from India. They had their own cricket and tennis clubs, tea parties and bridge, 'sixteen annas to the rupee'. The native bazaars never saw them, and even the Eurasians aped them to the extent of tabooing all Indian society.

So Fred Gaisberg had once more to take into his own hand the matter of artist recruitment:

I met the Superintendent of the Calcutta police, who placed at my disposal an officer to accompany me to the various important entertainments and theatres in the Harrison Road. Our first visit was to the native 'Classic Theatre' where a performance of *Romeo and Juliet* in a most unconventional form was being given. Quite arbitrarily, there was introduced a chorus of young Nautch girls heavily bleached with rice powder and dressed in transparent gauze. They sang 'And Her Golden Hair Was Hanging Down Her Back', accompanied by fourteen brass instruments all playing in unison. . . .

We now proceeded to attend a dinner party and Nautch dance in the home of a wealthy *babu*. We elbowed our way through an unsavoury alley, jostled by fakirs and unwholesome sacred cows, to a pretentious entrance. The host and his native guests eagerly welcomed the brave band of *pukka* Anglo-Saxons who bestowed such honour on his house. No native women were present excepting the Nautch girls, who had lost caste. We Europeans ate at a separate table; not even our host sat with us. After a rigidly European dinner we retired to a large salon and were entertained by the Nautch girls.

At this particular dinner we heard two popular dancing girls, one of them named Goura Jan, a Mohammedan, rather fat and covered with masses of gold armlets, anklets, rings, pearl necklaces, heavy earrings hanging from about ten piercings in each ear. Her crowning adornment was a large diamond fastened on the side of her nose. Her teeth were quite red from betel-nut chewing. Her chewing habit necessitated the presence of a bearer following her about with a silver cuspidor into which she would empty her mouthful, much to the distraction of her charms. She terminated each song with a most cleverly executed muscle-dance. This lady gets 300 Rupees an evening, and can often be seen driving in the Miadern in a fine carriage & pair.

Fred Gaisberg put Goura Jan at the top of his list of prospects for recording. Over the weekend they negotiated, and on the Tuesday she came to the improvised recording studio, accompanied by '4 musicians—2 esrag, 1 tambura, 1 pr. mandiers. Her other attendants were a bearer for her pipe & to prepare her betel-nut, I ayah or black girl attendant, one coolie to fan her, another girl to carry her cuspidor, and a coolie to carry the traps. Calvé came to our lab with far less cortege and required much less attendance. . . . The Mohammedan girl could lay considerable claim to a coloratura voice. She performed with ease some very difficult vocalising such as scales & a sort of guttural trill which she drew our attention to herself. But at the end of the session when we reproduced Suzanne Adams's record of the 'Jewel Song' in *Faust*, the little lady & her attendants were very much astonished by the rapid execution & trills.'

It was an early high point. Most of the rest was sheer grind, Sundays not excepted.

Sunday 16th. Today we made 30 records of the 'Classic Theatre Orchestra', consisting of two baritone horns, one cornet, two clarinets, two drums (native tambulas), and a set of triangles. They all play in unison.

And so it went on for three weeks—interrupted by one pungent reminder of Fred Gaisberg's home, half a world away.

> Thursday 27th. . . . I went to the theatre (English) with a young American, Mr. Lusk. . . . This young man is a Yale graduate and represents the General Electric Co. of America in the East. I have been in his company a great deal and have found him interesting and entertaining. I invited him today to a Thanksgiving dinner at the Hotel. I had ordered a turkey, cranberry sauce & mince pie, very good champagne, and also arranged the table prettily with American flags.

Christmas of 1902 was spent aboard the P. & O. ship *Chusan*, taking Gaisberg, Dilnutt, and Mr. and Mrs. Addiss toward China and Japan. The plan was to get on to the most remote point, and work gradually back from there. By mid-January 1903 they were waiting for the equipment to clear the Japanese customs and be sent on to Tokyo for the next phase of recording. After two days of sightseeing Fred was preparing to go off again when he was handed a telegram:

> Monday Jan 19th. I received Will's cable telling me my father was dangerously ill, and that Will was starting for Washington. The cable was dated Dec 29th. I immediately cabled for news.
>
> Wed. 21st. After passing two anxious days I received a reply that my father was dead. I cannot put into words my feelings. Words are too cold to express my sorrow at losing my good, loving parent. The immense distance which separates me and my family places me in a trying position. So far I have not received one letter giving details. The last letter received was forwarded from Calcutta and dated Wash. D.C. Nov. 29th 1902.

Alone, unable to communicate directly with his family, Fred sought the only consolation that offered itself: he gave his thoughts to his diary. He wrote page after page—all he could remember about his grandparents, what he had been told of his father's early years, their family life together in Washington during his own boyhood and youth. At last, when he had sat at the little table in his hotel room for hours and hours and could remember no more, he concluded:

With his death has gone one of the dearest wishes of my heart, I should have loved to lay my life and work at the feet of him who has sacrificed and struggled so much for my sake. To see him retired happy in our midst to spend his declining years was my cherished hope. We had so often talked it over—our ideal: we both leaned towards the country—the cottage, the farm, the vines, and so, where we could live a simple, natural life. My dear father, if we could only repay you for all you have suffered for us.

It took a fortnight for the recording equipment to be released, then at last life began to creep forward.

Wed. 4th [February]. We did our first work after a lapse of nearly 2 months. We made some 54 records. Japanese music is simply too horrible, but funny to relate, Europeans who have been long in the country profess to really enjoy it, and say that there is more in the music & acting than a casual observer would believe. . . .

Friday 13th. I am beginning to like their music a little. Today we had a Geisha band, and to see these little women with big European band instruments was the funniest thing imaginable. This band play both on Japanese & European instruments. I took a photograph of them.

So it went on for two weeks.

Saturday 28th. We made records of the Imperial Household Band. The orchestra was composed of 12 men and their music was weird & fascinating indeed. They had one Koto (harp-like instrument), one Beiwa (guitar-like instrument), two instruments looking like a very miniature church organ (blown by the mouth continuously), 2 reed instruments about 4 inches long sounding like an oboe, two flutes of bamboo wood, one large drum suspended on a standard, one small drum . . ., one cymbal or small gong. Though they played some 10 pieces it was impossible to distinguish one tune from another.

In Shanghai, Fred Gaisberg had his first close look at Chinese life:

A first visit to a Chinese city is so novel and the appearances so unlike any city one has ever before seen that one is amazed.

He cannot believe those narrow lanes—scarcely 5 ft wide—are main streets and thoroughfares and not alleys: roofs nearly touching each other and nearly excluding the daylight, artisans working right in the roadway, no means of transit except to walk or a palakin carried by two coolies . . . dense crowds of busy men, crying coolies bumping into you with their long poles, sickening beggars holding before you horrible deformities, vile smells of every rottenness from refuse-heaps in the road or a filthy sewer. . . .

We then went to the largest temple in the town. Arranged around the court were some 100 gods, one god for each year in 100 years. I bought an offering of some silvered paper & burnt it in front of God 31 (my age) and made a wish. . . .[1]

Wed. 18th [March] we made our first records. About 15 Chinamen had come, including the band to accompany. As a Chinaman yells at the top of his power when he sings, he can only sing two songs an evening—then his throat is hoarse. Their idea of music is a tremendous clash and bang. With the assistance of a drum, three pairs of huge gongs, a pair of slappers, a sort of banjo, a squacky fiddle of bamboo & some bagpipe-sounding instruments, besides the yelling of the singer, their idea of music was recorded on the Gramophone. On the first day, after making ten records we had to stop: the din had so paralysed my wits that I could not think.

Up to the 27th March we made 325 records, for which we paid $4 each . . . and there was not sufficient difference between any two to describe.

Every arrangement was difficult, everything accomplished took ten times the effort it should have done. Days were lost waiting for the *Chusan* to take them back to Hong Kong. When finally it did sail, the entire passage was accomplished with the ship's whistle blowing constantly through the fog-bound waters 'so thick with trading and fishing junks that it is almost impossible to escape running them down. . . .'

By the time they had set up in Hong Kong and brought in some performers, nearly a month had passed:

Thursday 23rd [April]. We made some 35 records. The artists were of a lower grade & dirtier than those in Shanghai, and their songs not nearly so interesting.

[1] This refers to his 31st year.

Friday 24th. We made 45 records.
Sat. 25th. ,, ,, 45 ,,
Sunday 26th ,, ,, 20 ,, before 12 o'c and by 3 o'c had packed our boxes and soldered the tins and were ready to decamp.

The proportion of actual work accomplished to time spent in preparation seemed absurd. But everywhere it was the same. It was nearly the middle of May before they could carry out the next stage of recording in Singapore. At the end of a week's work there they cabled London for money and instructions. The result was that George Dilnutt was recalled, 'there not being enough work to keep him'. Mr. and Mrs. Addiss remained, but Fred Gaisberg was left with all the real work. So it was when they arrived at Bangkok on 1 June.

I unloaded my outfit off the *Korat*. I had literally to do it myself. Set up plant.

Four days' work yielded a hundred records. Then back to Singapore to find a ship that would take them to the last city on the recording programme, Rangoon. But it was getting late:

Thursday, June 18. We sailed at daylight. . . . We are catching the first of the Monsoon weather. We are the only cabin passengers. . . .

Saturday 20th. Last night we ran into a particularly bad squall. One man was lost overboard. All day very rough.

At last they arrived in Rangoon, where Fred carried out a final four days of recording before turning homeward.

At Aden on the return journey, there was a last change of ships as Fred boarded the Australian *Oceana* to make the final passage northward. One by one the signs of familiar civilisation returned. As they moved quietly through the Mediterranean, Fred Gaisberg sought to put in perspective an unremitting year: 'Everywhere the invention aroused the greatest interest. The native and European press interviewed us and printed many columns about this amazing expedition. In my spare time I gave dozens of gramophone recitals to audiences who heard recorded sound for the first time. My selection of European records was worn to the bone. . . .'

But this kind of acceptance only showed the gramophone's capacity for extending its influence through a length and breadth of cultural geography where no single set of sympathies could possibly bear it constant company. Perhaps it might be different in some future time. But for a man of Fred Gaisberg's world, the voyage to the Far East had delineated another in the series of choices by which a career was to be shaped and a life lived. A real circumnavigation of the earth's diversities was a voyage too remote. Every city throughout the Near and Far East had its European and American waifs to show him—wanderers for whom the romance had vanished so gradually and so completely as to leave them without even the dignity of their disillusion.

When Fred arrived at Victoria Station on 5 August 1903, the contrast seemed complete. Here was Will to meet him, together with Ed Footman, B. G. Royal, and one or two other friends: 'We all had a nice dinner at the Trocadero & a look in a Music Hall afterwards.' Gradually through the conversations of the next days, Fred picked up the threads. Will had worked hard through the year to carry the main burden of London recording on his own shoulders. And he had followed up their capture of Caruso with another Italian triumph—the recording of Francesco Tamagno, creator of Verdi's Otello. 'Alfred Michelis carried out with stubborn persistence the negotiations with Tamagno's lawyer, and the document eventually signed was the first to give the artist a royalty on the sale of each record, a stipulated selling price of £1 each. . . . In addition he received a cash advance of £2,000—a great sum for those days plus a royalty of 4s. per record. . . . To carry out this recording my brother, as Tamagno's guest, spent a week in his mountain home at Sousa in the Mont Cenis pass.' And the records, despite the heavy financial commitment, had been a distinct success—especially the ones in the new twelve-inch, four-minute size introduced during Fred's absence. Since making the Tamagno discs, Will Gaisberg had recorded a number of these large plates, including some by two veteran English baritones—Richard Temple, one of the most eminent of all Gilbert and Sullivan singers, and the great Charles Santley, whose career extended back to the first English production of Gounod's *Faust* nearly fifty years earlier.

Chapter Nine

AFTER HIS year in the Far East, Fred needed to visit his family in Washington. He sailed in mid-August 1903, and was met in New York by his sisters.

> Saturday morning [22nd August] we took the 11 o'c train for Washington. A hot, dusty ride. Charlie met us at the station in the trap & drove us home. I found all the folks looking well & content, but my mother shows plainly the sorrow & trouble my father's death brought her. . . .

Afterwards Fred spent a few days in Philadelphia, where he saw Calvin Child. Then a week's visit with William Barry Owen and his wife, holiday-making on the Massachusetts coast, once again revealed Owen the sportsman: 'He missed the boat to Europe in order to watch a ball game between the Martha's Vineyard nine and his home team.'

Back in Washington before his departure, Fred assumed the role of responsible elder brother.

> Bought a Chase & Baker player[-piano] for the folks. Decided to take Louise to Europe with me to study violin, voice & languages.

Louise was the youngest Gaisberg. She was not yet fifteen, but she seemed to have the brightest musical talent of the family. Faced with Fred's proposal for Louise, Mrs. Gaisberg seemed unable to offer effective opposition. Louise herself could later recall no personal role in the decision. Fred had taken on the management of her 'career' just as he was beginning to 'manage' established artists in the recording studio. At the end of September, when the S.S. *Minneapolis* sailed from New York, her passenger-list included Mr. Fred Gaisberg and Miss Louise Gaisberg.

In London they joined Will in a two-room service flat in Gower Street. The large drawing-room at the front was converted nightly by means of a screen into a bedroom for Louise, while Fred and Will squashed into the tiny single bedroom behind. Louise remembered that their first guest was a twenty-year-old youth from Brooklyn called Louis Sterling who had crossed the ocean full of ambition to start his own record business in London. He struck Louise as 'the ugliest man I ever saw', but he was kindness and good fun personified, and he rapidly became a close friend in the young Gaisberg household. And there was Lillian Bryant, an expert pianist who often accompanied Louise's violin practices on the upright piano they had installed in the little flat. But it was still very lonely for a fifteen-year-old girl, coming in from the Royal College of Music at the end of a dark winter's afternoon, with only the housekeeper to make a cup of tea for her.

Both Fred and Will were much occupied with events at City Road. Now every effort was being made to capture the great Nellie Melba. Fred knew her of course by reputation: 'Melba was more than a prima donna. She was in the diva class, and well she knew it. . . . For long she doubted, or pretended to doubt, our ability to reproduce her voice successfully on the wax. Overtures were started by Landon Ronald . . . and continued over a long period.'

At the beginning of 1904 Melba was at last brought to the point of consenting to a Gramophone 'test'. Her conditions seemed almost wilfully difficult. First, the test session was to take place not in the City Road studio, but at her own house in the West End. Second, she was to be accompanied not by the usual piano but by an orchestra: fifty musicians must be fitted into her drawing-room. Third and most important, Melba herself was to have sole determination of the results.

The possibility of including the name of Melba in the roster of Gramophone artists proved inducement enough for the directors to agree to all this. And so dawned a day that Fred Gaisberg would not forget.

> Our equipment was set up in the beautiful drawing-room of her mansion in Great Cumberland Place. . . . The room was

filled with treasures and trophies. Landon Ronald had charge of the arrangements and also conducted the orchestra of some forty-five players whom we somehow managed to crowd into the room. The recorders were working under great disadvantages, and our nerves were keyed up to the highest tension. I had charge of [the recording] and a nerve-wracking experience I found it.

Melba was a Queen of Song no doubt, but as Fred soon had cause to realise, 'it was certainly a dominant, harsh Queen. When she addressed one, she made no attempt to clothe her speech with sweetened words. She was a woman who had risen to the top of her profession by sheer driving force. . . .'[1]

She was caustic enough about the process but sufficiently interested to keep everyone working hard through a long day as she made one record after another. When it was over, Melba announced that she had no special wish for any publication whatever. Of course nobody wanted the task of taking that answer back to the Gramophone directors. After a staggering display of Landon Ronald's tactical diplomacy, the most Melba would agree to was that they might send the *Traviata* 'Ah! fors' è lui' disc to her old father in Australia. If he could recognise her voice from the Gramophone then perhaps she might think further.

While the Melba records were despatched to Hanover for the pressing of samples, Fred Gaisberg saw all sorts of manoeuvres being mounted:

They involved a visit by our Sales Manager, Sydney Dixon, to Monte Carlo, where Melba was starring in opera. For one whole month he courted her with flowers, speeches and dinner parties; still she would not be convinced. Finally she fell to a ruse. While she was dining . . . with the great composer Camille Saint-Saëns, Dixon in the next room played a Caruso record. Saint-Saëns was enthusiastic, which had the desired effect on Melba.

The trap had been baited with care. Dixon had conspired with Alfred Clark in Paris to invite the elderly Saint-Saëns to make some discs of his own music, even though such 'documents' offered no better commercial promise than any other piano

[1] Typescript article '1909'.

recordings. But the main object was achieved: Saint-Saëns was well disposed to the Gramophone, and he co-operated beautifully.

If Melba's vanity was played upon at Monte Carlo, however, her shrewdness was not. She allowed them to play the 'Ah! fors' è lui' record at a reception for the press in March to test the reaction, and deigned to agree to some further recording in her drawing-room if the orchestra and equipment were brought round again. So the whole agonising process was gone through once more—still without the shadow of a contract.

In fact it was 11 May before Melba was finally brought to agreement. The lady was to be paid the sum of £1,000 immediately. Her records were to be sold at not less than one guinea each (a shilling more than Tamagno discs). She was to receive a royalty of five shillings on every copy sold. And all her records must bear a specially coloured label which would not be given to the discs of any other artist. But when the records appeared in the shops at the beginning of July, the entire first pressing was sold out within a few days. The only cloud on Fred Gaisberg's horizon was a clause in Melba's contract that she was to come to City Road for a further recording session within six months.

Meanwhile the doors of the Gramophone studio had opened to another Australian singer, a young baritone called Peter Dawson who had been in London for two years.

> 'To keep the pot boiling', Dawson accepted all and sundry engagements—'smokers', seaside concert parties, and phonograph recording.[1]

Peter Dawson's cylinders were made for two of Fred Gaisberg's friends. One was Louis Sterling, whose new phonograph business had begun to flourish. Sterling's colleague was none other than Russell Hunting. Hunting was still doing his 'Casey' sketches, and his interest in the Sterling phonograph business didn't prevent him from continuing to make Gramophone discs for Fred Gaisberg as well. They all agreed that disc-marketing and cylinder-marketing were separate concerns, since a customer who owned one type of machine probably would not own the other. So the three friends entered into what Fred described as

[1] *The Voice*, Winter 1948, p. 3.

a 'secret understanding': 'I exchanged with them certain non-contract artists, and we worked together to our mutual benefit.'[1]

As soon as he heard Peter Dawson sing, 'Russell Hunting . . . spotted the record-making possibilities of this youngster's voice and gave me the tip. Within a few weeks I had him making popular comic and serious ballads, oratorio and operatic arias, Gilbert & Sullivan solos, duets, trios, quartets, choruses, and so on.'[2]

Recording Peter Dawson marked the beginning of a new phenomenon—a career that could be made and maintained almost entirely through recordings, to which actual concert platform appearances would always remain secondary. Dawson was to enjoy a profitable life in the Gramophone studios over the next forty years and more, for he was a sunny personality with a sonorous, reliable voice.

A very different affair was the recording of a youngish Scot who had recently come into the limelight with his inimitable combination of balladry and Highland parody—Harry Lauder. The continuing demand for his records by 1904 had made him a frequent visitor to City Road. But Harry's record making had to be monitored very carefully. One of his favourites was 'Stop yer ticklin' Jock': it was the sort of thing that invited the slipping in of all sorts of variations and 'improvements'—some of them unobtrusive enough to pass unnoticed until after the records had been pressed and were being sold in the shops.

There was also another hazard where Harry Lauder was concerned. The indefatigable Peter Dawson had quickly spotted a good thing, as Fred Gaisberg was soon to realise.

> Peter is no respecter of persons and under the name of 'Hector Grant' he recorded, in perfect imitation, Harry Lauder's entire repertoire, a fact which Sir Harry never forgave.

In describing it, however, Fred forgot to define his own part in this genteel piracy. Peter Dawson recalled the origin of 'Hector Grant' as follows:

> At the Gramophone Company one day I gave an imitation of Lauder singing 'I love a Lassie'. I was astonished at the reaction among the recording staff. Fred Gaisberg, the chief, came up to me excitedly and said:

[1] Typewritten article on John McCormack.

[2] *The Voice*, Winter 1948, p. 3.

'Peter, can you do any more like that? I mean, can you sing Scottish?'

I was amused at the way the little American put it, and answered, 'Yes of course. I can sing all his songs, including "Stop yer ticklin' Jock". . . .'

A little later he asked me what I thought of the idea of singing Lauder's songs for the Zonophone Company (a subsidiary of the H.M.V. [[1]]) under another name. In response to my argument that it might ruin my future if it became known, I was assured that no one would suspect that a singer of Lauder's rollicking Scottish songs could be Peter Dawson.

I promised them a decision within twenty-four hours. At home, chatting it over with my wife, we both agreed that with a lean summer ahead it would help with our finances. And so I recorded Lauder's songs. They were a great success. . . .

They were such a success that Dawson, heavily disguised and in a kilt, was sent on a tour of public appearances as 'Hector Grant'. He recalled:

Some time later I met Harry Lauder at the recording studio. I was making a Peter Dawson record. . . . We chatted about old times, and he suddenly said, turning to Fred Gaisberg and myself:

'Did ye no ken a chap by the name of Hector Grant? He had a grrrand voice. He must have been killed in the war.'

Fred grinned, and in his quiet American way asked, 'Didn't you know, Harry, that Hector Grant was Peter?'

But with obvious disbelief he replied, 'Nah, nah, ye canna tell me that. I saw him in Glasgie. Yon was a much older man. And besides, I've come doon to mak' records an' no tae argue nonsense.'[2]

In the early autumn of 1904, Fred heard from Russell Hunting again. He had just made some cylinders of a ragged, twenty-year-old Irishman with a promising tenor voice. His name was John McCormack, and Hunting described his new acquaintance thus:

[1] The Gramophone Company had acquired the European rights of Zonophone in 1903, and thereafter used the label as an inexpensive subsidiary.

[2] Peter Dawson, *Fifty Years of Song*, pp. 42, 45–6.

I first met him through Jim White, who was manager for the Edison National Phono. Co. in London. Jim telephoned me one day, in effect, as follows:

'Say, Russ, our—and your—agent in Dublin wants us to record a chap who sings Irish songs in the real Irish manner, and wants to send him over here. He says he will sing for almost nothing but thinks we should, between us, pay him ten pounds.'

Well, I agreed to pay *half*, and although I don't know exactly what White paid him, I gave him £5 for one week's work . . . and I have never been thanked so much by anybody. (White told me, when we were arranging for him to come to London, that he sang for pennies along the *waterfront*. . . .)

John, when I first saw him at our Gower Street buildings, was wearing a coat that had seen many better days, upon which a few pieces of fur (on which the moths had dined frequently) were sewn.[1]

Hunting thought the young man had good potential, and Fred Gaisberg found it a good moment to try such a singer: 'No one was keener to welcome an Irish tenor than I, since I was alive to the commercial possibilities among the Irish Americans, who showed the most idolatrous worship of their bards.'

Fred was to remember all his life his first sight of John McCormack.

He struck me as an over-grown, under-fed, unkempt youth—loosely built, pale faced, disorderly dark hair, untidy clothes, very bad teeth, and worn down shoes . . . and he was drinking too much. . . . His eyes were piercing dark and he had very little to say, but that little showed him decidedly confident of himself—almost aggressive. . . .

We all took a serious interest in this rough diamond. . . . We recorded the very popular Irish songs, and I recall the difficulty he had when singing F's and G's. . . . I was particularly struck with this defect, and thought what a pity in so promising a voice—for the quality was truly beautiful. . . . While making his records he revealed to me that he would shortly be leaving for Italy to study with the well-known Maestro Sabatini.[2]

[1] Letter to Fred Gaisberg, 13 September 1933.
[2] Typewritten article on John McCormack, with MSS. additions.

The date fixed for the visit of Melba to City Road was 20 October. The session had been built up as an 'event' with invitations to the press. So when the day came, Melba displayed only her 'public' personality. In the description of one journalist present:

We are waiting in a small room at the top of an office in the City Road. We look out from the windows into a yellow fog, out of which dripping telegraph wires and drenching roofs struggle into a blurred existence. The room is lighted by green-shaded electric lights hanging from the ceiling. It is carpeted, and palms are arranged behind a table set with decanter and glasses. But obviously it is a place of business, a little chamber of commerce. From one of the walls, a mere partition of white wood and frosted glass, projects a trumpet. . . . On one side of this trumpet is a piano dizzy on a tall, rough wooden stand. . . .

Today we are waiting for Melba and Kubelik. The Chairman and the Manager of the Company, French composers, German musicians, and a few guests make up the knot of waiting people; half the languages of Europe are being talked together in a Babel of good spirits.

Enter Kubelik—wonderful little Kubelik, so thin, so slight, so serious. There are prim greetings for a few minutes, and then in a sudden rush, bringing merriment and fresh air in with her, Melba enters—Melba who can make honey vocal and waterfalls articulate, charming and delightful Melba—and we are all laughing and talking again in the best of spirits.

After this business, Kubelik opens his violin case, the accompanist climbs to the high seat in front of the piano, the Manager invites us to be seated, and Melba goes to the trumpet. The chamber of commerce is suddenly silent. Kubelik, slight and dusky at Melba's side, stands with his violin at his breast. The accompanist waits with his hands on the keys.

Then from behind the frosted glass an electric bell rings a sharp summons. The accompanist strikes the first chords of the *Ave Maria*, and in another minute Melba is heard singing. She stands with her back to us, her hands clasped in front of her, her lips a few inches from the trumpet. . . . Behind the frosted glass, which is cloudily luminous with electric light, the shadows of the operators pass as Melba sings. . . .

One wonders who will be listening to this music a hundred, two hundred, five hundred years hence. In the Venice, Paris, Berlin, and New York of that far day, people with a knowledge at which we cannot guess, with an outlook which we cannot comprehend, will be listening to the charm of this song even as we are now listening in a London office. Melba and Melba's life story will seem to them an ancient tale, Kubelik's toil and triumph will mean nothing to them; but the voice of the one and the violin of the other will be as real and as gracious then as they are to us now.

Test recordings for singers who had signed no contract, different Gramophone artists encouraged to compete in precisely the same repertoire, potted palms and press receptions, records of today to be heard in five hundred years: it was all too much for William Barry Owen, who by now could no longer resist his old suspicion that the popularity of the Gramophone was nearly exhausted. The typewriter he had introduced had not done well, and the electric clock was a failure. Despite all the apparent signs, the gramophone must be next. So at the end of 1904 he sold out his interest in the Company, resigned his directorship, and retired to the United States. Owen's racy, extrovert personality had given tremendous stimulation to the growth of the Company throughout Europe. But his departure now marked the passing of the Gramophone from childhood into adolescence.

In the first half of 1905 Fred Gaisberg was much on the Continent. In Vienna during the winter he recorded the operetta veteran Alexander Girardi and the distinguished Wagnerian *Heldentenor* Winkelmann, who had sung the title role in *Parsifal* at the first performance in 1882. And the younger Vienna Opera singers were eager to record for the Gramophone: Elise Elizza, Leo Slezak, Leopold Demuth, Wilhelm Hesch and Richard Mayr all came before Fred's horn in these months.

In Milan during the spring, Gramophone affairs were less satisfactory. Alfred Michelis had at last realised the dream of regularly using a small orchestra to accompany operatic records. Michelis had therefore hired a young pianist and conductor called Carlo Sabajno as a kind of operatic scout and occasional house-*maestro*. But this Mediterranean Landon Ronald had scarcely settled into his new role before Michelis himself departed from the Gramophone Company. Alfred Michelis had been tempted away by the promise of further recording advances to join a new firm called Fonotipia, which had the backing of the amateur composer and professional banker Baron d'Erlanger.

And so young Sabajno found himself in virtual charge of Gramophone recruiting in Milan. He was an energetic man, and given time would no doubt improve his connections. But the driving force of Alfred Michelis was meanwhile sorely missed. In place of Caruso, DeLucia, Tamagno, Bellincioni, and Marconi, they were now recording Teresa Arkel and a promising tenor called Giorgini. It wasn't that these singers were nobodies, but inevitably the Milan sessions of 1905 seemed to have taken a step backward.

Back at City Road in the summer, life was poised for another descent by Melba. And when it came on 4 September it proved to be the most excruciating session thus far. Fred Gaisberg remembered the elaborate preparations.

> There was the big Daimler to fetch her and her attendants—including Landon Ronald, Bemberg, Haddon Chambers (the writer then in high favour with Melba) and Mlle. Sassole, her secretary. . . . There was the youngest typist prettily dressed to hand the Diva a five-guinea bouquet of roses, the directors headed by Sydney Dixon in striped trousers, white spats, white waistcoat, cutaway black coat, squeaky patent leather boots that seemed to pinch as they danced in attendance on Her Ladyship as she cracked the whip with baleful glee.
>
> My recording studio was on the top floor, but the lift would stop first at the second floor where a long table was set up in the Board Room laden with good things to eat. Here light refreshments—including the ubiquitous champagne—were partaken of, and then the artists were sent on up to the studio where I would be anxiously waiting to get on with the job of making records—no easy task under these conditions in a cramped room. . . .

For this session a male trio of experienced Gramophone regulars were present to sing with the great lady. Melba took one look at them and it was clear there would be trouble. It began when she was too familiarly approached by Ernest Pike, whom

Fred Gaisberg remembered as 'a sweet-voiced but simple-minded tenor, the son of the baker at Sandringham House. Apparently he had once been commanded to sing for the Royal Family and would never let one forget it. . . . Attempting to "pal up" with Melba, he was met by the withering comment: "You're one of the bloody chorus!" '[1]

That set off the irrepressible Peter Dawson. As the trio pressed close around Melba to get near the horn for the recording of 'Old Folks at Home.'

Peter gave her that impertinent look of his. She turned on him saying,

'You're from Australia?'

He answered, 'Yes, Ma'am.'

She asked, 'What city?'

He replied 'Melbourne.'

Her retort was, 'What? that town of parsons, pubs, and prostitutes!'

By the end of the session Landon Ronald was shaking so badly that he could hardly play the accompaniment to his own song 'Away on the Hill'. What Bemberg thought of it all never emerged. He had stepped in to play the piano part for his song 'Sur le lac' and then discreetly faded into the background.

[1] *The Voice*, Winter 1948, p. 3.

Chapter Ten

THE CITY ROAD office was still reeling from the Melba afternoon when Fred Gaisberg received the news that early in December he and Will were to record the great Patti (now the Baroness Cederström) who lived in semi-retirement in her castle in Wales.

> From my earliest days I had had the name of Patti and her marvellous singing dinned into my ears. . . . To me she was a goddess enthroned beyond the access of ordinary mortals like myself. . . .
>
> Needless to say, to record the voice of Patti was the ambition of all talking machine companies, but both the gramophone and the phonograph were still too underdeveloped to warrant offering conditions attractive enough to overcome her prejudice against what she still regarded as a new-fangled toy. However, time was flying, and the moment could be lost for ever if delayed too long. So at last, when again approached by the Gramophone Company, she said:
>
> 'Well, if you will go to my solicitor, Sir George Lewis, and arrange everything with him, I will do whatever he advises.'
>
> The conditions Sir George Lewis made were simple: the entire recording apparatus should be taken down to Craig-y-Nos, made ready for immediate use, and the operator was to wait there from day to day until the Baroness said she was willing to sing.[1]

When my brother and I went to Craig-y-Nos Castle we travelled by a narrow-gauge railway to Penwylt, now called

[1] 'Adelina Patti', in *The Gramophone*, February 1943, p. 123. Fred Gaisberg based his account of the preliminary negotiations partly on material from Herman Klein's *The Reign of Patti*.

Craig-y-Nos. Here a bus met us and we drove to the sombre and imposing edifice where the singer lived. There we were greeted at the door by her agent, Mr. Alcock, and his wife. . . . I heard later that when my brother and I arrived Madame instructed . . . Mrs. Alcock to take a peep at these two suspicious characters and report to her what they were really like. When Mrs. Alcock returned and said we looked like harmless young men, she said:

'Well, look after them well.'

We soon discovered that every provision had been made for receiving us: two large bedrooms had been cleared and were placed at our disposal. Here we assembled our recording machine. We had a curtain over one of the doors, and through a hole projected the recording-horn. The piano was placed on wooden boxes, and when Madame Patti entered the room she was terribly intrigued as to what was behind that long horn. She had the curiosity of a girl, and peeped under the curtain to see what was on the other side.

Do not imagine for a moment, however, that when we set up the recording machine Madame rushed into the room to sing. Not a bit of it. She needed two full days to get used to the idea, during which she simply looked in every now and again and saw the ominous preparations for immortalising her voice. She did not know whether to be glad or sorry. To reward us for this long wait, she would say:

'Those two nice gentlemen—let them have champagne for dinner tonight to make up for their disappointment.'

Curiously enough, Landon Ronald had not been involved in the negotiations to record Patti, though he was well known to her. But when the Gaisbergs arrived, he was already on the scene. Ronald himself recalled the train of events.

On hearing that I was in some way connected with the Company, I received a charming invitation from her to stay for a few days, with the request that I should play for her. The whole scheme fascinated me, and I accepted the invitation with the greatest pleasure.

Those few days will ever remain impressed on my memory as amongst the happiest I have spent. She was a delightful hostess, and her husband (Baron Cederström) one of the kindest and gentlest of men. She was just a few weeks off sixty[-three], and her voice in a room was still amazing. After dinner she would get me to play her some of *Tristan*, which she had gradually learned to love, and would then, after a little persuasion, just see if she 'was in voice'.

And it was then that she sang divinely—for her husband, her brother-in-law, and myself. We were all quite overcome by her great artistry and agreed that the records must be made the next morning. She assented, and accordingly at [eleven] o'clock everything was made in readiness for the event.

Her first selection was Mozart's famous 'Voi che sapete'. She was very nervous, but made no fuss, and was gracious and charming to everyone. When she had finished her first record she begged to be allowed to hear it at once. This meant that the record would be unable to be used afterwards, but as she promised to sing it again, her wish was immediately granted. I shall never forget the scene. She had never heard her own voice, and when the little trumpet gave forth the beautiful tones, she went into ecstasies! She threw kisses into the trumpet and kept on saying:

'Ah! mon Dieu! maintenant je comprends pourquoi je suis Patti! Oh, oui! Quelle voix! Quelle artiste! Je comprends tout!'

Her enthusiasm was so naïve and genuine that the fact that she was praising her own voice seemed to us all to be right and proper. She soon settled down and got to work in real earnest, and the records now known all the world over were duly made.[1]

But it wasn't all so easy for Patti—or for Fred Gaisberg:

It was an ordeal for her to sing into this small funnel, while standing still in one position. With her natural Italian temperament she was given to flashing movement and to acting her parts. It was my job to pull her back when she made those beautiful attacks on the high notes. At first she did not like this and was most indignant, but later when she heard the lovely records she showed her joy just like a child and forgave my impertinence. . . .

She was used, in a queenly way, to rewarding any services or kindness that people showed her. She had a large and noble heart, but was decidedly temperamental; she would be calling

[1] Ronald, *Variations on a Personal Theme*, pp. 102–4.

everyone 'darling' one minute and 'devil' the next. But perhaps a woman who had sacrificed so much for her art and for her friends and relatives could be forgiven all these outbursts of temper.

> I have always instinctively felt that Patti was the only real diva I have ever met—the only singer who had no flaws for which to apologise. No doubt she had so mastered the art of living and protecting herself from the public gaze that she could plan her appearances for just those moments when she was at her freshest and brightest. I noticed that she never overtaxed herself, and her appearances were only for short periods of an hour. . . . She was very devout, and I was told she offered prayers in her beautiful private chapel to her patron saint for the success of the records. From 11 to 12 o'clock in the morning for four days in succession we made the records. . . . I shall never forget the delight of standing close beside the delicate source from which radiated those pure tones, whose message of delight will live and vibrate through the ages. It was as though one actually saw the spirit and soul seeking another abode.[1]

In the spring of 1906 both the Gaisbergs were away from London on recording trips abroad. Will took his turn at an extended tour in India and the Far East—assisted, as Fred had been three years earlier, by George Dilnutt. Fred himself went once again to Milan, where Carlo Sabajno had assembled a large roster of artists eager to make Gramophone records. There were numbers of 'promising' singers, of course, but also Boninsegna and Antonio Pini-Corsi. The great tenor DeLucia had agreed to make some more discs. And Sabajno directed a large number of choral extracts from the operatic repertoire, and even some orchestral records.

At the end of May Fred was back in London. Within a few days he was on his way once again to Patti's castle at Craig-y-Nos. His companion this time was Charles Scheuplein, who had until recently done much of Alfred Clark's recording in Paris. But Clark had made enough money from the Gramophone to retire at the age of thirty-two to a miniature chateau in the Loire Valley. Scheuplein was now a colleague at City Road.

Arriving at Craig-y-Nos, the arrangements were much the

[1] 'Adelina Patti', in *The Gramophone*, February 1943, p. 123.

same as before. But in the few months since Fred's visit in December, decay seemed to have set its hand on the enchanted castle.

> I and my assistant, Charlie Scheuplein, had meals with Mr. and Mrs. Alcock, and their conversation was mostly about the lively entertainments and gaiety of Craig-y-Nos when Signor Nicolini [Patti's second husband] was alive. Operas and concerts were staged in the small private theatre, and the two often appeared in the famous love scenes from the operas. It seems that Nicolini was keenly alive and kept the diva continually amused and entertained. The Alcocks contrasted those days with the sober and slow tempo of the Cederström regime.
>
> I can imagine that at the time of my visit life tucked away in the Welsh hills must have been somewhat dull for the little lady. She quite obviously welcomed the diversion of having her voice recorded and she was determined to enjoy it to the limit, although it must have entailed a lot of extra work to her establishment. She frequently looked in on us and seemed happy in exchanging conversation and watching us at our work. She was always sending us grapes from the big greenhouses, and when we left she loaded us with a basket of choice fruit for our return journey to London.

Great as Patti had been, however, and great as she still unquestionably was at the age of sixty-three, the Gramophone had now recorded virtually her entire active concert repertoire. Much as everyone might have wished for it, there would be no third visit to Craig-y-Nos.

Early in 1906 the three Gaisbergs had left their tiny flat in Bloomsbury for an apartment in Sutherland Avenue, Maida Vale. They haunted the auction rooms of Phillips Son & Neale to furnish it, and they laid down a crimson carpet throughout the main floor. The whole thing was on a grand scale—too grand for Louise: 'You could ride a bicycle in any one of those rooms,' she recalled many years later. Fred and Will had visions of elaborate hospitality with Louise as their hostess. But Louise, in the parlance of the day, was not domesticated. She did the shopping on her long journeys between Maida Vale and the Royal College of Music, but some domestic help was an absolute necessity. So Kate had come to them, a large, blonde girl who had her quarters in the basement.

It was a complicated household for a seventeen-year-old to supervise—especially when she was attempting to pursue a full-time course of professional music study. During the early part of the summer Louise had seemed wan and listless. Suddenly she was really ill with an infection that gathered itself into a gland in the neck.

Fred blamed himself. He had lightly assumed the responsibility of taking this brilliant little sister away from her mother and the family home to give her the benefits of a European musical education. But especially with Will's absence in the Far East for several months, Fred's attention had been all too occupied elsewhere. After some cabling back and forth it was decided that Louise must go back to Washington. Fred got leave to accompany her. It turned into an affair of many weeks.

As soon as they arrived Louise was sent into hospital, where an operation was deemed necessary. Recovery was slow, but Fred stayed with the family throughout this time. When she was well enough he took her to Capon Springs, where she could complete her convalescence with as much riding and outdoor exercise as she could manage.

In the autumn of 1906 Fred and Louise returned to London. Louise's illness had finished her chances of a career with the violin. She still had her remarkable voice, and after a successful audition she began vocal study with an excellent teacher of the day, Charles Acton. But Mrs. Gaisberg had been thoroughly upset by the whole affair, and during the next year she took the brave step of uprooting herself from the home her husband had built and coming with Carrie and Isabel to join Louise and the boys in London.

The interruption of the sudden journey to America had created another perspective in Fred's professional life. As a complement to his recording activities in the autumn of 1906, he began to make notes about some of his experiences and the people he had met. He was prompted especially by the thought of the ageing Patti, more or less alone with her memories in her Welsh castle. She would never make any more records, and therefore Fred would never meet her again. He began scribbling fragments about Patti and Craig-y-Nos on odd scraps of paper. Once begun, it proved a habit easy to continue.

Up to the time of Will's return from the Far East late in 1906, recording at City Road went steadily forward. There were some choral recordings which required careful marshalling, as reported by a journalist invited to see the process.

> When the Welsh Choir attend, these admirable performers first assemble in the practice room, where they rehearse their numbers while the orchestra are similarly engaged in the recording room. When each section has perfected its part, the chorus proceed to the latter department, taking with the orchestra assigned posts before the receiving horns. The number finished, the choir return to the practice room.[1]

They were in fact putting onto discs as many as possible of the celebrated sections from Handel's *Messiah*. The records were made piecemeal, whenever choir or soloists were available. It might one day amount to something like a complete performance: meanwhile they kept chipping away at it as opportunity offered.

The tenor solos from the *Messiah* were being sung by a young tenor called John Harrison. His rapidly mounting experience with the gramophone was already suggesting a sharp differentiation between music-making on the concert platform and in the recording room.

> John Harrison is perhaps the most nervous of Gramophone performers, particularly demanding that no others be present than the accompanist and the operator when he is recording. Before commencing, he looks suspiciously behind the doors and in the adjoining rooms to satisfy himself that no lurking listeners are there. And his wishes in this respect receive every attention, for it is under these conditions that this delightful tenor gives of his very best. Given his desired privacy, he attempts his extreme of vocal and artistic effects, and it necessarily follows that his first effort is not always successful; but the second or third will be, and it is only the perfect record which is given to the world. Other artistes are discovering the possibilities in this direction, and making use of them, with the result that seldom is such excellence attained in the concert hall as is registered on the magic disc.[2]

[1] *The Sound Wave*, March 1907, p. 74.
[2] Ibid., p. 76.

But there were still problems for which rough and ready solutions were often the order of the day. *The Sound Wave* reported an early visit of Mischa Elman to City Road.

> The youthful genius was playing a certain excerpt from Gounod's *Faust*. The number, however, could not in its entirety be got within the limits of the disc, and it was suggested—we think by Mr. Gaisberg—that at a particular point a cadenza should be introduced, and so obtain an effective finish. This was done, and we may say for ourselves that we were simply charmed with Elman's interpretation and the lingering beauty of his cadenza. But at the finish he turned sadly to Landon Ronald at the piano:
>
> 'Yes,' he said, 'it will do, but it is not *Faust*—it is *Faust* de-composed!'[1]

When Will returned from India, he and Fred were made joint managers of the Gramophone Recording Department. Fred welcomed this, for Will had a talent in mastering just those aspects of office-drill Fred himself longed to avoid. More and more clearly it was emerging for Fred Gaisberg that he was happiest only when dealing directly with the artists themselves: everything else seemed secondary to that.

During the next eighteen months the entire business side of the Company was to undergo a thorough re-organisation. The man in the forefront of all this was none other than Fred's old friend Alfred Clark. Trevor Williams had persuaded Clark to come out of his premature retirement, as Clark himself later recalled.

> I returned from Paris to London to become Managing Director of The Gramophone Company. My first step was to move the headquarters from the City Road to Hayes. The business had so grown that one could hardly move in the old headquarters. Hayes, with its numerous acres, offered itself as a spot where we could develop to our heart's content.[2]

The idea was to combine the head office, recording studios, and pressing plant in a single site. In February 1907 the distinguished

[1] *The Sound Wave*, March 1907, p. 76.

[2] *The Gramophone*, December 1929, p. 291. Clark's observations on the crowded conditions at City Road are more than confirmed by a report of the Gramophone Company's annual outing in June 1907 when over a hundred employees turned out. (*The Sound Wave*, July 1907, p. 220.)

Va Recording in The Vatican, April 1902: (*left to right*) William Michelis, the castrato Alessandro Moreschi, Will Gaisberg

Vb Caruso making a gramophone record: a self-caricature

VIa A Nautch girl and her musicians: a photograph by Fred Gaisberg, Calcutta 1902

VIb Laying the cornerstone of the new Gramophone factory at Hayes, May, 1907: Trevor Williams (Chairman of the Company) with Nellie Melba

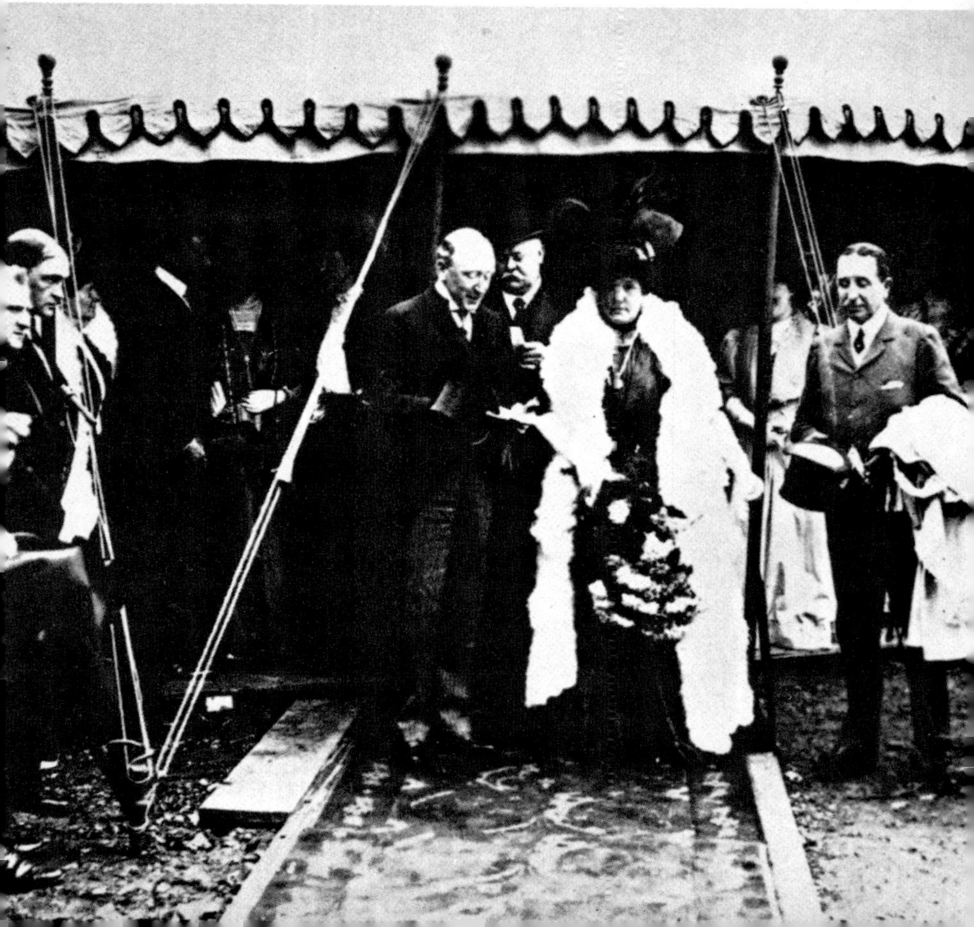

VIIa Fred Gaisberg in Egypt, 1907

VIIb Fred Gaisberg and Francesco Marconi drinking to the success of Marconi's new records, Frescati 1907

VIIIa Chaliapin recording in Russia with male choir, 1913. Behind Chaliapin stands the conductor Carlo Sabajno

VIIIb Chaliapin opening the new recording studios at Hayes, 1913. Fred and Will Gaisberg stand at the left

tenor Edward Lloyd cut the first sod for the enormous building project, and in May Melba laid the cornerstone. And the 'Typewriter' was soon to be dropped from the Company's name: from 1908 they would be known simply as The Gramophone Company.

One indication of the growing seriousness of the gramophone business was the atmosphere of grim purpose and even worry that now overtook even distinguished performers when they faced a recording session. In February 1907 Fred Gaisberg had witnessed a memorable exhibition of studio nerves from a very eminent singer at the peak of his career: 'The Van Dyke Opera Season was held at Covent Garden. This terminated suddenly and I engaged Vilhelm Herold, the Danish tenor, to sing for us some excerpts from *Lohengrin*. For this purpose I also engaged the German chorus. . . .'[1] *The Sound Wave* reported on the session:

> Herr Herold . . . put himself on a very sparing diet for two days previous, in order to record in best possible voice. He arrived with the full intention of finishing his six songs, but after two he pleaded that 'Gramo fright' had tired him, so that he was compelled to postpone the remaining songs.
>
> Apropos, it may be here stated that this peculiar form of nervousness is by no means uncommon. Many artistes who are perfectly at their ease on the concert platform seem to lose their accustomed confidence before the recording horn. No doubt they realise that the tiniest little fault will be permanently registered, and reproduced before the mighty audience of the talking machine public not only of today but of days to come.[2]

When the Herold records appeared in April, however, they elicited response from a very august quarter. *The Sound Wave* reported in May:

> It is well known that Her Majesty Queen Alexandra takes a great interest in The Gramophone Co.'s products. Recently a number of records were made by the celebrated tenor, Herr Herold . . . who is a countryman of our gracious Queen Consort. Her Majesty was so delighted with them that she

[1] Typewritten article entitled '1907'.
[2] *The Sound Wave*, March 1907, p. 76.

specially ordered a record of a song entitled 'The Fleeting Years', which had been dedicated to her. This special mark of Her Majesty's appreciation was given entirely from the gratification she had derived from the excellence of the Gramophone Co.'s reproduction of the famous Danish tenor's voice.

Immediately on receipt of the command the Gramophone Company approached Mr. [Edward] Lloyd to sing the song, and the great tenor was of course delighted to accede to such a request. As an instance of the company's prompt methods of business, it is interesting to note that the command was received on Thursday, and the record, duly finished, was delivered to the Queen on the following Saturday. . . . 'The Fleeting Years' appears in The Gramophone May list.[1]

Still, The Gramophone Company had no monopoly on the general talking machine success during those years. Fred Gaisberg received a sharp reminder of this when he met the young tenor John McCormack in the Irish Club in Charing Cross Road to try to persuade him to make some new discs for the Company. McCormack had recently returned from his many months of study with Sabatini in Italy.

In that short space of time he had made great progress in singing, and gave more attention to his appearance. One of the first things I understand Sabatini did was to insist he should have his teeth seen to, or he would stop his lessons. He was now married to Lily Foley, his boyhood sweetheart, and the miraculous improvement in John on the social side can be attributed to his wife, who from the beginning with tact and intelligence brought about a steady progress in the deportment and appearance of her youthful and uncouth husband.

When it came round to the question of further Gramophone records, however, it turned out to be too late.

Our rivals, the Odeon [Company, had] tied him up exclusively, and it was [not until] 1909 that our group bought him from the Odeon Company, paying the sum of £4,000, which at that time was considered a big price, but which proved in fact

[1] *The Sound Wave*, May 1907, p. 138.

to be a fine stroke of business for us, since under our trade-mark John climbed quickly to the first place as a record seller, and his royalty earnings for many years rivalled those of Caruso.[1]

Thus John McCormack would find his own way into gramophone immortality.

[1] Typescript article on John McCormack.

Chapter Eleven

MORE AND more of Fred Gaisberg's energies in these years were being claimed by recording in Italy. After the better part of a decade in which both Milan and Rome had given the Gramophone at least as many disappointments as successes, the enormous promise of operatic recording in Italy was at last beginning to be fulfilled. Fred had made one expedition in the spring of 1905 and another a year later. Now that he would be going more frequently, he found a way of Italian living that was highly congenial.

> My visits to Milan were generally for long periods, so it was more jolly to live in a pension than a hotel. I and my English friends usually put up at Rieger's Pension in the Via Boccaccio. Another well-known pension was Bonini's in the Piazzo del Duomo. Bonini was a huge woman, a former mezzo-soprano, and attracted many artists to her home. There was a lot of roulette and the pace was too hot for me, so I preferred the quieter Pension Rieger, run by a disillusioned Munich baritone and his wife. It was an excellently managed place, and because it was so quiet appealed to the more lady-like sopranos and their ambitious mothers or their protective aunts. There were always young American or English girls and boys there, sent over to be coached in opera. . . .
>
> There was also a large rosy-cheeked Canadian, who seemed principally engaged in strolling in the Galleria dressed in bohemian garb and telling people what a great Otello he was. I discovered that an elderly American lady was supporting him and was continually urging him to seek an opera debut. He had the biggest room in the pension, at one end of which was installed a platform. On this he would strut, emitting high

C's fiercely and frequently. But his protectress wanted results and threatened to withdraw her allowance. So he secured from a small impresario, by the payment of 15,000 lire, a chance to sing Otello in the provincial opera house of Brescia. Half-way through the opera his voice wobbled and he sang so flat that the gallery whistled, hooted and threatened a riot. The *carabinieri*, always ready for disturbances of this kind, stopped the show and insisted that the understudy should finish the opera. . . .

Besides these guests there were some great singers who loved the homeliness of Rieger's, amongst them Maria Galvany and Elvira de Hidalgo, both great Spanish coloraturas. . . . There never was such a jolly pension as Rieger's, with none of those frowsy old fossils found in Bloomsbury boarding-houses. The mixed Bavarian, Italian and French cooking would have done credit to the Savoy Grill, and the carafe of red chianti thrown in with the fixed lunch tasted to me in those days like the nectar of the gods.

Fred Gaisberg's long visits to Italy for recording owed much to the brilliantly deployed energies of the young conductor Carlo Sabajno, who was already becoming something of a character in Gramophone circles. One of the younger recording experts, Edmund Pearse, was to remind Fred of all this many years later: 'Maestro Sabajno and his love-affairs would be worth a book in itself—and be a best seller—if we dared to write all we knew, though everybody would think it fiction.'[1] This Don Giovanni could turn even his private affairs to account, as Fred very quickly found out:

He had a keen intelligence, and it was as well to know that in dealing with him every move had a motive. One of his business axioms was that every man could be reached through some woman.

Nevertheless Sabajno's greatest energies were reserved for the recording room.

Like most young Italian conductors, he adopted the tactics of every now and again disciplining the orchestra when he thought they were becoming careless or did not take him seriously. Any excuse was valid to open up an offensive.

[1] Letter to Fred Gaisberg, 12 December 1940.

In January and February 1907 Sabajno had gathered his most brilliant roster of Gramophone artists thus far. There were Boninsegna, Perello de Segurola, and Giorgini. There was the sensational baritone Titta Ruffo, whom Fred recorded right at the beginning of his visit on 22 January. And then, early in February, over several days of sessions, he made records of another baritone, a singer of fabled reputation, Mattia Battistini.

Battistini had made a few recordings for Sinkler Darby in Warsaw in 1902. Now, with Sabajno conducting the orchestra and assisted by singers of his own choosing, the great man made a series of discs for Fred Gaisberg embracing solos, duets, and ensembles from a variety of operas ranging from Mozart to Verdi. But behind them all stood the solid personality of Mattia Battistini.

> He was a man of great charm and distinction of manner, generous to fellow artists and a lavish host at his home in Rieti. His endowments of elegance and distinction led naturally to a marked preference for roles in which he could play the part of a cavalier or noble seigneur, such as Don Carlos in Verdi's *Ernani*, Rodrigo in *Don Carlos*, the Marquis de Chevreuil in *Maria di Rohan*, or Don Giovanni.
>
> In conversation Battistini never raised his voice, which had a soft, husky quality and was almost falsetto in pitch. Although he spoke Spanish and French fluently, he was mostly at home in his Roman dialect. His sentences were short and jerky, and his face lit up with a humorous smile about the eyes. Tall and handsome, he looked after himself well, enjoyed good health and, for a singer, was exceptionally bright and merry. His dress and taste were immaculate—almost dandified. . . .[1]

In an era that was beginning to lay more and more stress on bright, young dramatic successes of the moment, Battistini stood for something as permanent as the horizon of musical performance could reveal. He was already fifty years old, had behind him a long career of *bel canto* singing that all the experts acclaimed as perfection itself, and showed no sign of declining powers. Altogether as musician and man he was a most valuable artistic asset.

[1] *The Gramophone*, February 1944, p. 131.

The Gramophone directors in London certainly took this view when they arranged a Press Reception at the Savoy Hotel for 14 March 1907, to play some of the new Battistini records that Fred had made. There were three selections from *Un ballo in maschera* and one of Battistini's great show-pieces, 'A tanto amor' from *La favorita.* In addition the guests were regaled with recent discs by Ruffo, Boninsegna, and Melba.

In the late spring of 1907 Fred Gaisberg returned to Milan for operatic recording of a different kind. In several carefully planned sessions at the beginning of June, they would record a complete performance of Leoncavallo's *I pagliacci.* It was a complex business. Sabajno advised them that it would be best to arrange matters in such a way as to deal with all the music of each singer, the choral parts, and the orchestral interludes on separate occasions. Thus the recording order for the twenty-odd records bore no relation whatever to the actual order in which the music occurred in the score.

For all of these sessions the composer himself was persuaded to attend, so Leoncavallo's masterpiece achieved its first recording 'with the big maestro sitting by while Sabajno conducted. Thus we could advertise: "Recorded under the supervision of the composer".'

In addition to *I pagliacci*, the Gramophone did its duty by the latest contributions to the operatic repertory—*L'albatro* of Pacchierotti, Parelli's *Hermes*, and *Jana* by Virgilio. Today these titles are curiosities, remembered if at all through the discs Fred Gaisberg made with Taccani, Carmen Melis, and other young singers, the orchestral accompaniments conducted by the composers themselves. In 1907 they might well have figured as the '*Pagliaccis*' of the future.

All such recordings, as Fred had good cause to remember, were especially demanding:

> Our small studios were hard put to accommodate orchestra, chorus, and soloists during these sessions, and it was especially trying in hot weather. Most of our recording had to take place during the late spring and the summer, when La Scala had closed and the artists and *professori* were free. Also, in the winter the heating of the studios was impossible. (Heating was always Italy's problem until the development of water power and the electric generating stations of later years.)

Year after year the same orchestral players attended, and I got to know them well as friendly and good-natured fellows, always smiling. Every year I would give them a supper in a modest but honest restaurant, when they would fall to on great steaming bowls of spaghetti and large flagons of chianti.

Our oboe was Giorgio, the buffoon of the orchestra and the butt of their jokes, but an extraordinary player. He really believed them when they told him just before a performance of *The Barber of Seville*, 'Watch out that you play your best tonight because the composer himself will be conducting.'

There was another mad but excellent musician, the first horn, whose virtuosity was amazing. He had an uncanny musical memory—so certain that during the long rests in an opera he could busy himself with reading or looking around the house but never miss his cue. He had to be under the constant escort of his wife.

I must not forget Nardi and Nastrucci at the first desk of the violins: both still remain[ed] pets of Toscanini notwithstanding the proverb that no master remains a hero to his valet. They were fine players and most pleasant companions.[1]

A part of Fred Gaisberg's Italian time was also spent in Rome. Here in October 1907 he was joined by his colleague Edmund Pearse to make records of the great tenor Francesco Marconi. Marconi would not record at the improvised studio they had set up in rooms in the Hotel Laurati, but only at his own palazzo 'with its terraces of palms and azaleas interspersed with fragments of Roman and Greek sculpture'. Marconi had the reputation of a close spender, but he was charming to the young men. Pearse wrote to Fred years later: 'I recall a Sunday we spent at Marconi's villa at Frescati where he, the erstwhile bootmaker, was very much the Grande Signor.'[2] He genially allowed Pearse to take photographs of himself drinking a toast with Fred to the success of the new records.

During the late autumn of 1907 a new Italian star arose—ironically in London. Her name was Tetrazzini, and the reverberations quickly reached Fred Gaisberg in Italy.

It was in the autumn and not the Grand Season [at Covent Garden] otherwise it is doubtful whether the managing direc-

[1] 'All Roads Lead to La Scala'.

[2] Letter to Fred Gaisberg, 12 December 1940.

tor, Harry Higgins, would have braved the wrath of Melba, who at that time was the reigning prima donna at Covent Garden. Higgins first heard of [Tetrazzini] through Campanini. He signed her up for ten performances during the autumn of 1907. Before the ink was dry he wanted to call the season off, and when she refused he offered her £300 to cancel the contract. Tetrazzini stood firm and threatened legal proceedings. Higgins then decided to go ahead with it.

Hearing about this engagement of a new soprano, my directors cabled to Carlo Sabajno . . . to secure the lady at once for record making. So he obtained an appointment and presented himself at the Tetrazzini apartment, hat in hand, only to be told that she was still occupied with her toilet. It was a humiliating experience for a *maestro* to hang around, waiting like a lackey, and he made some remark to that effect, which the maid repeated to her mistress. Whereupon he left, slamming the door after him. (I once asked Tetrazzini why she always refused to let Carlo conduct for her, and she told me that she seethed with anger when she heard that message from her maid, and vowed she would get her own back. This trait of never forgetting or forgiving was most pronounced in the lady.)

A month later she was in London. She had never sung there before and was still unheard of in England. Even to Higgins she was X the unknown quantity, and his tilt with her naturally prejudiced his outlook.

The season opened on Sat., Nov. 2nd. The night was foggy, and one could barely see the stage. The House was only ¾ full & most of that was paper. The opera was *La traviata* with Carpi as tenor, Sammarco the baritone, & Panizza the conductor. Harry Higgins told me that when he heard the first note of 'E strano' & then the brilliant cadenza with those clear, ringing attacks on the C's—a real *legere-spinto* with breadth & purity of tone such as he had dreamed of all his life—he rushed to the telephone to call up Fleet St. to rush down to the Garden their reporters to hear this phenomenon.

Sunday morning the papers carried front pages devoted to the new discovery. Tet became the rage of England, & it spread to America. The Autumn Season, starting as a failure, had turned into a huge success because of one little woman. In haste the Opera placed her under a long contract, and even ran 4 or 5 Albert Hall concerts to sold-out houses that autumn, so great was the public clamour to see & hear Tetrazzini.

On Monday, bright and early, our manager was on her doorstep, awaiting her pleasure. She made him wait. She had not forgotten the Sabajno episode and took it out of us, not only by keeping our representative in the cold, but by dictating her own terms for recording. . . . The market price for prima donnas had gone up, and instead of a few hundred pounds we had to pay a few thousand pounds. But even so it resulted in good business, as her name was on everyone's lips & she was necessary to enable us to maintain our lead.

On 20 December 1907 Tetrazzini appeared at City Road with the conductor Percy Pitt to make a dozen records. It was the beginning of a long and brilliant association with the Gramophone Company in which Fred Gaisberg was to play a great part. But the Tetrazzini discs of that first session were supervised by Will Gaisberg, for Fred was still in Italy recording with Ted Pearse.

Italy seemed to offer the Gramophone more and more that season. Early in 1908 Fred Gaisberg renewed his association with another important young artist.

At the Teatro dal Verme, Italy's great actor-baritone Titta Ruffo appeared eight times as Hamlet in Thomas' old-fashioned opera of that name. His acting and singing, as well as his costumes, made such a deep impression that he was the talk of the town: [it] placed him in a class equal to Chaliapin and Caruso as a world artiste. He was quickly engaged by the Colon Theatre, Buenos Aires and the Metropolitan, New York at a fee equal to that which Caruso was receiving.

We gramophone people were equally intoxicated by the magnetism of this handsome young baritone (he was barely thirty years old), and it was not long before he began making visits to record the Hamlet, Rigoletto, Tonio and other arias, as well as those duets from *Rigoletto* with Maria Galvany that had such popularity in those days. By the old method of preparing a bourse, he cleverly induced my Company to sign him up on a five-year contract at a total guarantee of a million lire—a fee unheard of at that time. . . .

I remember him as over medium height, muscular yet well-proportioned, never putting on weight, and with a grip that could bend an inch steel bar: he exuded strength and virile force. He was a friend of Chaliapin, whose acting had a great influence on him—as it did on all acting on the opera stage of Italy. As a *raconteur* of stories, especially in the Tuscan dialect, he was superb and, in my opinion, equalled only by Chaliapin (who also enacted whilst narrating his stories).

The Ophelia of that season was the beautiful seventeen-year-old Graziella Pareto. Of a height equal to Titta's, she was slim and of delicate features, yet with a voice of lovely quality and of sufficient power to make an ideal partner for him. These performances also marked her for a celebrity.[1]

Fred Gaisberg promptly carried off Pareto for the Gramophone as well, and there began another association that was to last the length of her career. He was less fortunate with another young soprano, Claudia Muzio. She paid a visit to the Gramophone studio that season, but soon deserted in favour of the rival Pathé Company.

Sometimes it seemed easy for Fred Gaisberg to forget such disappointments in looking toward very grand possibilities.

Chaliapin [had] appeared at La Scala in 1907 in some eight or ten performances of *Mefistofele*, Toscanini conducting. And in 1908 occurred his sensational series of performances of *Boris*. His reading of this role at the age of 35 was at its most perfect point and combined maturity of acting with youth and beauty of voice, all of which had a profound effect on the future of Italian opera singing and acting.

Frequently he came to our recording studios, and I carried out for him a series of experiments in voice-placing and tone-colour, principally in those *falsetto* effects of which he later became so fond. In those days of exuberant youth, he fascinated all of us by his charm and good nature.[2]

But by no means all of Gaisberg's time was spent in Italy during those years. Scandinavia in September and October of 1908, Calcutta in November; two months in Egypt and Syria at the beginning of 1909; thence to Constantinople and Salonica

[1] 'All Roads Lead to La Scala'.
[2] Ibid.

before arriving in Italy for yet another two months of recording to begin in April—so it went on. Spending so much of his time away from the Gramophone Head Office and the centre of recording in London, Fred was denied his brother Will's more continuous experience of gramophone progress in art and industry. And Fred found he could not quite get over the feeling of the old days that all this success and expansion was ephemeral. So it was that in the midst of a rich programme of recording in Milan, Fred could write to his brother on 14 April 1909.

> Say Will I have been doing a good deal of thinking of late and have come to the conclusion that the Gramo. business is *finished.* The novelty is gone and days of big profits are over. Gramophone will never see 40/– again and the Co. will settle down to a basis of 8 to 10% dividends. They will be handicapped with those big factories which will be sinks for dropping money and it will be retarded by barnacles and clinkers like all old concerns. I tell you it is an impossibility for the Gramo. Co. to show a profit with their habit of extravagance. Clark and Dixon have a hopeless task before them. It will be better for them to liquidate right away than to drag on indefinitely. . . .
>
> I feel very discouraged generally about the outlook of things generally (Gramophone) and only warn you that this is your last chance to save money. The salary you are now making is the highest you & I will ever get out of the business. The income from Gramo. stock you can *discount* as it will disappear in 2 years and with it your shares. So what you have saved & put away now is all that you can count on. It is only what I looked forward to all along.

If these were some of the accents of the elder brother advising the younger, the roles had also begun to reverse, for Fred was showing himself clearly in need of encouragement. When Will sent telegrams of reassurance, Fred wrote a week later: 'I am going right ahead merrily making records. . . . I made orchestral solos this morning—35 players.'

The roles of the two brothers meanwhile had also been quietly reversing themselves within the family home. Fred may have been depressed at Gramophone prospects in the spring of 1909, but the atmosphere of Milan still exercised its perennial magic. In the midst of the southern wealth of music and art, Fred found himself longing to see their youngest sister Louise as somehow part of it all—pursuing her singing studies in Italy even towards a triumphant debut at La Scala perhaps. But when he wrote to suggest the idea, there came a reply from Will couched in the terms of a man who knows the world better than his correspondent.

> As to Louise going from Frankfurt to Milan before you get there, I do not like that at all and will not let her go. I do not mind Louise being in Milan as long as you are there or her sister, but alone, no. I have seen quite enough of this Bohemian life, and I do not think the game is worth Louise risking the discomforts and hardships to which she would be put if she remains alone in Milan. Singing is all right, but they are a rotten lot, and I hate to think of Louise going through what some of them have to go through. If you are really in earnest about her singing, make arrangements in Milan so that Carrie can stay with her if you are not there. If it is worth anything it is worth a great deal. Louise is not strong, and I always [regret] the length of time we allowed her to stay in London without her sisters or anyone except you and I with her, and I always felt that it was on this account that she had trouble with her glands, and had to undergo an operation for them. Louise is a girl that has to have someone with her, because she gets very blue.[1]

In the end it was arranged just as Will suggested it should be: Louise went to Milan, where Fred arranged for her to stay at his favourite Pension Rieger—but only when another sister, Isabel, agreed to stay there with her. None the less the talent of the Gaisbergs' little sister was at last to have its full opportunity and test.

[1] Letter of 20 September 1909, now in E.M.I. archives at Hayes.

Chapter Twelve

BY 1910 the Gramophone Directors thought that what Fred Gaisberg had accomplished in Italy might be repeated in that land of vast but still largely unrealised talking machine potential, Russia. And so, during the next years, Fred's notebooks were to be filled with details and experiences of uncounted journeys across northern Europe. His United States passport for 1910–12 survives, so full of Russian visa-stamps that it looks as if the paper itself must have been used up before the document's validity expired.

At the beginning of 1910 they had signed the famous lyric tenor Sobinov to a new contract which provided for twenty records to be made during the next three years. In February Fred Gaisberg recorded the first ten of these in Moscow. They were marvellous discs in every way, and they included duets with the brilliant young soprano Neshdanova.

Then, after years of short-term understandings and disappointments, they were at last able to negotiate a ten-year contract with Chaliapin on 13 May:

> Advance 1st year £3,000 for 15 records.
>
> Royalty after sale of 1,000 of each title: if Co. continue the sale they agree to pay Chaliapin R.1.80 on each record sold over that number.
>
> Should Chaliapin be asked to make more than 15 records the Company agree to pay him R.2,000 for each additional record.
>
> Chaliapin will also sing in the year 1911–12 a further ten selections *not in Russian* for an advance of R.15,000 on royalty which is to be paid at the rate of R.1 for these records only. All 12″ in size.

Until Chaliapin actually signed his name under these terms, Fred remembered that all their efforts had seemed more than once at risk through the great man's rivalry with Sobinov: 'These negotiations were unnecessarily protracted because of the lifelong jealousy between these artists, each being afraid the other was getting the larger fee from us.' In fact there was only one aspect of the agreement which did not present any difficulty where Chaliapin was concerned, and that was the question of who should conduct the orchestra at the recording sessions.

> [I] consulted him, asking if such and such a director would be agreeable.
>
> 'Yes, yes,' he replied, 'anyone will do, for it is I who will direct.'[1]
>
> I remember that on the night when Chaliapin signed his contract he invited us to a party at Yar's Restaurant and engaged the largest *chambre séparée*. With his cronies from the chorus he sang Russian and gypsy songs the whole night through. It was a tireless night: no women were present and Chaliapin was as happy as a school-boy.

In the late autumn of 1910 Fred Gaisberg returned to Russia to make the first of the records provided for in Chaliapin's contract. Feodor Ivanovich greeted him like a long-lost little brother, and then proceeded to appropriate Fred as though he were some diminutive but essential article of personal property.

> At the height of his achievement in 1910 he drove me in a sleigh around the great Bolshoi Opera Square to proudly show me the long line of people queued up to buy tickets for a performance announced that morning of *Boris*, and he pointed to the cavalry patrolling to keep the line in order.[2]

He also gave Fred a personally conducted tour of the living accommodation a great singer could ordain for himself in those final days of Czarist Russia.

> His vast apartment in St. Petersburg was of the most up-to-date and *de luxe* type. The music room alone contained a Persian carpet 30 ft. by 45 ft. On the walls were eight enor-

[1] 'Recording Chaliapin in Moscow', MS. dated 14 May 1913 in E.M.I. archives.

[2] Typescript, 'Chaliapin'.

mous Gobelin tapestries which he valued at £10,000, and a great collection of paintings of the best Russian artists.

In Moscow, the guides used to point out his home. It was an important building standing in its own grounds, and was designed in a lavish style which permitted him to entertain Grand Dukes and great celebrities.

Each of these establishments was run by an army of servants and retainers, which was the usual thing in pre-war Russia. Besides that, he had a very extensive estate in the Crimea, where he looked foward to living when he retired. All of these possessions he had amassed notwithstanding the fact that he lived in a most lavish and extravagant manner.[1] To get the records made, however, was a very different affair.

It was always difficult to find halls in which to carry out recording in Moscow, St. Petersburg, or any other Russian town. Well heated rooms of any size were hard to come by. The Gramophone Company were fortunate in securing ample offices in the Middle Market of the vast building known as the Chinese Bazaar, on the Red Square facing the brilliantly ornate St. Basil's Church and the picturesque walls of the Kremlin. The large room in which the recording took place was heated by a large porcelain stove reaching the ceiling. A small workshop attached was not heated, and the plating baths would frequently be hard-frozen of a morning. The Russian assistant had his own method of heating it up. He punched holes in a tin bucket and started a fire in it, leaving the door closed. Once he was found there in a coma from the gas, and his life was saved only after quick and drastic treatment. On another occasion I called two janitors to assist in moving the piano, which was always raised three feet from the ground. In this case they shoved so strongly as to topple the piano over on me. I was sore for days.

. . . It frequently occurred that the accompanists had to be kept waiting for one to two hours; but this did not prove so expensive as it did with an orchestra. No law of punctuality was valid where Chaliapin was concerned: it was the duty of the world to wait for him. If the session was set for 5 o'clock and his voice was not warm or set up, he would demand:

'What is the use of coming until it is?'

[1] 'Chaliapin as I Knew Him', in *The Gramophone*, 1938.

When I explained this to my directors, they would wax indignant and say they would not tolerate such behaviour. I would have to tell them that the Opera often waited, and even Grand Dukes thought nothing of it. After all, the whole scheme of the Gramophone was to obtain the artist when he was at his best, and not when the factory whistle blew. It was not wilfulness on his part: he was as happy making good records as we were to obtain them. He was only waiting for that moment of the day when that great voice was velvety and pliant (*morbido*).[1]

Explanations were all very well, but even Fred Gaisberg had to admit that Chaliapin was a recording man's nightmare.

He never made a gramophone record willingly; he had to be coerced and almost kidnapped. He went to the grave without discovering the most propitious hour of the twenty-four in which to record.[2]

Eventually I learned that it was useless to call a Chaliapin session before 8 in the evening or even later. Before that time his big voice or frame was not tuned up. To assemble musicians and Chaliapin before that time meant they would get on each others' nerves as he tried to warm up his voice with coughs, grunts, scales, and squeals. Sometimes this wound up in a free fight for all. All worthwhile records were rushed in in the last twenty minutes of a session—when conductor and instrumentalists were tamed to zero and Chaliapin had sand-papered his voice to a flexible, velvet tone.

His first recording session [in the autumn of 1910] is an unforgettable memory. We persuaded him to enter the waiting sleigh, and when he entered the recording room he was greeted boisterously by the choir and orchestra, who had been patiently waiting for some hours.

His chest stripped and bare like a prize-fighter, he starts his recording. As on the stage and everywhere else, he takes full direction of orchestra and laboratory. . . . When he stands before the trumpet and expands that great chest of his and at ten yards' range attacks the recording diaphragm, the chances are the recording expert will be overwhelmed by a great and sudden fear for his delicate recording diaphragms.[3]

[1] 'Chaliapin'. [2] 'Chaliapin as I Knew Him'.
[3] Typescript, 'Recording Chaliapin in Moscow'.

We worked on one record after another until one o'clock in the morning. His pleasure was so great that he invited the choir and myself to finish the evening at the *Strielka* Restaurant, listening to its gypsy choir. This entailed hiring six sleighs or more and undertaking an hour's journey over the hard frozen snow through the biting Russian night winds.

On arriving at the *Strielka* we were received with a noisy welcome, and the show literally began all over again, with Chaliapin standing in the midst of the performers, singing and conducting the combined choirs of the nomadic gypsies and of the members of the Opera House choir who had come with us. Several hours passed in hilarious music-making. Chaliapin was truly in his element.

Trouble was occasioned by a certain Prince D. who, being more than a little tipsy, became annoyed when our combined choir overwhelmed the efforts of an impromptu choir he had organised and was conducting. There were hot arguments and bitter words, and the hostess and her attendants had difficulty in maintaining peace.

We returned to our hotels completely exhausted by one of the most riotous nights I personally have ever witnessed, at about eight o'clock in the morning—not at all an unusual thing in the Russia of pre-war days.

Chaliapin tended to swamp every other Russian Gramophone experience. But Fred Gaisberg and Ted Pearse accomplished a great deal of important recording during those late autumn weeks of 1910.

Among the artists recorded upon my arrival in St. Petersburg was Maria Michailova, whose record of Gounod's *Ave Maria* had become world-famous. In my pocket I had a commission from Lionel Powell, the concert impresario, to engage her for a concert tour of England if my impressions upon hearing and seeing her were favourable. My friends in Russia marvelled at my enthusiasm for her, since she had remained only a second-line artist at the Opera House and had never made a concert tour even of Russia, in spite of her successful records.

Indeed I received a shock when I met the dumpy little creature, then over fifty, after the picture my imagination had painted from hearing her golden records.

At that point Fred's tact achieved a small masterpiece of compliment. The little lady's fame had gone round the world by means of her recordings, and so it would have to remain. But as Fred's Gramophone colleague George Cooper was to remind him of Michailova years later: 'You will remember how pleased she was when you called her "the Recording Angel".'[1] This had a delicate significance: in most of Europe the Gramophone Company had recently abandoned their established trademark of the Recording Angel in favour of the dog-and-gramophone of Barraud's famous painting 'His Master's Voice'; the Russian Company, however, had kept the Angel.

A year later, in the autumn of 1911, Fred Gaisberg was in Moscow again.

> . . . I had two unusual records made that had enormous popularity. I had often visited the Kremlin, where the guides showed you the biggest bell in the world and impressed on you that Moscow was a city of a thousand churches. This encouraged me to make a record of Moscow bells. In the open, the cold was far too severe for our waxes, so I had to arrange for the bells to come to us. One morning a well-known bell-founder brought a peal to our hotel. The largest, weighing several tons, being unable to pass through the door, had to be hoisted up through the window. When these five monsters were installed in the room our concert began. Heavens, what a din! Their vibrations almost brought down the house. These records [were to have] an immense vogue with Russian soldiers, mainly perhaps because they reminded them of the familiar echoes of their village chimes.
>
> The other unusual record was one of the Lord's Prayer, sung by the priest Rosoff with the Iuchov Choir. The soloist, a magnificent creature, tall and massive, with long wavy hair and a patriarchal beard, had a pedal-bass voice recalling the tones of a 32-ft. organ stop. He began the first phrase, 'Our Father Which Art In Heaven', on the lowest note of his voice, gradually ascending, semitone by semitone, with steadily increasing volume until the high C was reached, and with that the choir burst out into harmony with 'For Thine is the Kingdom, the Power, and the Glory for Ever and Ever, Amen'. It was a superb climax.

[1] Letter to Fred Gaisberg, 5 July 1940.

Rosoff was proud of his breath control, and would lie at full length on the floor and invite me to stand on his diaphragm. Then, taking a breath, he would easily lift me up seven inches in the air.

Our uncovering of this rich new gramophone field was by no means unchallenged, and we had continual fights with competitors—some scrupulous, but most of them the reverse. Russia was one of the countries where international patent and copyright laws did not hold good.

As early as the spring of 1909 Fred had been writing to his brother Will in London about this latest Russian difficulty.

It seems that Rodkinson was interested in a dubbing plant in Russia that dubs our own records, and as he held notes and mortgages on the businesses of most of our Russian agents he could easily force them to buy the dub-records of this factory. He now openly owns this dubbing plant, and it is this that is ruining our trade there. It seems also as though Rodkinson had some hold on Birnbaum, and this is why Birnbaum got the Co. to give Rodkinson £750 per year for 3 years when he left the Co. and negligently allowed this bonus to be called 'for past services rendered', so R. can claim it as salary even though he is in direct competition against us.[1]

In the spring of 1912 . . . I was recording in St. Petersburg in our studio on the Fontanka when Joe Cummings, a colleague from a competing concern, dropped in to see me. I was, of course, surprised at this visit. He was a little Englishman and, in answer to my query, went on to tell me that he had signed a year's contract with the [Rodkinson] Company. After having worked for them for six months, he was still without any salary and was very anxious to get back to England to his sick wife, to whom he was unable to send money. It was for this reason that he had come to ask my assistance.

I had known that there was a [Rodkinson] Company operating in St. Petersburg. They were pirates in the gramophone trade. In other words, they were forging our Chaliapin, Sobinov, Caruso, and other Red Label celebrity records and selling them at reduced prices. Naturally a hue-and-cry was raised by the artists who were being cheated out of their

[1] Letter of 14 April 1909 in EMI archives.

royalties, and for some time we had been trying to take legal action against this firm. They were, however, too wily and our only hope was to get evidence somehow that they were pressing records from our own records.

Joe Cummings's appearance offered me the solution to this problem, and I told him I just wanted a little favour from him, and then he could have the money for his wife. He asked what it was, and I replied:

'Give me a signal when Chaliapin records are actually in the press and being stamped in the [Rodkinson] factory.'

It was arranged that the signal should be the dropping of a handkerchief. The time and place were agreed upon and we notified the police. The plot moved successfully, the police raided the factory and obtained all the evidence we wanted. Their action enabled us not only to confiscate all the forged matrices but also to destroy their entire stock of accumulated records of our celebrity artists and to close down their plant.

In the autumn of 1913 Fred Gaisberg was in St. Petersburg again, this time to record a great and familiar singer far away from his home ground—Mattia Battistini.

Italian opera was well supported in St. Petersburg, Moscow, Kiev, and Odessa before World War No. 1, and Italy's best singers bravely endured the rigours of the Russian winters to earn the big fees offered by zealous impresarios. Each winter at the time of my visits to St. Petersburg, from 1900 to 1914, there was usually a season of Italian opera at the Grand Theatre du Conservatoire. Here I saw Battistini at his best, for during this period he was at the highest pinnacle of his work, although he was then fifty years of age [and more]. He was the star of the season, and the assisting artistes, who were all first class, gave him no mean measure of support. . . .

[In 1913] I was in the company of Carlo Sabajno, Battistini's great friend, and this enabled me to be frequently in the great singer's company. Battistini fitted well into the *haut monde* of St. Petersburg life, and counted many admirers in Court and aristocratic circles.[1]

When on tour . . . Battistini's regime was modified: he saved up all his energy for his public performances, rising only

[1] 'Battistini and others', in *The Gramophone*, February 1944, p. 131.

at mid-day after a kind of reception at 11 a.m. in his bedroom, recalling the royal *lever* of Louis XIV. I like to remember attending his morning receptions in the old Hotel de France, with its big rooms heated with great porcelain stoves and furnished in old-fashioned red plush. Carefully shaved and groomed, lying relaxed in a big four-poster bed, Battistini would exchange gossip and trivialities with his visitors while the valet would serve chocolate all round.[1]

Battistini made a long series of records in St. Petersburg during that autumn with Sabajno conducting. Vocally they were perhaps the finest representations on disc yet made of the great baritone. But Sabajno was unhappy in Russia, as Fred soon realised.

Here he found himself out of his element. The musicians would not submit to his discipline, and frequent outbursts of passion made our sessions the joke of St. Petersburg. He made a great pal of Chaliapin, however, who spoke excellent Italian, and they larked and joked like boys until one of the jokes turned on Chaliapin, who was notoriously touchy. He spied over Sabajno's shoulder while the conductor unsuspectingly sketched a comic caricature entitled 'Boris on the Battlefield'; then the fur flew.

It was a demanding existence—continual journeys across the entire breadth of Europe at a moment's notice, contracts to be negotiated, artists to be placated, and every smallest expense carefully reported. No one had realised quite how demanding it was until Fred Gaisberg's health had suddenly broken down in March 1911, when he was forced to go into a German hospital for six weeks.

When at last he returned to London, it seemed the moment for the Gaisberg family to look for another home. Since the arrival of Mrs. Gaisberg with Carrie and Isabel, the family had been living in a smallish house in Rudall Crescent—one of the 'new' streets of Hampstead, but rather dingy. Now they purchased a much larger property near the top of Fitzjohn's Avenue. This was also a 'new' road, running up the hill from Swiss Cottage into Hampstead, but the houses were all detached and of rather grand sizes, set behind trees. Opposite the Gais-

[1] 'Battistini and Others.'

bergs, near the corner of Netherhall Gardens, was a Norman Shaw house which had been built for the Royal Academy painter Edwin Long. It was at the moment unoccupied; rumour had it that it might be bought by Sir Edward Elgar.

But Fred was never long in London during these years. When he was not in Russia the incessant recording demands were likely to take him to any one of a dozen European capital cities. In January 1912 he crossed to Paris to make records of the great Polish pianist Paderewski.

> My brother Will had personally negotiated the contract, obtained Paderewski's signature, and left me with the job of making satisfactory records of this giant's playing. . . . He was then at the zenith of his artistic career, with twenty brilliant, all-conquering years at the back of him. Was my awe and worship to be wondered at?
>
> Of all the musicians I have known he was the most inaccessible, and in his presence one had always to be on one's guard and use the utmost tact. A clumsy act, and he could humiliate one in the most withering way.
>
> I remember arranging a session in our Paris studio. Without asking Paderewski's permission, the Company's very enterprising Paris manager invited a journalist friend to be present. This was bad enough. But when the scribe, with a patronising manner, began to interview Paderewski, he sat there on the piano-stool frigid and white. It slowly dawned on the company present that a most awful blunder had been committed, as Paderewski stalked majestically from the room, leaving us looking at each other in blank amazement.[1]

Later that day they heard that Paderewski had left Paris altogether and returned to his home in Switzerland.

Anxious diplomacy was carried on over the next forty-eight hours. The result was that Fred Gaisberg would have to follow the great man to his home, set up all the necessary equipment in the music room there, and in that suitably protected atmosphere persuade Paderewski that he might be able to get on with the task of making his records.

On 26 January Fred piled four recording horns, stands, cutting machine, and wax blanks into a hired automobile and was driven into Switzerland.

[1] Typescript article, 'Paderewski as I Knew Him'.

Paderewski, from the first, diffidently consented to record and never completely reconciled himself to the ordeal. He always doubted whether a machine could capture his art. . . . His art involved such broad and unrestrained dynamics—the faintest *pianissimo* crashing into a great mass of tone. In other words, he painted on a vast canvas, and the gramophone could only reproduce a miniature of his mighty masterwork.

Against the experience of hearing Paderewski play, the records made during the visit seemed pale indeed: one had to remind the great man at every other moment to modify his dynamics for the recording machine, and the unwonted restraints worried him. Altogether it stood out in Fred Gaisberg's memory as 'one of the most arduous weeks of my recording experience': 'Neither I nor anybody else ever made really satisfactory records of Paderewski. . . .'[1]

Yet the company of the man himself represented something quite new in Fred's widening experience.

I look back on the week spent at 'Riond Bosson' and that tall, vigorous man with the world at his feet. What an opportunity to study him at close quarters! Had I been a musician, he would probably have been more constrained in the selection of topics of general conversation. So he spoke on many and varied subjects covering a wide range of interests. I did distinctly get the impression that he was indignant that his status as a pianist should handicap his ambition in the field of politics.

In the end Fred Gaisberg was overwhelmed as he had only once before been overwhelmed. Near the end of his own career he was to reflect: 'Of the greatness of Paderewski and Chaliapin neither gramophone nor film can give anything but a faint suggestion. It is only when I hear a record of either that I realise the futility of trying to reflect their genius by mechanical means.'

When Paderewski appeared in London during the summer of 1912, however, he went out of his way to show his gratitude for what Fred Gaisberg had tried to accomplish:

In my autograph album on August 3rd 1912 Mr. Paderewski wrote three bars of the *Andante con moto* theme from his Symphony op. 24, and added the words:

[1] 'Paderewski as I Knew Him'.

'To Fred Gaisberg, with the very kindest regards of I. J. Paderewski.'

Paderewski had the reputation of refusing requests for autographs and I remember my intense satisfaction as I watched him write those precious lines. It was the first entry in a handsome new album my father had given me many years ago; otherwise I could never have summoned up the courage to ask him for his autograph in a book already scrawled over by lesser lights. . . .

My mother always knew when Paderewski was in London because a bouquet of roses was sent to her. Often the ever-thoughtful Paderewski and his equally charming wife Helena would send my mother, then an invalid, baskets of fruit from their farm in Switzerland.[1]

Then Fred Gaisberg's recording of instrumental music found encouragement on a different front—that of the orchestra.

My first experience with a great symphonic conductor was in 1912, when Artur Nikisch and the London Symphony Orchestra, fresh from a grand concert tour in Canada and the United States, recorded a part of their touring programme. It was virtuoso playing which was unique at that time. . . . Nikisch, a trim, dapper little man, exuded a magic which made the players anxious to obey his slightest behest.

He set about his rehearsals in a quiet yet whimsical way. The men nevertheless knew that sooner or later he would let fall one of those steely, satirical remarks for which he was famous. Such was his phrase concerning the jealous quarrels amongst the musicians, that 'The only time they are united is when they are united against me.' . . .

When we recorded the *Hungarian Rhapsody* [No. 1 of Liszt], for which Nikisch was famous, one of the players reminded him that Dr. Richter always took a certain passage quite differently. He replied: 'Richter was a German–Hungarian; I am a Hungarian–Hungarian.'

Nikisch used to explain to his men, when he attempted an extremely attenuated *rubato*, that he permitted unlimited licence, but always within the framework of the bar, and he insisted on maintaining throughout the strictest rhythm. He

[1] 'Paderewski as I Knew Him'.

will go down in history for his wonderful readings of the Weber Overtures, which he made into jewels. Records of some of these [were made then]. . . . He always conducted from memory. He would commence the *Oberon* Overture by merely raising his eyebrows, and frequently gave directions by a nod.

But the limitations of orchestral recording in those days were severe. The size of the band could be no more than about forty, and still there was an unmerciful crush to get them all close enough to the horn. Even so, there were some instruments that simply would not record—lower strings in particular. These parts had all to be re-assigned to trombones and tubas. The result on the records sounded like exactly what it was—a brass band to which woodwind and a few violins had unaccountably been added. The Gramophone Company were to keep the Nikisch records on the catalogue for more than a quarter century, but hardly anyone outside the Company itself ever took them seriously as musical documents during Fred Gaisberg's lifetime.

In the summer of 1913 there was a season of Russian opera and ballet in London the like of which had never been seen before. Thomas Beecham took the Drury Lane Theatre for several weeks, and there he directed the first performances ever given in England of Mussorgsky's *Boris Godunov* and *Khovanchina* and Rimsky-Korsakov's *Ivan the Terrible*. Beecham brought the finest Russian singers to London for the performances including Sobinov and Chaliapin. Sobinov, in Fred Gaisberg's opinion, 'had passed his prime'. But the Gramophone Company took full advantage of Chaliapin's presence to sign him to an additional contract for a session of songs from his concert repertory. And Chaliapin opened the Gramophone recording studios just completed at Hayes that summer. Fred Gaisberg found himself spending as much time with Chaliapin outside the recording room as inside it.

His songs nearly all deal[t] with drama, tragedy, and unrequited love—which might lead one to believe he was an apostle of gloom. On the contrary, his normal mood was boyish exuberance, and only two things could depress him, which were: to be in bad voice on days when he was to appear in public; and being crossed by conductors or stage-managers.

Of course he had to have his own way, but so many little things could make him as happy as a child—such as a new necktie, a fine painting, a well-grilled chop, a good London smoked salmon or a fine bit of cheddar. He was a joy to a chef or to a good tailor.

He was inordinately fond of clothes, and when he arrived in London in 1913 he bought himself an ascot grey high hat and outfit to match.[1] We walked from the hatter's to Drury Lane, he watching his reflection in shop windows. We arrived somewhat late at the theatre and had to hurry over dressing.

. . . The Russian chorus struck just before the Coronation Scene in *Boris Godunov*. It was a command performance and the Royal Family were in the house. The scene took place without the chorus, who were obdurate. After the scene, Chaliapin rushed to the back of the stage and remonstrated with the ringleader, who argued back. I saw Chaliapin strike him one blow which completely knocked him out. With that, the choristers threw themselves on Chaliapin and bore him to the ground. They would have mauled him badly if the mezzo-soprano Petrenko had not covered him with her body. Finally I and the stage-hands were able to draw him into his dressing-room and lock the door. How it all ended after this serious interruption I am not quite sure, but I remember. . . . Thomas Beecham's treasurers arriving with a sack of gold and passing out a golden sovereign to each chorister, after which the show continued.

Those Russian choristers were an unruly crowd, rather spoilt by success and steeped in revolution even then. They and Chaliapin had many tilts. They were certainly a wonderful chorus and made history, in that they received encores for their acting and singing like any *prima donna*, and afterwards took their curtains.

Beecham's second season of Russian opera and ballet at Drury Lane in the summer of 1914 brought first British performances of Borodin's *Prince Igor*, Rimsky-Korsakov's *May Night* and *The Golden Cockerel*, and Stravinsky's *The Nightingale*. Chaliapin was in London again, and demanded Fred Gaisberg's presence on all occasions as a sort of combined guide

[1] 'Chaliapin as I Knew Him'.

and mascot. He was again much drawn to Savile Row, and there were continual passages-of-arms in rehearsals and performances.

> But his greatest pleasure was to sit with his cronies round a table after a show, exchanging stories and singing part-songs. He could keep that up until 6 or 7 o'clock in the morning. He was a supremely good mimic and story-teller and used to act his stories, playing each part in turn. He could 'take-off' an *izvozchick* or Russian cab-driver, a drunken man, an old woman, a young lady, or a policeman. I have seen him hold the attention of an audience for ten minutes whilst he tried to sew on a button with a needle and thread. . . . I was nearly always in his company in London in the summers of 1913 and 1914, when he was the outstanding figure of those memorable seasons.[1]

[1] 'Chaliapin as I Knew Him'.

Chapter Thirteen

WITH THE close of the 1914 season of Russian opera in London, Chaliapin departed with his family for a motor tour of the Continent, and Fred Gaisberg turned to the preparations for his sister Louise's wedding in September. Having studied singing in Italy for several years, Louise had made her debut during the previous winter at La Scala as one of the Flower Maidens in *Parsifal*. But then in February 1914 Mrs. Gaisberg had died quite suddenly: she had been a martyr to diabetes for years, but the end came almost without warning. Louise seemed more shaken than anyone, and her professional ambition seemed to evaporate. It had not been a surprise when she became engaged to Camillo Valli, a young Italian business man whom she had known for several years.

Then on 4 August came the declaration of war. Everything was suddenly at risk. Within a week The Gramophone Company accepted its first government munitions contract: that meant the beginning of some grim re-tooling in the Hayes factory. On the domestic scene there were some anxious moments. But Louise's wedding could take place from Fitzjohn's Avenue before young Valli was called up for military service. Fred gave his sister away, and two days later he, Will, Carrie, and Isabel saw the couple off to Italy with mingled wishes and worries.

Almost immediately after that the war reached right into the Gaisberg household itself, as Fred remembered.

> Coming home one evening I found the entire [Chaliapin] family assembled in my drawing room. . . . Motor and trunks confiscated as they toured Europe, [they were now] refugees on their way to Newcastle to travel to St. Petersburg.

Chaliapin said that he had just accepted an advance of $150,000 for performances at the Chicago Opera House to take place in

1915. The entire sum had been sent to the bank in St. Petersburg, and he was now beginning to wonder whether he would ever see a penny of it.

The Gaisbergs did what they could to improvise hospitality. Since their mother's death, the duties of hostess had devolved upon Carrie—a tiny person of impeccable dress and her full share of Gaisberg self-effacing charm. She was not musical, but she knew how to make a musician comfortable—in this case a very big musician with the whole of his family. 'And for the next few days', Fred recalled, 'I busied myself expediting their return by the long northern route.'

The same problems were soon making themselves felt throughout the far-flung organisation of The Gramophone Company. Fred Gaisberg's travels in peace-time years had shown him all too clearly what the problems would be: 'The First World War naturally played havoc with an international business like ours. The Company had the major part of their matrices stored in the Hanover factory in Germany, which supplied most of Central Europe, Scandinavia, and the Balkan States with records. Hardly completed was the transfer of all master-shells from Hanover to the Hayes pressing-plant, started in 1908. This plant was intended to house the central archives for all master-negatives. A large factory in the friendly Hanseatic town of Riga had just been completed in 1913, and was capable of supplying all Russia with records. At that time Riga was a premier city for manufacturing on modern lines, and its products were the equal of any in Europe for price and finish.'

The new plant at Riga had a special importance, for during the pre-war years Russia had led the world markets in classical records. Perhaps the best hope of maintaining contact and control was to carry on frequent recording trips there. So Fred Gaisberg and Sinkler Darby were asked to go once more to Russia—this time by the unfamiliar route which the Chaliapin family had travelled a few weeks before.

> On November 14, 1914, I started on the first of the journeys I was to make to Russia during the war by way of Bergen, Stockholm, Trondheim, and St. Petersburg. With my American passport I had very little trouble, and I received a royal welcome from our marooned agents, Albert Lack and George Cooper, when I arrived in St. Petersburg.

I shared a flat with Cooper in a newly built apartment house of vast dimensions: the walls were three feet thick and the foundations were built like a concrete vessel, to float on the marshland upon which the city of St. Petersburg stood. That winter there was no fuel to feed the great central-heating system, so our rooms were as cold as a refrigerator.

Four months after the war broke out, I saw the birth of that pathetic and unhappily permanent feature of Russian life, the queue. What can ever compensate for the billions of hours weary women and children have so patiently endured in cold and rain, standing in those dismal processions?

There were already plans in existence to dismantle the new factory in Riga should the Germans threaten the city. In that case the Company would have to fall back on the hope of improvising pressing arrangements in St. Petersburg or Moscow, as supplying records from England was a clear impossibility over such long routes in war conditions, and Hanover of course was alienated. Meanwhile, however, the record business thrived in Russia, and so did the pirates:

> As in England, I found that there was a great increase in the demand for records from both soldiers and civilians. The hits of the war period were 'Hai-da, Troika' and 'Black Eyes'. . . . As Russia was not a party to the Berne Copyright Convention (1908),[1] the composers and publishers of this music could claim no royalties on the millions of copies sold outside that country.
>
> Inside Russia there was a copyright law covering national music, and our copyright department decided that 'mechanical rights' were payable on all arrangements. Faced with this decision, Mr. Suk, our artists' manager of that day, founded a shadow publishing firm, and I soon discovered that it claimed every popular and folk song as its copyright because of some inversion of chords or some other simple change. I did not let him enjoy this Eldorado for very long.

And there was a full programme of recordings to carry out.

[1] An agreement to protect copyright among the signatory nations. There was at the time no other international copyright law to cover gramophone recording.

The success that stood out in Fred Gaisberg's memory of this visit was that of Lidia Lipkovskaya.

> Some outstanding records of coloratura arias were recorded in St. Petersburg in 1914, which show the extraordinary agility and perfection of her voice. . . .
>
> It was shortly after I made these records that things began to happen in Russia, and I like to remember her then in the zenith of her beauty and power.[1]

The year 1915 began badly and got steadily worse. The Gaisbergs had decided to sell the house in Fitzjohn's Avenue. Since the death of Mrs. Gaisberg it had seemed larger and larger. After Louise's marriage and departure for Italy, Isabel had returned to the United States. Domestic help was difficult to get. In February the house was sold, and Carrie, Fred, and Will went into an apartment in the Avenue Mansions, Finchley Road.

It was a disappointment in many ways, but Fred hardly had time to think about it. He was being posted to and fro across war-torn Europe with such frequency that it seemed as if the Gramophone directors had come to the conclusion that all the separate parts of their industrial empire might be held together through any eventuality if only Fred Gaisberg could be kept moving rapidly enough amongst them. Near the end of January he was in Paris and Monte Carlo. Then almost immediately he went to Milan to make the first complete recording of Mascagni's *Cavalleria Rusticana.* This was a welcome chance to visit Louise and Camillo Valli, but in the existing conditions it proved very difficult to organise the recording. From Milan he journeyed to Belgrade, and then early in March to Budapest.

> In [the] sleeping-car between Belgrade and Budapest, whe[re] most stringent controls at the frontier were in force to prevent the escape of capital, I was asked if I owned some thousands of dollars uncovered by the frontier guards between the mattresses in the adjoining compartment. My American passport led them to suspect me of the ownership. The occupant of the compartment, an Austrian Jew, denied that they belonged to him, but I could see him turn a sickly grey as the officers took possession of those lovely dollars.

[1] Battistini and others'.

With his American passport, Fred was even able to get to Berlin for a week of talks with his colleagues at the end of March, though of this he has unfortunately left no recollection.

During the summer Fred Gaisberg was sent again to Russia, and the impressions of this trip were to remain with him all his life.

In the middle of July 1915 the prospects of Russia were still considered good enough to venture a recording expedition. There was a large demand for goods, and high prices and a market free of German competition were tempting. The objective was to obtain records of the new hits, especially war and soldier songs. The Riga pressing factory was in full swing, and the menace of the German offensive against Warsaw was not considered serious.

I embarked from Newcastle for my second recording trip to Russia during the war, with all my papers in order. My route was via Bergen, Stockholm, Petrograd. My kit was light, as my recording outfit was already in Petrograd. On the 800-ton steamer, a thorough examination of the small party of travellers was made by the British authorities. Letters and documents were sought for principally. After this I went below to write a letter to my folks, and gave it to a sailor to carry ashore and mail. I then retired to my cabin, thinking to get some sleep before the ship started, because the night was stormy and I am not too good a sailor.

It was not long before I was aroused by a banging on the cabin door. Opening it, I was confronted by a British officer holding in his hand my letter.

'What does this mean?' he said.

I replied that it was only a farewell to my folks.

'Don't you know that after the examination you are not allowed to send letters ashore? Open it up, and let's see what it says.'

I did so, and was then asked to destroy it. Again my passport and credentials were examined, and after the officer was satisfied I was permitted to retire. (One can hardly criticise the precaution, as Stockholm was the clearing house of spies during the war. After 1915 it was impossible for civilians of any nationality to leave England for Norway.)

Our ship started with all lights off, for enemy submarines

were thick in the North Sea: the ship preceding ours had been stopped, mail bags taken off, and British subjects of military age taken prisoners.

After a stormy passage of fifty-six hours, during which our little steamer was mercilessly buffeted, I arrived more dead than alive at Bergen. What a relief it was to walk through this new world, secure from the turmoil of war preparations.

Early the next morning we arrived in Christiana and changed trains for Stockholm, reaching that city in the evening in time to connect with the small packet that ferried us across the Baltic to Abo. (Shortly afterwards the ferry across the Baltic was stopped, as the Germans dominated these waters and their submarines continually stopped the neutral ships, arresting British subjects and confiscating the mails.) . . . Russian officers made a thorough examination, but by nine o'clock in the morning we were safely aboard the train for Petrograd, where we arrived late the same evening. The entire journey [had] lasted 136 hours, as compared with the pre-war time of 60 hours. . . .

Petrograd was quite normal and the summer—usually so dead when the wealthy fly to European resorts—was this year animated and interesting. (This was the last summer that the beautiful capital could boast of comparative happiness. In the winter that followed, the pinch of food and fuel caused by the German campaign against Poland and the rupture of transportation, began to be acutely felt.)

Gathering my recording outfit together, I left Petrograd after a few days and headed straight for Tiflis via Moscow. . . . In Moscow Chaliapin offered me hospitality, as the hotels had been taken over by the government. We dined regularly at the well-known Hermitage restaurant, where he seemed to command the best in the house. . . . His family . . . were truly happy and cheered to see me so soon again, after giving up all hope of setting eyes on anyone from the outer world until after the war.

I stopped long enough to go over the city and see the devastation caused by the pogrom of May—a truly sad sight to see entire sections of the city (including many magnificent buildings that might have served as hospitals) razed to the ground. I remember passing by the magnificent building of a former Gramophone agent on the Kusnitsky Most: from the fifth storey windows rioters hurled Blüthner pianos, harps, organs to the cheering crowds below, and then set fire to the building. Another dealer, Aabel, told me how the hooligans stopped before his shop intent on destruction, and how his daughter rushed into the street and on bended knees swore they were good Russians and devout Christians, and showed their baptismal certificates as proof. They brushed her aside and went on with their work of destruction.[1]

It was when I succeeded, after a struggle, in finding a place on the train that was to carry me to Baku and Tiflis that I realised what chaos one year of war had produced, and that I began to have doubts of ever being able to travel back again. The train was crowded, packed tight to overflowing—which means the passengers were even clinging to the platforms and roofs, quite a normal state of affairs since the war. As it was summer, the heat, dust and stench were overpowering. Our locomotive burnt wood, so it had to stop every twenty miles and raise its steam pressure. Then begging peasants appeared with outstretched hands—not aggressive, like professional beggars, but with the mute appeal of a sick animal.

The station restaurants would still serve travellers with simple food. . . . Sitting at a table, eating a bowl of borsch, a neighbour would take from his pocket a wooden spoon (with which everyone travels) exclaiming,

'Ah, *tovarich*, your borsch smells very good; is it as good as it looks?'

He would then help himself from your bowl and add, 'Ah, yes, it *is* good soup.'

The farther south we went the hotter and more uncomfortable it became, and we suffered from a thirst in a country where, because of cholera epidemics, one was warned against drinking unboiled water.

I was joined at Baku by my old friend Fred Tyler, who was glad enough to see me. Everything was at a standstill, but food was more plentiful. . . .

I was surprised to receive an urgent note from a Mr. Leslie Urquhart to come and see him. Full of curiosity and flattered to be taken the slightest notice of in such strenuous times, I went to the imposing office building of a large petroleum

[1] Typescript article, 'My last trip to Russia'.

company, and was shown into an up-to-date office that might have been in New York City. Urquhart was a business man on the grand scale, as his modern office equipment would indicate. But there he was stranded, with all his technicians called up for military service and all his intricate dictating phonographs and calculating machines gone wrong. He had heard of my arrival at the club, where I had been described as a 'talking machine expert'. Here, he thought, was a chance to have his machines put right. It was ironical to see this high-pressure business man trying to carry on in spite of war and famine with no helpers; but I could do nothing for him.

In the beautiful town of Tiflis I set up my recording equipment, and in company with Fred Tyler proceeded to collect our artists for recording. . . . Most of the recording in the Caucasus was done in Tiflis, where we found Georgian, Armenian, and Tartar artists. But we also used Baku, Kutais, Petrovsk for Daghestan singers, and Georgievsk in the northern Caucasus for Tcherkess artists.

We also recorded in Tiflis the choir of the Viceroy's bodyguard of Cossacks—a fine body of men with some remarkable soloists. . . . This recording was carried out in the Orient Hotel in Tiflis. With the Hotel Europe in Baku . . . this was the best hotel in the Caucasus at that time. For the recording of the Cossack choir we arranged a huge side table laden with *zakuska* (hors d'oeuvres), which rapidly disappeared during the intervals, washed down by copious draughts of vodka. In fact the last few numbers must have been taken in the proper atmosphere, and no doubt registered the true Cossack spirit.[1]

After completing recording in the Caucasus, I packed up and despatched the records and equipment to Moscow. I should think they are still shuttling between Baku and Batum, because we never saw them again. My journey back was a repetition of the discomforts I had already experienced, but this time I knew what to expect.

So Fred Gaisberg made his way back across northern Europe by the long route he had travelled out, with nothing to show for

[1] A MS. note states that about 200 records were made at Tiflis beginning on or about 26 July 1915.

those weeks of discomfort beyond the memories he would write down.

No sooner had Fred safely returned to London than he had to go back to Russia once more. The German grip in the East had begun to tighten, and it was now less a question of making new recordings than merely of organising the preservation of what already existed. And so it was that early in October 1915

> . . . I happened to be in St. Petersburg when the order was given to evacuate the machinery from our plant and destroy the buildings. We searched St. Petersburg and Moscow for a suitable location to which to transfer our large stock of thousands of copper matrices and our pressing-plant. St. Petersburg itself was threatened at the time by the German armies, and Moscow had . . . undergone [the] destructive pogrom in May, which had left the most modern of its buildings in ruins. Even railway stations, schools, and churches were filled with wounded soldiers retreating from Warsaw, the parks and boulevards taking the overflow of refugees and their belongings.
>
> It was the search for these factory sites that opened my eyes to the terrible housing conditions then only too prevalent. I remember driving to the outskirts of the city, where we were shown a loft. On opening the door we were nearly knocked over by the stench. Lying body to body were two rows of snoring droshky-drivers. There was no ventilation, and no light of any kind except our torches, which revealed walls crawling with vermin. Bad as it was, and badly as we needed the premises, I declined to give the word to the agent which would have sent the occupants packing.
>
> Our next visit was to a brewery that in normal times produced a brew which held its own with the finest on the European market. It was most depressing to see such a splendid, up-to-date equipment of aluminium and copper vats and electrical apparatus being wantonly sabotaged.

But events were now beginning to move forward with such swiftness that travel across northern Europe was becoming every day more dangerous and difficult, even with an American passport. It was imperative for Fred to leave Russia while he could, so at the beginning of November 1915 he turned homeward with a heavy heart. There was now no ferry across the Baltic:

I was still able to return to England by way of Finland. At the frontier I was searched and relieved of thirty gold sovereigns, for which I received and still possess a cheque on the Imperial Bank of Russia for 450 Rubles. This secret reserve of gold I had carried in a belt worn next to the skin. I had not intended to declare it, but the presence of bloodhounds sniffing around, and the warning of a fellow-traveller that every passenger was being stripped, made me hastily change my mind. Other passengers less discreet were detained. They lost the train and their money as well. . . .

The Finnish railway ended at the small town of Tornea, and the gap of some twenty miles to Haparanda, the Swedish rail-head, had to be made by rickety country carts in summer, or in winter by small low sleds drawn by little shaggy horses and carrying one passenger each. Wrapped from head to foot in folds of sheepskin robes, the traveller reclined cosily in the cradle of the straw-filled sleigh. The feeling of comfort lasted about ten minutes—until the zero cold penetrated your protection. When you were just about feeling the numbness that precedes freezing to death, your driver stopped and bundled you out at the jolliest and warmest of inns, built of wood and smelling of pine-log fires. Another perfume was that of coffee. The sight of good things to eat, spread out on a long buffet, turned you into a ravenous wolf. In fact this one moment compensated for all the trials endured in Russia.

A twenty-four hour journey on the single track railway skirting the Gulf of Bothnia, dodging in and out of pine forests, brought me to the flourishing city of Stockholm—and by contrast to realisation of the absolute chaos I had left behind me in Russia. A week later, when I arrived in London, I acquired the reputation of a prophet among my friends by foretelling a revolution in that unhappy country.

George Cooper, who was to remain in Russia until early in 1918, told the sequel in a letter written to Fred long afterwards: 'The Riga Factory machinery, as well as that of other factories, was transferred by the Russians to St. Petersburg & Moscow before the Germans arrived in Riga, and a very thorough job was made of it. The Germans didn't get much in Riga. . . . Ohsolin was able to start a small factory in Moscow with 40 presses, and kept us supplied with records the whole time of the war.'[1] This was running smoothly when the revolutionaries arrived, took over the plant, and began to operate it for themselves. It was the end of The Gramophone Company's fortunes in Russia—the richest market for classical recordings that any of them had ever seen.

[1] Letter to Fred Gaisberg, 14 June 1940.

Chapter Fourteen

AT THE beginning of 1916 Fred Gaisberg found himself momentarily settled at home, helping his brother Will with recording at Hayes, where the Company's entire English office had been moved soon after the outbreak of war. And thus it happened that Fred came to meet the musician whose interest was to do more for the status of the gramophone as a musical instrument than any other British influence during those years—Sir Edward Elgar.

Elgar had begun to conduct records of his own music in 1914, having been introduced by Landon Ronald. In the following year his new recitation with music, *Carillon*, had caught the wave of English sympathy for occupied Belgium, and the records he made of it enjoyed considerable sales. At the end of 1915 Elgar had produced an elaborate score for the West End production of a children's fantasy play by Algernon Blackwood, *The Starlight Express*. A new Gramophone contract was then negotiated, envisaging a steady programme of composer-recordings over the next several years. The series was to begin with *The Starlight Express*.

On 18 February Sir Edward duly arrived at Hayes with Charles Mott (the baritone of the stage production) and Agnes Nicholls (one of his own favourite singers for many years). And Fred Gaisberg spent the whole day with them making *Starlight Express* records with an orchestra of thirty-odd players squashed into the largest recording room they had.

Some of the orchestral instruments, such as the lower strings, still remained unrecordable in an ensemble of that size. This necessitated a certain amount of re-arrangement amongst the parts. And a few of the longer numbers had also to be cut so as to fit within the four-minute compass of the gramophone disc.

Elgar himself had undertaken all this work, and in the studio he proved to be fascinated with the process of making the records. A keen interest in mechanical things, it seemed, gave him a ready insight into the problems.

Elgar was accompanied, during those early visits to Hayes, by his wife. Lady Elgar was a small, deceptively gentle woman who seemed to hang on her husband's every word and gesture, and stood waiting to bundle him into the large fur coat she held ready for him the moment a record was finished. Fred Gaisberg found his initial impressions confirmed by later experience.

> Meeting Elgar for the first time, one would hardly take him for a composer, and I have a sneaking idea that he relished this deception. When he first came to our studio I thought I had never seen anyone who looked less like a musician. The Elgars seemed a prim and comfortable family of the county class, very provincial and sheltered—a product of some cathedral town of England where afternoon tea was the chief social ceremony of the day. . . .
>
> My brother Will had instructed me to make these recording visits a ceremony and to 'build up' the event. I usually had interesting people to meet Elgar, and often he himself liked to invite to a gramophone session his friends. . . . Invariably Alfred Clark, the managing director, would welcome him, and during the break for tea enjoy some of Elgar's tales.
>
> [Elgar] took a real delight in conducting, and I noticed that he seemed to enter another and distant world when he took up the baton. As he approached the climax of the *Cockaigne* [*Overture*] he became a giant of pent-up energy that seemed to galvanise players and audience alike. At the end I would look at this god in awe and ask, Is this the man who was telling funny stories a few minutes ago?[1]

Yet Fred's awe did not prevent his enjoyment of hospitality in the Elgars' home at Hampstead when it was extended to him. His first visit to Severn House took place three weeks after the *Starlight Express* session, and the description in Lady Elgar's diary is graphic:

> Mr. Gaisberg (brother of former) to lunch. Very interesting talk: Tiflis & places out in the Caucasian regions, one where

[1] Typescript article, 'Elgar'.

72 languages are spoken. Admired altered pianola—'a talking point' he called it.[1]

In the spring of 1917 Fred Gaisberg was asked to go to Italy for an indefinite stay 'to carry out the recording of war songs and to make contracts with artists, and also to erect a local pressing and matrix-making plant'. The last was the real objective. The wartime disturbance of shipping routes had made the supplying of records in the Mediterranean nearly impossible, and much potential business was being lost. So Fred packed his bags once again.

The Southampton–Havre route was open for civilians during the first three years of the war, so although the passport control hesitated and ransacked their index-cards, they passed me through with the usual careful search and a final rubbing of lemon on my bare back, which I really enjoyed.

My experiences in Russia had so tempered me that although Italy was literally scraping out the corners of her grain bins I found the scarcity of food endurable. The staple diet of *pasta* and *pane-unico*, dark and full of straw bits, was palatable if eaten with morsels of tunny fish, hare or horse meat. The glorious water from the mountains and, in season, the ever abundant grapes, peaches, tomatoes, cheese, and chianti were obtainable at reasonable prices.

But Italy was sadly altered in other ways: 'The war was not only an interruption, but also changed the old, happy Milan to a new and less pleasing city in which to live.'[2] He looked for Rieger's Pension, but it was no more: 'Swept away by the war, I heard that . . . demonstrators threw the furniture and pianos from the windows and set fire to them.'

The main task for Fred in Italy was to build the factory, and it was to occupy him for fifteen months. 'I enjoyed the excitement of creating a pressing-plant out of parts scavenged from the junk heaps of the Porta Magenta. Since new machinery could only be had for armaments, and hardly a scuttle of coal for raising steam could be found in all Milan, some ingenuity

[1] Quoted in Jerrold Northrop Moore, *Elgar on Record* (Oxford University Press, 1974), p. 16.

[2] 'All roads lead to La Scala'

had to be used before I could press records in the summer of 1918 in our first Italian factory.'

Thus Fred Gaisberg's war divided into two parts—that in Russia and that in Italy. And as had so often happened in his career, his own assignments caught and focused in a remarkable way the general concerns of the gramophone. In this case they also reflected two of the fundamental issues over which the war was being fought. His first two war-years had been given over to a series of attempts to shore up what proved to be an inevitably eroding empire in the East. Then after an interval at home in England, the moment had come to seek and express some sort of faith in a future within which the good things of the world might somehow re-emerge. But as with everyone caught in that war, Fred Gaisberg found it more costly—of money, of effort, of time—than could ever have been thought possible.

During the two years in which Fred was, as he thought of it, 'marooned in Italy', he was more fortunate than many. He was able to make a home with Louise and Camillo Valli and their young family in Milan. And there was Luisa Tetrazzini. During those years she became a close friend, often entertaining Fred in Milan and Rome. In the last year of the war the two of them conspired in a most unlikely project—'to entertain Major Mackenzie Rogan and the Coldstream Guards in their first visit to Italy'.

These were old friends. Before the turn of the century, at a time when orchestral records were a total impossibility, it had been recognised that the sounds of a military band might be captured for the gramophone with some success:

> The Band of the Coldstream Guards appeared to me to answer the requirements for gramophone records completely, so I hunted out the leader, Lieutenant Rogan, in his Streatham home, and started him on his long career of recording which spread the fame of the Coldstreams to the ends of the world. . . . [Now] as Major Mackenzie Rogan he was in command of . . . the full bands of the Guards and the band of the Garde Républicaine, totalling over two hundred players . . . sent to Milan and Rome to cement goodwill and friendship between the three countries. . . .

Tetrazzini organised a reception on a lavish scale for them.

It must have cost her a pretty penny, but it went a long way towards fostering goodwill among her English admirers, and its value was reflected in the very successful series of recitals she gave in England after the war. (I can take the credit for arranging her return to the English concert platform and was also responsible for fixing up her first broadcast in England.)

But all that remained for the future. As the war ground mercilessly forward, the authorities recognised in Fred Gaisberg's presence in Italy an undoubted opportunity.

Lord Northcliffe, extending his scheme of propaganda behind the enemy lines, had sent Colonel Baker to work on the Italian front at the Isonzo, where the Slavs, Jugoslavs, Croats and Serbs, Hungarians and Czechs were manning the mountain trenches on the Austrian side, sometimes a few hundred feet from the Italian lines. I was sent to Vicenza, whence I would make excursions in army lorries, under military escort, to various prison camps. Deserters of these nationalities would record their folk-songs, dances, and spoken words, urging their listeners to desert without fear as friends would receive and care for them. These records were played back at points in the trenches, opposite the places where those nationals were known to be posted and, according to Colonel Baker, resulted in a fine harvest of deserters.

Those days will live in my memory for two things: the reckless, untamed driving of the Italian chauffeurs, who seemed bent on imitating the comic films of motor racing, and the blood-curdling mountain thunderstorms with their blinding flashes of lightning and torrents of rain. Still, I survived and managed to return to Milan with a mixed booty of bully beef and white bread and butter, exchanged for gramophone records with a section of English gunners.

Despite this interruption, however, and despite all the difficulties of trying to construct a pressing plant with almost no materials, Gaisberg was nonetheless able to make his presence count heavily in his Company's favour over the long range as well: 'The last two years of World War I, which I spent in Italy, prepared me to resume recording activities with a full knowledge of the most promising singers and their value to me for records.'[1]

[1] 'All roads lead to La Scala'

So it happened that Fred was able to meet and secure the singer who was to assume a few years later the mantle of Caruso.

In the spring of 1918, I made a contract with the twenty-eight-year-old tenor, Beniamino Gigli, who, dressed in the uniform of a private in the infantry, sang his first ten records.

Thus began one of the longest and happiest of all Gramophone careers, a relationship that would continue virtually for the remaining forty years of the singer's life.

During that final year of the war, the Italian pressing plant at last began to function. Overseeing its first activities and dealing with its growing pains kept Fred very busy through the summer and autumn. Then, as if by the waving of a wand, it was announced that peace was practically upon them. There would be an Armistice. At a certain moment of a certain day, the fighting would stop. Perhaps it had been, in the words of the American President, 'a war to end war'.

From London Will Gaisberg wrote that he had been asked to go out to the front lines to try and record some of the sounds of war before they vanished forever. The expedition set out on 8 October. Will wrote:

> . . . Capt. F. Warlock, Mr. Clayson, my assistant, and I left Charing Cross for the purpose of recording the Royal Garrison Artillery's heavy gas shell attack on the German lines in front of Lille just before the town was entered by the British. . . .
>
> At every stage of the drive from Boulogne—where we were instructed in the use of gas masks and provided with steel helmets—to the Front, 'the mark of the beast' became more and more apparent. Destruction was everywhere; large towns and villages were levelled to the ground, and here and there a mass of masonry, that once was a home, still standing in a grotesque and pathetic attitude of desolation. Already the returning inhabitants were seeking among the ruins for their homes and many a rough cart loaded with broken household effects was making its difficult way over the rough roads. Progress became difficult through the country just vacated by the enemy, where thousands of German and Turkish prisoners, and Chinese Labour Battalions, were engaged in repairing the roads.
>
> Gradually we came within the sound of the guns, and eventually, when only a short distance from Lille, we pulled up at

a row of ruined cottages, in one of which the heavy siege battery had made its quarters. In the wrecked kitchen we unpacked our recording machines and made our preparations before getting directly behind a battery of great 4·5″ guns and 6″ howitzers, camouflaged until they looked at close quarters like gigantic insects. Here the machine could well catch the finer sounds of the 'singing', the 'whine', and the 'scream' of the shells, as well as the terrific reports when they left the guns.

Dusk fell, and we were obliged, very reluctantly, to pack up our recording instrument and return to Boulogne—and to England; but we brought with us a true representation of the bombardment, which will have a unique place in the history of the Great War.[1]

The history of the Great War may have been nearing its end, but this was still a dangerous undertaking. Despite the instruction in helmets and masks, Will himself had been severely gassed during his day at the front. Back in London he fell victim to the terrible influenza epidemic then raging, and less than a month later he died.

Fred and Carrie (who had come out recently to be with him in Milan) could hardly believe it. Louise of course joined in their grief, but the presence of a family of her own softened the blow. For the others, nothing stood between them and their loss. Carrie said over and over again that if only she had been with her youngest brother, she might somehow have saved him. Their large, far-flung family had come virtually through the war unharmed. Louise's husband Camillo had survived his turn at soldiering, and back in the States Emma's eighteen-year-old son Warren had covered himself with military distinction. Now the circle was broken—at a most painfully unexpected point.

For Fred it was almost worse. Perhaps he had been tempted to feel the fortunes of the gramophone shining with a special brightness upon anyone who bore the name of Gaisberg. If so, the fates had now extracted full measure: Will might probably never have fallen victim to the influenza if he had not been sent on a foolish expedition to try and extract the last ounces of gramophone commerce out of the war. Fred wrote to Emma's

[1] 'Recording the Guns on the Western Front', in *The Voice*, December 1918, p. 4.

husband Rudolpf Forster in Washington that he felt himself on the verge of chucking in his career.

Forster was one of the few people who might be in a position to help Fred and Carrie at that moment. He was employed in the White House as a presidential secretary: so it was possible that he could assist in getting immediate visas for Fred and Carrie—American citizens still—to get quickly back to England. But throughout the entire dreadful business there was not a glimmer of good luck anywhere. Due to the imminent cessation of hostilities, wire services throughout the world were hopelessly congested. Fred's cables did not reach Forster for days, and Forster could only write back:

> The cables you sent were delayed a week or ten days—the first reaching me only a few minutes before one from The Gramophone Co. in London announcing dear Will's death. These both reached me on the 11th of November—six days after he had died and in the very midst of the first outburst of rejoicing over the signing of the armistice.[1]
>
> When your cables reached me, days after they were sent, it was impossible for me to cable back to you, for the cable companies would not accept private cables of any sort, the government business completely monopolising at that time all cable facilities.[2]

When Fred and Carrie did finally reach London, they found a mass of condolences, including a letter from Sir Edward Elgar: 'His loss was a great shock to me as our friendship and esteem had become a very real thing in our lives. . . .'[3] But practically there was nothing left to do but to approve a note of Will's career that had been written by Alfred Clark for inclusion in The Gramophone Company's new magazine *The Voice*.

> Our readers will, I know, learn with the deepest regret of the death from pneumonia of Mr. Wm. C. Gaisberg. For over 17 years he has been connected with the recording work of the Gramophone Company, and ten years ago was appointed chief of the department which controlled record making throughout the world. . . .

[1] Letter to Fred Gaisberg, 10 December 1918.
[2] Letter to Fred Gaisberg, 9 January 1919.
[3] Quoted in Jerrold Northrop Moore, *Elgar on Record*, p. 27.

He was a dreamer of dreams who had the ability to make them 'come true'. But apart from our admiration of his ability it was probably his genial lovable nature that so endeared him to us all, that to-day makes us feel his loss as that of a brother. His circle of friends extended far into the world of art, and he gained the respect and affection of all the world's greatest artistes. They, too, will feel his loss bitterly.

In our grief we ask his brothers and sisters to accept this expression of our heartfelt sympathy.

These words were read out at the annual meeting of Gramophone Company shareholders by the Chairman, Trevor Williams. It was just twenty years since his success in raising European capital for Emile Berliner's invention had brought Fred Gaisberg to England, where Will had quickly followed.

Chapter Fifteen

At the beginning of 1919 Fred Gaisberg was forty-seven. How seriously did he think of leaving The Gramophone Company altogether after Will's death? There is no later reference, however oblique, to the state of his thinking about this question in any known writing of his. But the final answer proved to lie in the extraordinary relation of the man to his work. One of his colleagues described Fred Gaisberg thus: 'He was one of the rare people who are completely dedicated to their work. I doubt if he thought about anything else for long. His family recognised this, and surrounded him with the care and devotion which such a man needs. Both his sisters Carrie Gaisberg and Mrs Valli understood him well, and of course Carrie more or less ran his private life for him. I suppose he could have existed on his own, but it is hard to imagine his doing so and giving time and thought to the thousand and one daily trivia which take up so much valuable time.'[1]

At various times in the past Fred had been offered Gramophone 'promotion'—advancement to administrative responsibility. Will had accepted a certain amount of this, and so had become in the end Head of the Recording Department. Fred had always side-stepped, avoided, and if necessary refused such opportunities: they would have stifled him, and he knew it. After Will's death those opportunities presented themselves once more: again Fred's answer was no, but again he stayed in his job.

Company directors do not as a rule go out of their way to be understanding towards an employee who refuses their offers of promotion. But in the case of Fred Gaisberg the Gramophone directors—especially his old friend Alfred Clark, the Managing Director—were understanding. They must have recognised that

[1] Bernard Wratten, Letter to the writer, 20 October 1972.

by allowing Fred to remain in a secondary position to someone inevitably very much his junior in the recording world, they would be acceding to a situation which might prove unstable. On the other hand, it could hardly be denied that the unique experience and sophistication Gaisberg brought to the job of recruiting artists and helping them to make their records must count heavily in whatever post-war world might emerge for 'His Master's Voice' and for the industry as a whole.

And so, in common with the world around him, Fred Gaisberg struggled to find his way out of the immediate past, to turn his back upon the losses of the war, and to pick up as many of the old threads as might be woven into new patterns. At the beginning, it seemed that a great portion of the old design itself lay ready to be taken up and continued. In the year after the war's end, Fred was travelling more than ever at the Company's behest—recording here, negotiating there, and everywhere assisting the local Gramophone managers to get their businesses back to some state of equilibrium. Thus he spent April of 1919 in Italy and much of May in Paris.

The Paris visit embraced a heavy programme of recording. And as this was going forward, Fred Gaisberg met the first in a series of brilliant young men he was to attract to The Gramophone Company during the next few years. His name was Piero Coppola:

> Born in Milan in 1888, he was already giving piano recitals at the age of eleven. When I first met him he had a trunk-load of compositions in manuscript—to which labour of writing must be attributed the fact that the youth was nearly bald. His work comprised operas, symphonies, and concertos of great length. In spite of his short stature, watery eyes, a fringe of hair surrounding an almost polished dome, and an almost shrinking modesty, his ambition was conducting. In the French capital he forged his way to the front rank of conductors, and much to my surprise and pleasure I observed him commanding the respect and dignity of artists and public alike.

In Coppola Fred saw just the man he needed to plan and oversee the Company's recording in France. Coppola was a keen Francophile, which Gaisberg himself was not. A colleague recalled: 'Fred had his likes and dislikes. . . . He was never exactly at home in the French repertoire and was apt to find many French artists frivolous. . . .'[1] Coppola, however, combined wide cultural sympathies for all things French with an undoubted ability to conduct an orchestra. And so, as Fred Gaisberg summarised it:

> I secured the engagement of the youthful Piero Coppola as house conductor for our Paris studio, and he held the position until the outbreak of the Second World War. His enthusiasm for French composers and modern music generally gained him a prominent position in Paris, and this was reflected in his recording of many important works of Debussy, Ravel, Berlioz, Fauré, Honegger, etc., with which he enriched our catalogue. He recognised very early the genius of Francis Poulenc and Serge Prokofiev; the latter he personally brought to London to record his C major Concerto, Op. 26, which Coppola conducted with the composer at the piano.

The restoration of something like an international programme of recordings after the interruption of the war also acted as a reminder for Fred Gaisberg of the incredible strides the gramophone had made since its earliest years—since the beginning of his own career. So it seemed natural to begin in a desultory way to set down some thoughts about these parallel histories—the machine's and his own. Scribbled into odd corners in notebooks and diaries of this time are rough notes of jumbled history and recollection.

> Sir Wm. Preece first exhib. Edison's Phono before the R. Scientific Soc. . . . 27 Feb 1878. . . .
> Phono sold to King Ed VII Prince of Wales. . . .
> B. Shepard. . . .
> Auction sale of a piano
> Departure of a Troopship
> Leslie Stuart. . . .
> Jacobs . . . Trocadero
> Maurice Farkoa. . . .
> Chas. Tainter, Graham Bell, Volta Laboratory—paper cylinder coated with wax. Chicago World's Fair slot machine. . . .
> Recording rooms with a battery of 25 phonos. . . .

[1] Letter to the writer, 20 October 1972.

John York Atlee . . . Billy Golden. . . .
Experiment for a talking doll. . . .
Easton & Cromlin, stenographers to the Senate. . . .

As Fred Gaisberg sat in those post-war railway carriages taking him from one heavily capitalised European Gramophone centre to another, his mind seemed to find its way back again and again to those times of primitive adventure which had been the beginning of it all. He wrote to old Emile Berliner in Washington to ask for his memories. Berliner replied with a long, affectionate letter that also gave personal news.

> I am sure you can write a more perfect and a more interesting book than MacFarlane's and I shall be glad to give you every assistance. Just put your questions, or what might be still better, come over here and pay us a call. . . . I still have that photograph taken at 1410 Pennsylvania Ave. with you, Sinkler Darby, Gloetzner, Suess, Joe, Zip, and myself. . . .
>
> Thanks, we are all well. . . . I am not going to tell you all the things that I am engaged in just now but I am going to make another hit, this time in the literary line and it isn't a book like 'Conclusions' either. . . .
>
> I rejoice with all other Humanitarians that Germany was downed. I was not two months in this country, in 1870, when I changed my German 'Emil' into the French Anglo-Saxon 'Emile', which showed how early I recognised the difference between the two points of view. But I would have never thought that Germany would have been so stupid as to begin this War: they might have owned the World practically in another ten years.[1]

But if Fred Gaisberg wanted to write a book then, there was simply no time. For in addition to everything else, his presence was beginning to be in requisition by a number of the international celebrities he had befriended in the recording studio. They had started to demand Gaisberg's personal services in areas which had nothing to do with record-making. But the reason for this trust was exactly the reason for his success with them in the recording studio. One of his colleagues, Bernard Wratten, was to see it thus:

[1] Letter to Fred Gaisberg, 21 February 1919.

I think that in the final analysis it was Fred's complete integrity that enabled him to deal so successfully with artists. Complete integrity implies so many things: an absence of self-consciousness, of conceit, of pompousness. Fred was transparently honest, and although he could and did speak out in no uncertain way, he had an instinctive tact which prevented the plain, unvarnished truth from being offensive. He never shrank from a situation, and the artists knew he was telling them the facts.

Of course to most international artists he *was* His Master's Voice: Fred and HMV were indivisible in their minds, and that carried a great deal of weight. Fred dealt with them on equal terms: he might be short of stature and slight of build, but he 'compensated' by sheer force.

One secret of his success was that in awkward situations he could always imagine himself in the other man's shoes and think as the other man did. Perhaps this is what people call insight. There never were head-on collisions.[1]

The earliest renewal of post-war associations on these lines was that with Tetrazzini. Since Fred Gaisberg had been in more or less constant touch with her during the last two years of the war, when she wanted to make her *rentrée* into England it was naturally to Fred Gaisberg that she turned. He put her in touch with the concert manager Lionel Powell (who before the war had entrusted to Fred's judgement the question of touring the Russian soprano Michailova).

But Tetrazzini was always turning back to Fred to solve this or suggest that. It happened, for example, when Powell decided to take advantage of Tetrazzini's enormous pre-war reputation with the British public by arranging press conferences.

She was news, and therefore her press conferences were well attended. She always asked me to act as interpreter at these affairs, and I found them great fun. One had to serve up discreet news and guide the scribes away from private affairs which sometimes seemed the only things that interested them.

The stock question was, 'What do you think of London?' They could have answered it better themselves, since the diva lived hermetically sealed, for the duration of each visit, in her

[1] Letter to the writer, 20 October 1972.

private suite at the Savoy. Her only outdoor experience was the journey to and from the Albert Hall in a closed conveyance.

The woman reporters would ask her views on English cooking, when they might have known that she remained faithful to her Italian dishes. To another question, 'What do you think of Englishmen?', she might truthfully answer: 'Apart from my manager and my accompanist, Ivor Newton, I have never met any.'

In the autumn of 1920 Tetrazzini asked Fred for his help in the writing of her memoirs, and his contribution was such that he was promised a share of the proceeds from the book's sale. In fact the writing turned out to be rather like managing a Tetrazzini press conference: 'I helped her with her book *My Life of Song*, but felt, as she related the various episodes of her crowded career, that she was only showing the façade to the gaze of the world.'

Twenty years later, after Tetrazzini herself had disappeared from the scene, Fred could not resist the temptation to include one juicy story in his own book—still suitably cloaked in anonymity.

When I told a journalist friend that I was working on my first book, he said I should include some sensational stories about prima donnas. One international artist whose memoirs have already appeared omitted this saucy episode, in which she played the role of misleading lady.

Imagine a gala night at the end of a brilliant opera season. Many floral tributes were taken to the apartment of the leading star, who was giving a supper party. In the course of the evening she succeeded in encouraging her husband, the conductor, to drink until he was so overcome that he fell asleep. Whereupon she and her lover, a handsome basso, laid him stretched out on the floor, surrounded him with masses of flowers, and, like La Tosca after bumping off Scarpia, placed a lighted candle at each end of him and a crucifix on his breast. Then they eloped together.

Eventually the betrayed husband caught up with the lovers at Buenos Aires, and accepted a monetary consolation of some size from the misconductor to resign his claim on the lady. I never heard the sequel.

Of course he didn't have to. The light of Tetrazzini's friendship was to brighten many a day in Fred Gaisberg's life through these later years of the great singer's career.

Not all the celebrities who applied to Fred Gaisberg for help after the war were blessed with Tetrazzini's temperament or her luck. To the end of his life Gaisberg was to be haunted by the recollection of Titta Ruffo, who in his great days before the war had always seemed a young man (he was in fact younger than Fred himself by several years): 'I helped him to appear in a Queen's Hall recital in 1922. It was not very successful. There was something pathetic about a former great singer . . . reduced to impotency through loss of voice while yet a young man. . . .'[1]

But then Battistini, the oldest singer of all who had survived as an active performer on the post-war musical stage, made an eminent success when he appeared in England in the same year. Battistini's coming to England at all in those years, however, had been due entirely to the enthusiasm of Fred Gaisberg:

> Battistini's last London appearance in opera had been in 1906, and it looked as if England would not again hear one who was considered to be the greatest exponent of *bel canto* of his day. My enthusiasm for this artist was so great that I made every attempt to interest the English impresarios in promoting concerts for him in England, but I could make no progress until I ran across L. G. Sharpe and we came to an arrangement to go fifty-fifty in the expenses and profits.
>
> Three Queen's Hall recitals were given. . . . Their artistic and financial success was very gratifying to us, but beyond this there was the satisfaction of having our convictions substantiated. Battistini was then over sixty-five years of age, and the press filled enthusiastic columns with praise of this great artist and his demonstration of the authentic Italian school of singing. I am certain that to many young singers and teachers those performances were a revelation.
>
> There was no assisting artist, and the programme consisted of up to twenty of the most difficult arias and romances. . . . The baritone seemed to get better as his voice warmed up, and the remarkable thing was that he finished each concert absolutely fresh. Afterwards he would relax and say, 'Now I will indulge my one remaining vice.' He would then produce a

[1] 'All roads lead to La Scala'.

large Havana cigar, light this up, and lie back luxuriously in perfect ease and contentment.

I remember escorting him to a luncheon at [which] Ben Davies was present, and there was a great discourse on voice production with many illustrations and countless 'Ahs' by each of the old gentlemen, followed by examinations of throats during emissions. They were both masters at their jobs and understood what the other was explaining, yet neither spoke the other's language.[1]

Other vocal careers had been interrupted by the war at their most sensitive points.

[One] glorious singer who, had she been born a generation later, would have sent all Hollywood clamouring to her doorstep, [was] Maria Jeritza, or Baroness Popper. In her heyday, Jeritza was a most attractive woman with a head of real flaxen hair, and had a superb dramatic soprano voice, which she exploited particularly well in *Tosca* and as Princess Turandot. Jeritza reigned supreme in Austria in 1914 when the Vienna Opera was the first in Europe, and among her admirers was the Emperor Franz Josef.

Her name was forgotten in England after the war because as Baroness Popper, the wife of an Austrian nobleman, it had naturally not been mentioned during hostilities. In 1920 I was the only one who still knew her when she arrived in London on a visit with her husband. By frantic telephone calls I managed to get Harry Higgins along in time to discuss plans with her. This meeting resulted in a sensational performance of the role of Tosca at the Covent Garden Opera. . . .

These activities were not at all unconnected with the gramophone, which during those post-war years was beginning to play its part in what Fred Gaisberg saw as a remarkable era.

The four war years were not productive of any advance in music or the recording art. It was a sterile period of suspended animation. At best it left the appetite whetted for a feast—a feast that came with the big boom in gramophone records in 1920–22. Those years produced a veritable harvest for the various companies and their artists.

[1] 'All roads lead to La Scala'.

The amazing appetite for music and entertainment immediately after the war can be gauged by the average earnings from record royalties in 1923. Three top violinists each averaged £15,600, two sopranos each £17,900, two contraltos each £6,400, three baritones each £4,400. Of course the average earnings of two celebrated tenors of that epoch far exceeded £30,000.

During those five years following the Armistice . . . we recorded usually two complete operas [in Italy] each year. They would cost from Lr.50,000 to Lr.120,000 each in the post-war depreciated currency. Such standard operas as *Traviata*, *Rigoletto*, *Il Trovatore*, *Carmen*, *Pagliacci*, *Cavalleria Rusticana*, *La Bohème*, *Aida*, *Madame Butterfly*, *Faust*, etc. sung in Italian were sold in most countries, but sales in Italy alone covered the initial outlay. As we usually made use of the lesser-known singers, carefully chosen for this work, it gave us a good general knowledge of the younger artists and those hidden in the provinces. Some of our discoveries later turned out trumps and have since made fine careers.[1]

[1] 'All roads lead to La Scala'.

Chapter Sixteen

AGAINST THIS flourishing background, the most intense experience of the post-war years came for Fred Gaisberg once again, as so often in the past, from Russia:

> H. G. Wells, invited to Russia to observe the success of the Revolution there in 1919, was a guest at the home of Chaliapin in Petrograd. As he returned, Chaliapin handed him a personal letter to me which is now in the archives of The Gramophone Company. This letter begged me to look out for a further communication from him in which he would inform me of his attempt to leave Russia, and asked for my assistance. It suggested that our place of meeting should be Riga; he would be entirely without funds which I was to provide and he also asked me to plan a proposed programme, so that he could resume his concert and operatic activities in Europe and make further gramophone records.
>
> I was not surprised, therefore, when I finally received a further request to meet him in Riga at a certain time and place, and through the courtesy of The Gramophone Company I was able to keep the appointment.[1]

Before any of this could happen, however, it was necessary to assure Chaliapin's entry into the West.

> On account of the universal fear of the contagion of Communism, the obtaining of visas to enter England and America was a long and difficult matter. Eventually these were assured (principally through the good offices of The Gramophone Company) only on condition that he limited his activities solely to giving concerts for the Famine Relief Fund.

[1] Typescript article, 'Feodor Chaliapin'.

This was in 1921, when there was a famine raging in Russia so great that the Americans had organised an extensive Relief Fund with Hoover at the head. In Germany the mark was falling to the billion point. To get across the Polish Corridor meant being challenged and often indefinitely held up: in fact, the passengers in our train had to descend, and a number were detained. Most towns were rabidly Communistic, including our meeting point Riga. . . .

We met in the early days of September. . . . His wardrobe was in rags and tatters and he looked most forlorn in his threadbare clothes. His world in ruins, bewildered and stunned, I saw a very humble Chaliapin laying plans to rebuild his world in foreign lands at the age of fifty. He told me how all his possessions had been taken from him by the Government, and the money I was able to hand over to him—representing the royalties earned on his records during the War period—comprised his entire capital on which to start life over again.

After the Revolution in 1917, things [had] got increasingly difficult, and during this period he had many conflicts with the Russian Communists, who were jealous of the fees and kind that he was able to extract for his appearances. I . . . heard him describe how instead of Rubles—which by that time everybody scorned—he demanded his payment in flour, potatoes, bacon, and butter. On one occasion the doorkeeper complained:

'Why should you receive these gifts when you are a worker just like ourselves?'

Chaliapin replied, 'Well, to-night I am going to stand at the door, and you can go on and play the part of Boris.'

All this time he had to exercise the greatest of restraint to prevent himself from making physical attacks on the personnel of the theatre, which was appointed by the Committee. They tried to force him to act in propaganda operas but this he steadily refused to do, at the same time attempting to preserve a sympathetic attitude towards Communism while laying his plans for making his earliest escape from Russia. . . . Years elapsed before this could be accomplished—years of real hardship and anxiety, with long periods when his home was without fuel and the larders very short of rations. . . . At last he was given full permission to go abroad on the strength of a scheme he put forward to further the interests of Communism and raise funds for the Famine Relief Fund. . . .[1]

On eventually arriving in London, he fulfilled the conditions of his visa and gave five Famine Relief concerts, retaining for himself a certain proportion for expenses. His opening concert at the Albert Hall was filled to the last seat by an enthusiastic and fashionable audience, and he was fêted and lionised by a host of the friends he had made in 1913 and 1914.

After his bitter experience in the Russian Revolution, Chaliapin's first post-war visit to London must have come as balm to his despairing heart, since everywhere he met with the warmest reception and sold-out houses. I shall never forget the simple pleasure he took in studying the types and characters of the down-and-outs that we encountered in our midnight strolls on the Embankment, or his delight in the homely food at the coffee stalls and the shelters of the taxi-drivers. He had a theory that where the taxi-drivers ate, there one would get the tastiest food; sometimes he was right.

He spent a great deal of time, with evident delight, in the Savile Row tailors' shops, where he replenished his wardrobe, spending close on £400. He insisted on fraternising with the cutters and fitters and toasted them with champagne on the last day of fitting, telling them how he honoured an artisan who took pride in his work. He would say that in a sense they were equally as great in their art as he in his.[2]

When these Albert Hall concerts were given in 1921, it was the first time London had heard Chaliapin in a recital programme; hitherto his appearances were always in opera. He had created quite an original concert technique that immediately found favour with his audience. His programmes favoured dramatic songs and *Lieder*, which he dramatised, each of which was a rare cameo portraying love, sorrow, or joy in lyrical and dramatic pictures. He provided librettos with the translation of the words, and after announcing the number of the title selected he would pause for a few moments to enable the audience to scan the lines.

I assisted him in preparing his libretto, and was in attendance both at rehearsals and on the concert platform in the

[1] 'Feodor Chaliapin'.

[2] Typescript article, 'Chaliapin's accompanists'.

early days, to give him the English pronunciation of the titles and numbers.

The question arose of finding suitable songs for encores—songs which would appeal to non-Russian audiences. We had put down on our list Schumann's *Two Grenadiers*, Mussorgsky's *Song of the Flea*, and *How the King went forth to war*. It came into my mind that Chaliapin's early experiences as a boy—(he was born at Kazan on the Volga River, and had played on the banks and swum in the waters; and as a restless youth, become a member of a wandering opera company, frequently sailing up and down its course, seeing the toilers on the banks of the river hauling great barges upstream to the accompaniment of a monotonous chant)—comprised a good deal that was picturesque and also close to both the traditional and the everyday life of the Russian masses. I knew that this early experience was the foundation of his intense sympathy with the life and the aspirations of the Russian worker, and therefore suggested that he should give the outside world an impression of that early environment by singing the Song of the Volga Boatmen. Its simple melody, with the refrain 'Ei ukhnem', was already well known to the Russian public, but he objected that it was nothing more than a chorus, and had only one complete verse, which only Russians could appreciate. I said that we would write others and get his friend Koenemann to prepare an appropriate piano accompaniment. This Koenemann was commissioned to do, and he made several attempts before Chaliapin finally accepted the version as it now appears.

I was present at the first performance of the song . . . and was gratified by the fact that it at once made a hit. From that first post-war concert until the last, it . . . always found a place in Chaliapin's programmes, and if omitted the gallery would shout until he did sing it![1]

I also acted as interpreter in all Chaliapin's newspaper interviews. And I am certain that Gerald Moore and Ivor Newton were grateful for my presence and assistance during the concerts.

A whole article could be written on the heroism of his accompanists. His demands on these gentlemen were exacting,

[1] 'Chaliapin as I knew him', in *The Gramophone*, May 1938, pp. 508–9.

and only the most experienced and talented could hope to survive. They had to sense his every mood and his liberties with the music. This gave them little time to bother about the technique of piano playing. If they were at all sensitive they were bound to be confused before the public when they missed his cue.

When he was not in particularly good voice he would be in a highly charged nervous state, and the poor pianist was then bound to have embarrassing moments, when Chaliapin would beat on the piano top for the pianist to increase or decrease his pace. This frequently happened in the . . . 'Madamina' from *Don Giovanni*, or in the rubato he would employ in *How the King went forth to war*. When singing the *Persian Love Song* (Rubinstein) he would adopt a fine *mezza-voce*, which he would spin out to such an extent that we would all be on tenterhooks for fear his voice would break. (Of course when he attempted this in the gramophone studio, record after record would be made until he got this fine effect to his complete satisfaction. . . .)[1]

After the War his voice seemed to be more sensitive to colds, due to the hardships of the Revolution; and his abnormal vanity always to sing up to his highest standards sometimes inclined him to postpone concerts that should have taken place. In Russia—and in fact all over Europe—it appears a simple matter to cancel a concert on the morning of the actual day, by merely pasting the words 'Concert cancelled' across the *affiche* in front of the opera house or concert hall. By some magic this news spreads and within a few hours reaches the ears of practically everyone. This however cannot be done in the big cities of England and America, and the concert managers always suffered agonising moments until Chaliapin actually made his appearance on the platform.[2]

The Revolution had certainly left its traces on Chaliapin, and he was in a somewhat shattered and nervous state. I had to assist him a great deal in business affairs which had suddenly developed when it was known that he had entered Europe.

When the time came for him to leave for America, he begged me to accompany him, and this I was fortunately able

[1] 'Chaliapin's accompanists'.
[2] 'Feodor Chaliapin', pp. 7–8.

to do.[1] In November 1921 we embarked on the S.S. *Adriatic*, and our voyage across the Atlantic started under good auspices, for the ship carried perhaps the most distinguished contingent of passengers it had ever held, including a number of the members of the Disarmament Congress and operatic celebrities returning for the Metropolitan Opera Season.

. . . Richard Strauss, then fifty-seven years old, and [Elisabeth] Schumann [were going over to tour] America, Strauss himself accompanying her recitals of his *Lieder*. On board the S.S. *Adriatic* I played poker every evening with them, together with Chaliapin and Lucrezia Bori. Egged on by Elisabeth, who tipped us off about Strauss's parsimony, we all played against him one evening. The 'ante' was only five cents, and every now and again she would flick one of the coins from his pile into hers. This would go on until he spotted her. Then the game would be interrupted while he laboriously counted out his money. The smoking-room, led by the boisterous Chaliapin, would rock with laughter. Strauss is not witty but he has a sense of humour, and when he laughs his nose goes white. This peculiarity would set us off again.

Elisabeth contributed to our hilarity by disclosing her odd gift of imitating bird-calls without moving a muscle of her roguish face, so that it was almost impossible for the hearer to trace the source of the sound. If she had not laughed, we should have persisted in thinking there were canaries in the salon. (A few years later, much against Schumann's will, I utilised this gift of mimicry and made her record Zeller's *Viennese Nightingale's Song*, in which she whistles the refrain. This happy thought not only netted her several hundred pounds but endeared her to the masses.) . . .

The usual concert was organised, in which all the artistes participated; and it is doubtful whether such a coterie of celebrities has ever appeared at one concert in such happy fellowship. When Chaliapin sang *How the King went forth to war*, the deckbeams fairly shook. He was in his most happy and boyish mood, and for the sheer pleasure of the thing sang song after song to Dr. Strauss's accompaniment.

Upon arrival at Ellis Island, the *Adriatic* was besieged by

[1] In fact 'Chaliapin refused to sail for America . . . unless Gaisberg accompanied him.' (Mrs. Alfred Clark, letter of 18 September 1965.)

an army of reporters, journalists, and 'picture-men' who cornered first one and then another of the celebrities, and did their utmost to draw out of Chaliapin his opinions on the political situation in Russia, a topic which he insisted on avoiding.

Among those to meet us was Solomon Hurok, the well-known impresario, a man of great enterprise but of very limited schooling. In fact, although Russian-born and raised in America, both his Russian and his English were of the sketchiest kind. However, he insisted on installing himself as interpreter for Chaliapin. Surrounded by the reporters hungrily waiting for copy and firing questions at Chaliapin, Hurok said:

'Just wait, boys, and let him talk.'

Thereupon Chaliapin, in beautifully intoned Russian, eloquently held forth . . . gesticulating with those eloquent arms and fingers of his:[1]

'I myself have known the meaning of hunger. I well remember when our little family, consisting of my mother, father, and brother, were forced to leave Kazan and emigrate to Astrakhan in search of work. On arriving there, I believe I sent in some scores of written applications to various official departments and personages, but to this day I have never had a single reply. We had no money, and we quietly (but none the less surely) starved. . . .

'I remember walking one day in the fields with my father, when he sank to the ground, unable to go any farther. I sat beside him for a long time, overcome by despair. Somehow or other we got back to the town, and then I went to a shrine and prayed with bitterest tears. If only you knew how humiliating is the sensation of hunger! You would treat the hungry far differently if you only knew what it was!'

He stopped, and with one voice they cried out to Hurok, 'What did he say?'

Hurok briefly summed up the whole thing by tersely saying, 'He says he thinks America's fine!'[2]

Chaliapin's foreboding of misfortunes awaiting him in New York was partly realised. He had no sooner arrived in New York than he was attacked by severe laryngitis, which

[1] 'Feodor Chaliapin'.
[2] 'Feodor Chaliapin'.

IXa Tetrazzini arrives at Victoria Station for her first post-war tour, November 1920. Fred Gaisberg is on the left, with his niece Isabella Valli presenting flowers

IXb On board the S.S. *Adriatic*, November 1921: (*left to right*) Richard Strauss, H. G. Wells, Chaliapin, Elisabeth Schumann, Strauss's son. Photograph by Fred Gaisberg

Recording in the 1920's:

X The great *bel canto* baritone Battistini

XIa Fred Gaisberg in his office at Hayes

XIb Yeḥudi Menuhin

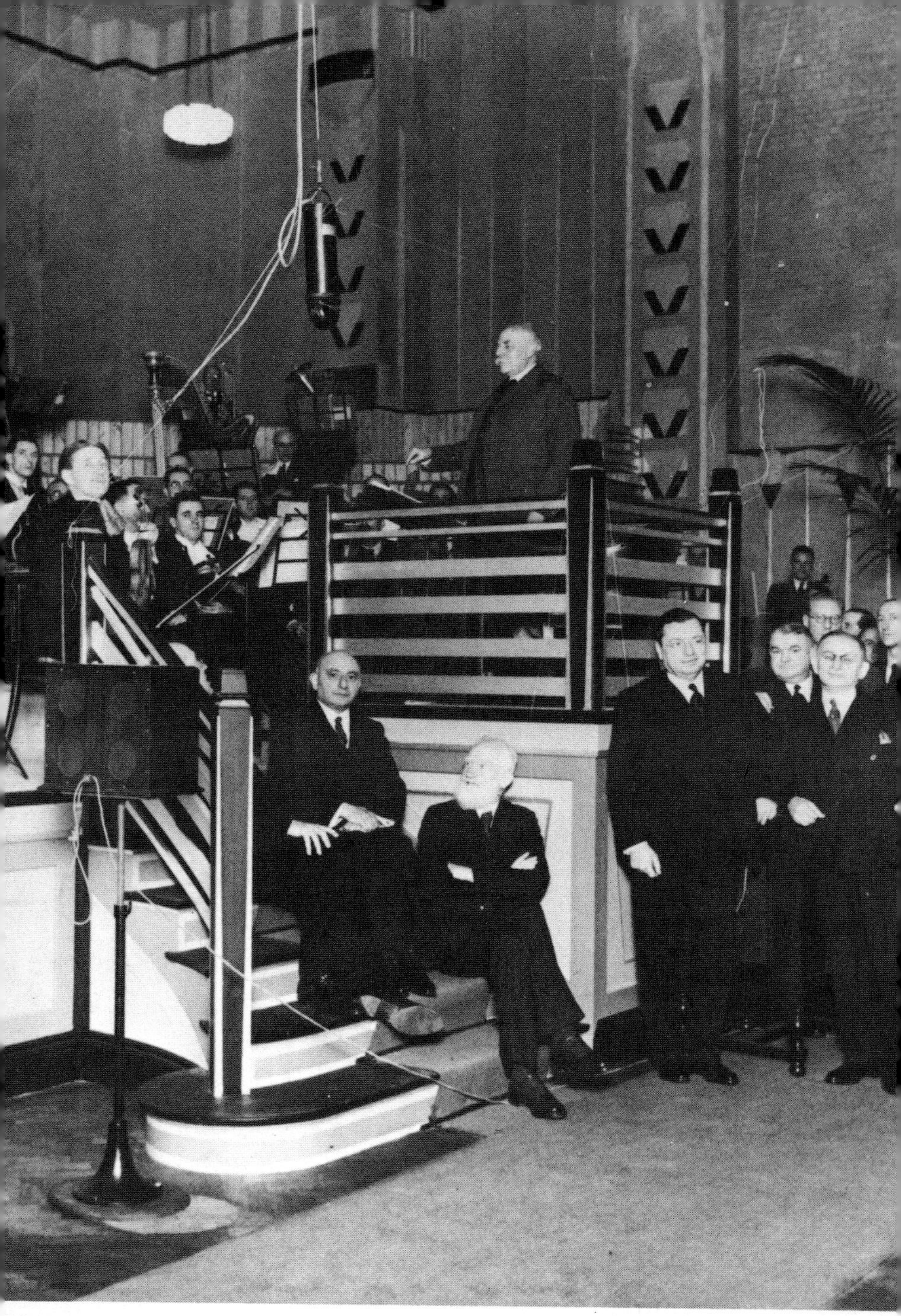

XII Opening of the new EMI studios in Abbey Road, November 1931. Sir Edward Elgar is on the platform with the London Symphony Orchestra (leader: W. H. Reed); seated on the steps (*left to right*) Sir Walford Davies, Sir Landon Ronald, George Bernard Shaw; the EMI group on the right is headed by Alfred Clark (Chairman) and Louis Sterling (Managing Director)

necessitated him postponing three times his first concert. In an agony of self-pity, he was quite unlike himself.

Titta Ruffo breezed in like sunshine from heaven, and for two hours they exchanged stories. I sat there spellbound and realised that these two overgrown schoolboys were probably the greatest raconteurs living. They were entirely satisfied with the effect they were producing on one another, and as the stories became more and more ribald they gesticulated to each other until in the end Chaliapin had to get out of bed to illustrate his points. . . . I can never forget the richness of those two magnificent voices—even in speech. They were simply trying to impress each other, and had they been paid a fee of a thousand pounds for their performance, they could not have been more assiduous in their anxiety to create an effect.

But when the time came for a concert appearance it was a different story.

The scene is Chaliapin's bedroom at the Waldorf-Astoria Hotel on a Sunday evening half-an-hour before he is due to commence his post-war debut in New York. . . . He is surrounded by the impresarios Solomon Hurok and Frederick Coppicus, his accompanist Rabinovitch, and myself. The air is charged with anxiety. Chaliapin with his laryngoscope, seated in his chimie before a mirror, is inviting us to look down the instrument to convince ourselves that those inflamed spots on his vocal chords make it impossible for him to sing. The concert has already been postponed twice on account of his laryngitis. The two American impresarios are wringing their hands, saying they will be ruined by another cancellation, and begging him to go to the concert if only to apologise to the audience.

Chaliapin in despair threw himself on the bed and moaned: 'Borga, borga, what have I done to deserve this?' He paced the room, knocking his head on the wall, and again cried to God: 'Why should I be so punished?'

Then suddenly Nicolai, his little Russian valet, said: 'Feodor Ivanovich, go to the concert. God will give you back your voice when the moment comes.'

Chaliapin stopped short, and with a look of scorn at the valet said: 'What the hell has God got to do with my voice?'

It was already past the hour for the commencement of the

concert when we made a combined effort and started to dress him in spite of his continued resistance. I put on his socks and tied up his boots, Hurok tied his tie, and we dragged the protesting giant downstairs, thrust him into a taxi, and started for the Manhattan Opera House.

Driving up to the stage-door, we could see by the commotion that the house was sold out, and that the restless audience had worked itself up into a fever of impatience. No sooner did we enter the artistes' room when the ballerina Anna Pavlova, who was waiting there for him, threw herself on his neck and they both cried together, she in greatest sympathy for his plight.

Chaliapin tried to persuade the doctor in attendance to go on the platform and announce that Chaliapin was going to appear—in spite of his warning that his septic throat made it impossible to sing, and if he attempted to do so he would probably lose his voice forever. This he was too shy to do. Then we tried to induce Solomon Hurok to make the announcement, but his English was so imperfect that he lacked the courage to face the howling audience. The task was eventually imposed on me, and in my innocence I accepted.

I was placed in the middle of the stage with the curtain down alone on that vast space. I could hear the yells of the audience from the other side like hungry lions in a den. In a moment the curtain quickly rose, and I looked out on that sea of faces. There was a hushed silence. Closing my eyes I cried out the apologies of Chaliapin and asked the indulgence of the audience. There was a great roar as I retreated to the wings.

Then Chaliapin strode forth followed by his accompanist, and for the next five minutes the cheering was continuous. Through his superb acting he made it plain that he was suffering; he even produced tears to win the sympathy of the public. Then he literally barked out in that sick voice five songs. It was indeed a pitiful performance, but the audience had to be satisfied, as there certainly would be no money returned.

By a back door he and I fled from the theatre to a quiet Harlem speak-easy, where I did my best through the long evening to console him. Early next morning I hustled him down to a secluded farm in the heart of New Jersey, on the outskirts of Jamesburg, before reporters could get at him, and I kept him there until his throat was well.

But in the end Chaliapin's American visit was an extraordinary success. Fred Gaisberg analysed it thus:

> At every concert in America there was a large percentage of his fellow-countrymen, who clamorously and enthusiastically cheered him to the rafters. It is difficult for anyone but a Russian to appreciate the deep emotion with which Chaliapin fills his countrymen. He is so typical of 'Mother Russia'—his tall blond figure, the real peasant type; his boyish and almost childlike nature, deeply moved by impulses of the moment. He is like a breath from the woods and fields of the good old Russia that they cherish in their memories.
>
> He was hailed as the greatest artist in the world, both lyric and dramatic, and it would seem that the resources of language had been exhausted by the critics in their search for words to praise his performances.[1]

In February 1922 Chaliapin and Gaisberg sailed back to England. Chaliapin gave two further concerts in London before returning to Russia to try and bring out his entire family. Gaisberg reported to a friend in New York:

> Your letter of the 2nd March came to hand the day before Feodor Ivanovich left London. He has given two concerts in all, both of which were great successes, and the Albert Hall concert established a record, as the house was sold out and contained the highest amount of money ever taken in by one artist, and he received the highest fee ever paid for a single evening's performance. . . . His former impresario was very much annoyed that he did not act for him on these occasions. The reason of this was that he did not accept my judgement that Chaliapin could fill the Albert Hall.
>
> Chaliapin sailed on the S.S.*Baltanic*, and left London docks at 7 o'clock on Thursday morning for Danzig and Libau. . . . We succeeded in getting his 31 pieces of luggage on the ship with the loss of only one case; and as this happened to be Nicolai's personal luggage, consisting of old socks and an old pair of shoes from his wife and some threadbare trousers, this did not affect Feodor Ivanovich's spirits, but it seemed to depress Nicolai. Nicolai left 120 dollars with me to buy monthly food check remittances.

[1] 'Feodor Chaliapin'.

Chaliapin will arrive in Libau on Tuesday the 14th, and expects to be in Petrograd by the 25th March. He was armed with all sorts of papers to give him safe conduct and to enable him to return to England. He hopes to bring his entire family out in June, and I have orders to secure a furnished house for their reception. . . . He tells me that he left a nice little lot of money in America, and here he also has in the bank a good nest egg, so I think his immediate future is well provided for.[1]

Everything went according to plan, and the Chaliapin family arrived in London and stayed for several months in the house Fred Gaisberg had found for them. But in the end they were attracted to France, that never-never land of Russian exiles. Gradually Gaisberg realised the extent of the change that had come into his friend's life:

Chaliapin was Russian to the core, and it was a cruel fate that sent him to live and die in exile. Transplanted so late in life, he could never adjust himself to be other than an alien. He always lived in the hope that a political change would enable him to return again to Russia.

One cannot blame him for refusing Maxim Gorky's offer on behalf of the Soviet Government to return there. I was present in the Kaiserhof, Berlin when, after dinner, Gorky pleaded with him for two hours, setting forth honours, position, and rights the Soviets were prepared to guarantee him if he would return. Gorky urged that it was his duty as a Russian to go back and put his shoulder to the wheel, rightly or wrongly.

Chaliapin replied that he had suffered too much at their hands. He was not in sympathy with the leaders, and was not young or resilient enough to risk the change. It was no good.[2]

[1] Letter to Miss Catherine Wright, 11 March 1922.
[2] 'Feodor Chaliapin'.

Chapter Seventeen

IN 1925 the electrical broadcasting microphone was introduced into gramophone studios. Because of its enormously greater range and sensitivity the microphone revolutionised gramophone recording overnight. Thinking about recording methods as they had been during his entire career up to 1925, Fred Gaisberg wrote:

> In some ways acoustic recording flattered the voice. A glance at the rich catalogue of that period will show that it was the heyday of the singer. . . . The inadequacy of the accompaniments to the lovely vocal records made in the Acoustic Age was their great weakness. There was no pretence of using the composer's score; we had to arrange it for wind instruments [largely] . . . and all *nuances* (such as *pianissimo* effects) were omitted. . . .
>
> Acoustically recorded sound had reached the limit of progress. The top frequencies were triple C—2,088 vibrations per second—and the low remained at E—164 vibrations per second. Voices and instruments (especially stringed instruments) were confined rigidly within these boundaries, although the average human ear perceives from 30 to 15,000 vibrations per second, and musical sounds range from 60 to 8,000 vibrations.
>
> Electric recording encompassed this and more. A whisper fifty feet away, reflected sound, and even the atmosphere of a concert hall could be recorded—things hitherto unbelievable. On this revolutionary sound-recording system the Western Electric people were secretly at work. One of the most alert of talking machine personages of that day was the old pioneer Frank Capps, inventor and associate of Edison. . . .

He and his friend Russell Hunting were then in charge of the Pathé recording plant in New York City, and to this plant the Western Electric people arranged to send their wax records for processing.

Capps and Hunting were curious enough to play over the sample pressings before sending them to the Western Electric people. What they heard coming from the records took them completely by surprise. For the first time they heard sibilants emerging from the trumpet, loud and hissing!

One day in the autumn of 1924, I received a telephone call. It was from Russell Hunting, who had just arrived at the Hotel Imperial, Russell Square. He said:

'Fred, we're all out of jobs. Come down here and I'll show you something that will stagger you.'

When I reached his rooms he swore me to secrecy before playing the records. They were unauthorised copies of the Western Electric experiments and, as Hunting predicted, I saw that from now on any talking machine company which did not have this electric recording system would be unable to compete with it.

When the Western Electric achieved electrical recording as a side-line to their research in telephone communication, a mine was sprung in my world. My colleagues, versed only in the simple acoustic methods of recording, had to begin all over again by studying electrical engineering. With dismay they saw young electricians usurping those important jobs of theirs, the reward of long apprenticeship. However, a few of my old associates were equal to the emergency and mastered what was to them a new science.

Nevertheless this wind of change had come late in the careers of the first generation of gramophone men. Inevitably it brought to an end a part of their way of life, and Fred Gaisberg wrote a private note about this.

There were many technical secrets in recording and matrix-making which were only known to me. I was under contract to my Company from 1898 continuously to 1925, when my day of glory departed with the invention of electrical recording.

Gaisberg himself was to enjoy another quarter century as an active participant in the recording world. Those years were to provide in many ways the culmination and summit of his career. One of his younger colleagues, Bernard Wratten, made this comment:

> To understand Fred's remark about the departure of his 'days of glory' with the coming of electrical recording, you must think back to the early days. . . . Having grown up with the industry Fred remained keenly interested and *competent* in recording techniques so long as they related to acoustic recordings. Acoustic techniques were personal and subjective: recorders used their own favourite 'sound-boxes'; they might even have several, one for each sort of assignment—piano, voice, orchestra, etc. They developed a sixth sense to guide them and the really great men like Arthur Clarke and George Dilnutt could often make a fairly reliable assessment of a wax just by looking at it. (I have many times seen Fred check up on a test pressing by examining it in just that way, though with the coming of electrical recording it was no more than a rough check.) Controls were elementary.
>
> When electrical recording came along the art of recording introduced a whole new technology. Things took a big jump forward and it was no longer possible to be guided by the feel of the thing. Most of the old methods in the studio and recording booth went by the board overnight. A recorder had to be a competent electrician as well as everything else and, of course, in one sense the job of the recording engineer was greatly narrowed down.
>
> . . . With the coming of electrical recording the expansion was at a breathless pace. . . . Fred, once the physical act of recording passed out of his hands, had a roving commission and he remained the undisputed impresario assoluto he had become on the death of his brilliant brother Will.[1]

The electrical revolution focused everybody's attention on the possibilities of recording large ensembles. At the top of Fred Gaisberg's list was Wagnerian opera.

> In 1925 [Albert] Coates, who was recognised as England's greatest conductor of Wagner, joined with me in the endeavour to satisfy the eager appetite for Wagner music which had

[1] Letter to the writer, 20 October 1972.

> been denied throughout the war. He is responsible for a valuable nucleus of records of *Tristan, Parsifal, The Valkyrie, Götterdämmerung*, and *Siegfried* in English. . . .

Within a month of the introduction of electrical recording, that nucleus had begun to form. But there was a drawback, and it quickly became apparent: as the records were sung in English, they had no appeal outside the English-speaking community.

Making Wagner records of international scope meant finding the singers. And this was where Gaisberg's own experience and friendships proved invaluable, for Wagnerian opera had just made its first important re-appearance in London since the War.

> After the First World War several years elapsed before musical activities resumed their stride. It might be said that the Covent Garden Opera season of 1924 started music once more on the upgrade. For that season a company of comparatively unknown artists was collected from Central Europe and the Wagner famine was relieved with a diet of truly superior performances given by an exceptional cast of singers. We heard the greatest Wotan, Brunnhilde, Sieglinde, Fricka of our generation, Friedrich Schorr, Frida Leider, Lotte Lehmann, Maria Olczewska. . . . The greatest *Heldentenor* of our times, Lauritz Melchior was to join the galaxy of immortals a few years later. To these add Germany's best opera conductor, Bruno Walter, then in his forty-eighth year, in charge of that youthful company eager to give London its first German season in ten years. It was a feast for the gods.
>
> I was kept busy at the Garden and became very friendly with all of them, including the managing director Harry Higgins and, a year later, Eustace Blois. . . . Elisabeth Schumann, whom I had met in 192[1] while crossing the Atlantic, was my sponsor and as her dressing-room was usually the meeting-place for the whole company, we quickly became acquainted.

The key to any successful Wagner performance or recording, of course, was the *Heldentenor*. And that was Lauritz Melchior.

> I cannot claim to have discovered him . . . but I did at least realise that he was the only Wagnerian tenor who could help

us to build up the vast series of Wagnerian opera records which the newly discovered electrical process made possible, and I acted promptly.

Melchior and I have worked in complete harmony to achieve this great library of Wagnerian classics. We found that we had at last got a tenor who could sing and rehearse record after record without stress and without his voice going husky or becoming strained. The risk of this happening is no joke with a Wagnerian orchestra of one hundred men, costing £200 a session, and expensive singers as well.

Gaisberg was therefore at special pains to cultivate the great man. His young niece Isabella Valli (the daughter of Louise and Camillo) would recall:

> We saw a great deal of Melchior and 'Kleinchen' during the great International Season when Frida Leider, Lehmann, Schorr, and Olczewska were singing. I went to the entire *Ring* twice through with Uncle, and the great job was to go round and amuse Melchior in the intervals. He used to get bored, and when he was bored he was hungry. 'Kleinchen' always had open Danish sandwiches for these times, in a picnic box with champagne, whisky, and coffee. But in order to prevent him eating too much, we had to play Bridge with him. It was very funny. There we were in Melchior's dressing room—he so big and colossal in nothing but his bear-skin and make-up, and the rest of us all very small by comparison—solemnly playing Bridge for the hour and a half of the Dinner Interval.[1]

From recording opera in the studio by means of the microphone, it seemed only a short step to allowing the microphone to enter the opera house itself. But there were all sorts of hidden traps.

> We opened up negotiations with Signor Scandiani of La Scala, Colonel Blois of Covent Garden, M. Rouge of the Opéra, and Gatti-Casazza of the Metropolitan each in turn. Great and lengthy documents were drawn up to cover the royalties opera managers dreamed would accrue when records of their opera productions would be available to the world. For the chronic losses of their ventures which were the nightmare of their lives, gramophone records were welcomed as a cure and panacea.

[1] Conversation with the writer, 1973.

Having come to an agreement for recording during a performance with the opera house management, tedious negotiations had then to take place with each and every artiste, the chorus and orchestra taking part. This type of recording particularly lends itself to hold-ups at the pistol point. Disgruntled, dissatisfied, and 'clever' artistes find it difficult to resist such a heaven-sent opportunity to revenge their grievances. A form 'giving their permission to be recorded' and the fee to be paid had to be signed before the work could be carried out.

Further, if the opera was of recent years and still in copyright, the consent of the owners had also first to be obtained. The artists involved had to be those already under contract to my Company, or free from obligations to competitors. The conductor would have to be friendly, as his sympathetic help was of paramount importance.

When finally all these details were arranged, we would be assigned a small room near the stage in which to set up a pair of recording machines and control panels. One machine would be revolving and receiving the sound while the other was being loaded up. The actual recording would be in charge of a chief operator. In close touch with him by telephone would be a 'controller', usually a good musician[1], seated before a switch-board, and spread out before him a score of the opera in which 'cuts' and probable time duration of records was marked off.

The opera-conductor, with pre-arranged signals, would indicate to the 'controller' by a buzzer the 'get ready' and the 'start' of the Overture and each Act. That was all we required of him. The 'controller' did the rest, which consisted of following the score to advise the 'operator' of the loud and soft spots to warn him to increase or decrease the amplification. Especially had he to be alert for sudden *forte* timpani attacks, as these would have a fatal effect on the sound track: the effect would be that the blow would traverse three or four sound tracks and could not be reproduced by a pick-up. The way to deal with these 'whacks' was to cut off the lower frequencies.

Three microphones equispaced between the columns of the

[1] More often than not it was Fred Gaisberg himself.

proscenium would be placed in the footlights, hidden from the view of the audience. A difficult situation arose when a solo voice was back scene or off-stage. For instance, in the first act of *Otello* the tenor sings his entrance aria from the deck of a ship far from the microphone. When we attempted this recording the artiste was Zenatello, and before the show started I asked him to approach slightly the centre and direct his head down to the microphone. But when the moment arrived, he most accommodatingly dismounted from the poop deck of his ship and stood directly over the microphone and then burst into his 'Esultate! l'orgoglio musulmano sepolto è in mar.' He had exceeded my wishes, and I had to face an infuriated Colonel Blois who said I had messed up his production and threatened to throw us bag and baggage out of the opera house.

On another occasion, after tedious bargaining and planning we were set to record the complete *La Bohème*, when the Mimi, thinking to take every advantage of this God-sent opportunity, demanded at the eleventh hour a fantastic fee—to which we had to accede. In a similar way we were held up by a conductor at the moment of beginning, as he said he would not conduct unless we removed our microphones.

There was the complete recording of a Flagstad and Melchior performance of *Tristan und Isolde*, comprising fifty twelve-inch records. They were full of wonderful moments as well as blemishes—principally stage noises and the whisperings of the prompter and coughs in the audience. When I played the records for the artistes they were nearly inclined to pass them, but Melchior decided that in places his voice was under-recorded—especially in those big 'A's' of which he was so proud and sensitive.[1]

With the advent of the electrical process, certain recordings of popular Wagner selections . . . sold in tens of thousands. Consequently, when Siegfried Wagner and his wife, Winifred, came to London in April 1927 to raise money to carry on the Bayreuth Wagner Festivals, then in difficulties, the various companies were ripe and ready to overrate the commercial value of the Festival records.

I secured one recording session, the programme being of

[1] 'Notes on Actual Performance Recording'.

course the *Siegfried Idyll*. . . . After this we adjourned to the Langham Hotel for luncheon and to discuss the Bayreuth proposition. This was that we were to have the exclusive rights to record at Bayreuth, the terms being a royalty on the sale of each record plus a substantial guarantee. Siegfried agreed to everything and seemed most pleased, but we soon spotted that the last word was with his wife. She had already started negotiations with Arthur Brooks of the Columbia Company and withheld her reply until Brooks could obtain from his director, Louis Sterling, then in America, his company's confirmation.

In fact the Gramophone Company directors had begun to grow wary of on-the-spot recording.

Executive Minute No. 15589, 6–5–27.
Bayreuth Festival

. . . The matter was very carefully considered, and in view of the fact that we understand the majority of the leading artistes in Germany are under exclusive contract with the competition, the uncertainty of being able to make terms with the conductors, also that we have not been able to test the hall and coupled with the fact that our experience of recording at La Scala has so far proved unsatisfactory, it was

DECIDED

to advise the Artists Dept. that until we knew the leading artists engaged for the Festival, we were unable to make any offer.

So Fred Gaisberg watched from the side-lines while his old friend Charles Gregory directed Columbia's operations at Bayreuth. 'Charlie reports that the Bayreuth assignment was the most arduous and tiresome he has ever had. The artists and instrumentalists were difficult to assemble. They had come to look upon the Festival as a holiday and resented the extra rehearsals and performances that robbed them of their spare time, even though the Columbia were paying good fees. The orchestral players were particularly difficult, and were always going on strike. . . . These sessions started at any time they could be fitted in, but usually in the evenings when the theatre was free.'[1]

[1] Typewritten notes on Charles Gregory's career.

In the concert hall, however, the possibilities of on-the-spot recording were more favourable.

Some of the biggest sellers in the late 'twenties were a series of records recorded with the Royal Choral Society, eight hundred strong, during their regular concert performance of the *Messiah*. I sat at the feet of Dr. Malcolm Sargent, operating the signals to the recording studio in a remote part of the building. When the Doctor raised his arms to bring the choristers to their feet, I signalled 'Let down the cutting stylus.' I remember especially what fine records were 'Behold the Lamb of God', 'Glory to God', and the 'Hallelujah' Chorus. . . . The Royal Choral Society enjoyed handsome royalty earnings that tided them over many a lean year.[1]

One of the first innovations to follow electrical recording was a mobile van, with which we could realise the dream of recording [in places not accessible for running land-lines]. We used it with all the gusto of a new toy. . . .

The Temple Church Choir . . . came into great prominence, but it was their gramophone recording of 'Hear My Prayer', one of the early commissions of the Mobile Van, that brought it international fame and caused the dusty old 'church of the lawyers' to be so overwhelmed by visitors from the Dominions and the U.S.A. that tickets of admission had to be issued.

The recording took place . . . at a special private session in the Temple Church. Thalben Ball was the choirmaster and organist, and Ernest Lough, then between fourteen and fifteen, was the solo boy. A happy combination of chance helped to make this record: the soft, acoustic resonance of the church, a boys' choir with a fine discipline, a choirmaster who was a first-rate trainer, and a gifted boy with a musical sensibility and a silver voice just then at its prime. A year later the moment would have passed, for the voice had changed.

The fame of record C 1329 spread like wildfire, and in a few years close on one million copies were sold. The royalties payable to the Temple Church really embarrassed the lawyers, so unexpected was their sum total. After bonuses to each member of the choir there was sufficient left over for a fine holiday. With the balance they founded a scholarship.

[1] 'Notes on Actual Performance Recording'.

Chapter Eighteen

THUS THE pattern of Fred Gaisberg's career developed after the coming of the electrical process. The mechanics of recording had been taken from him, but the broadening scope of recorded music and the virtual redefinition of its role throughout the musical world drew more and more heavily on the other talents he had developed. And so he was described in these later years by his secretary at The Gramophone Company, Gwen Mathias.

> No matter how temperamental an artist may prove, Fred Gaisberg has the invaluable gift of recognizing the real cause of any trouble. . . . On countless occasions a highly charged atmosphere has been miraculously cleared by one of his quick shafts of wit. . . . His desk may not be a model of neatness, and if you ask him for somebody's telephone number, he will probably tell you that it is written on the lining of his hat. All the same, he has a remarkable knack of getting things done, and will crowd an incredible amount of work into one day without any sign of rush or hurry.
>
> He [will spend] two or three hours in his office [at Hayes] in the morning, giving his opinion of new recordings and dealing with masses of correspondence. More often than not he will return to London to keep a lunch appointment with some artist or impresario. . . . Probably the afternoon will be devoted to superintending a recording session, anticipating every demand and maintaining complete harmony. . . . Invariably one or two appointments will be fitted in during the course of the afternoon. Not content with all this, he may be seen almost any evening in the London concert halls or at the

opera, and this often involves entertaining visiting artists after the performance.[1]

In the evenings Fred Gaisberg was an inveterate observer of the musical scene. One never knew what prospects might turn up in this way. In December 1927 Sir Thomas Beecham (who had for years been firmly contracted for recording to the rival Columbia Company) had to relinquish a London Symphony Orchestra concert at the last moment owing to indisposition. In his place was a young man called John Barbirolli. The programme had not been altered: it consisted of two works by Haydn (which the young man knew) and Elgar's Second Symphony. This he had had to learn almost literally overnight.

Gaisberg went to the concert to see how Barbirolli would fare. It turned out to be a creditable performance of that complex and subtle score. The youngster obviously had the ability to work with an orchestra and gain their confidence in a very short space of time. As the applause began, Fred Gaisberg made his move. Barbirolli remembered: 'When I was walking off the platform after taking my bows, a man standing among the first fiddles attached himself to me and said, "My name's Gaisberg. Don't sign any contracts—I'll 'phone you in the morning." '[2]

What Fred had seen and immediately grasped was the possibility of an English Piero Coppola. 'I pursued John Barbirolli assiduously, as I needed a first-class orchestral accompanist for opera as well as concerto recording. I knew that in him I had found a gifted and practical man. He was elusive in negotiations and I very nearly lost him, as my terms were below those offered by a competing company which, however, could not give him the world-wide publicity that I was able to offer. I made [contacts] for him with such celebrities as Heifetz, Rubinstein, Elman, Kreisler, Schnabel, Chaliapin, and Melchior. . . .'

Soon Barbirolli was to be seen in the HMV recording rooms almost daily carrying off assignments of heavy responsibility.

> Imagine the recording of the Quintet from *Die Meistersinger* with Melchior, Schorr, and Schumann, conducted by Barbirolli, with some ten rehearsals and three attempts to make a satisfactory record. It needs a [nerve] of iron to stand the strain and costs over £600 in salaries and expenses.

[1] Typescript article, 'Fred Gaisberg'.
[2] Sleeve note to HMV ALP 2061.

The same judgment which secured Barbirolli in London was in equal demand abroad, as Gaisberg's secretary had good reason to know.

> Having travelled so widely, he is quite at home in all countries of Europe. News may be received of difficulties in one of the foreign recording centres, and a quick decision will be taken that he should proceed there immediately to use his influence in straightening out the matter. No elaborate preparations are involved: a telephone call is put through to his home asking for a small bag to be packed, and he starts off on a five hundred mile journey with as little concern as he travels the fifteen miles between the office and his home.[1]

His home was now at 42, Crediton Hill, West Hampstead. It was a smallish semi-detached house which he had purchased with his sister Carrie, and it was to remain their home for the rest of Fred's life. Their niece Isabella Valli would remember: 'Aunt Carrie's relationship with my Uncle Fred was discreet. She was very, very intelligent, and she was completely feminine. She asked him questions that a man wants to be asked without worrying him. She ran a most comfortable home for him, and she entertained his artists.'[2]

The neighbourhoods round Hampstead contained the homes of many of the artists with whom Fred Gaisberg was in contact. It was within easy reach of Hayes by means of a railway line that ran almost door-to-door. It was immediately accessible to all the West End halls, theatres, and recording sites in which so many hours of Fred's life were now spent. And another advantage lay in the fact that the Valli family had now come to live close by. Isabella remembered:

> On Sunday evenings my parents would entertain at our house in Hampstead. Usually there were about twelve or fourteen people, and supper was set out on our huge table with all the extensions put into it.
>
> Uncle used to ask the artists who were visiting London. When Marek Weber was in London he was always there, and he would bring his violin. John Barbirolli would sometimes bring his 'cello. Chaliapin came, Tetrazzini came. They both

[1] Typescript article, 'Fred Gaisberg'.
[2] Conversation with the writer, 1973.

adored animals, and one of their great passions was to tease my naughty little Pekingese, Shi. He used to sit at my feet with his little cross face in his paws, and if any of them dared to come near me he would attack their ankles. Chaliapin was merciless with him, making doggy-noises and cat-noises to tease him by the hour.

After supper we had music. Uncle would be at the piano, while we stood round him to sing. He was an excellent sight-reader, had a phenomenal musical memory, and could also improvise by the hour. And he would play anything—Viennese waltzes, jazz, opera, *Lieder*.

One of the things I remember most about Uncle at home is the amount of work he did at the piano. He was always using it to study unfamiliar works.[1]

All of Gaisberg's work for The Gramophone Company remained under the nominal supervision of the Head of the International Artistes Department. Soon after the introduction of electrical recording this position was occupied by a remarkable man, Trevor Osmond Williams. The smallest of Osmond Williams's qualifications was that he was the Chairman's nephew, and that fact had probably only very little to do with his appointment. For the younger Williams was one of those golden personalities before whom all doors seem to open—a man of formidable intelligence, tact, and charm who was held in respect by all who knew him, and in affection by those who knew him well. Outside The Gramophone Company, his managerial interests extended to the Boards of Covent Garden and the London Symphony Orchestra.

At 'His Master's Voice' Williams and Fred Gaisberg (who was twelve years his senior) made a very powerful team in the International Artistes Department. Their junior colleague Bernard Wratten was to describe the relationship thus: 'Osmond Williams allowed Fred complete freedom, though he kept an eye on the financial basis of the Department's recording contracts and generally maintained some sort of order and system—something Fred was quite happy to leave to him as it was not really in his line at all.'[2]

One of the Gramophone problems which Williams addressed

[1] Conversation with the writer, 1973.
[2] Letter to the writer, 20 October 1972.

with typical success was that of outmoded recording studios. The old acoustic rooms at Hayes were not well adapted for many kinds of music now being recorded with the electrical microphone, and they could not accommodate large orchestras. Since 1925 many recordings had been carried out in the Queen's Hall, where a permanent 'His Master's Voice' laboratory had been installed. With the great expansion of musical life in London during the later 1920s, however, it became more and more difficult to find the Hall itself free. They were having to fit in recording sessions often at odd and inconvenient hours, sandwiched uncomfortably between public events. And so, as Gaisberg wrote: 'Trevor Osmond Williams was working tirelessly on a plan to build a group of studios adapted for recording orchestras, large and small, and solo players and singers.'

The younger Williams's vision in making this plan had outrun Fred Gaisberg's own, and Fred was at first very dubious that the state of the industry even then would support such a capital expenditure. But Osmond Williams's drive, charm, and personal authority carried the day. A sizeable house was purchased in St. John's Wood. No. 3, Abbey Road was no more than a ten-minute taxi ride from anywhere in the West End. If it was even closer to Osmond Williams's elegant flat, it was not so much farther from Gaisberg's home in Crediton Hill. And the property had a large garden which could be built over to accommodate an orchestral recording studio that would duplicate the scale and acoustics of a big concert hall, with smaller studios and many offices adjoining.

The great plan was only just under way when, early in 1930, there was an incident which gave everyone concern. Osmond Williams and Fred Gaisberg were being entertained by Rosa Ponselle. Gaisberg wrote:

> [We] escaped from a super-heated salon in the Savoy . . . in the middle of a lavish supper party to which she had invited us. While we were taking the air on the Embankment my poor friend, already ill, collapsed. For half an hour Rosa, seated at the base of Cleopatra's Needle, bathed his head and soothed him until he recovered. There was an air of tender solicitude in her nursing that I shall never forget.

Williams seemed to recover. But in July 1930, in the midst of a visit to Vienna, he was struck down again, and this time it was fatal. The affection he had inspired amongst musicians everywhere was shown in a letter from Sir Edward Elgar: 'I cannot yet feel I can write about dear Trevor Osmond Williams: I think you know what I feel—I cannot get over the loss.'[1]

It was already a time of heavy change within the Company leadership. At the Shareholders' Meeting the previous autumn the old Chairman, Trevor Williams, announced that he had requested the Board to find a successor. He had virtually founded the European Company in 1898 and had been its Chairman ever since. The new Chairman turned out to be Williams's Managing Director, Alfred Clark. He was one of Fred Gaisberg's oldest friends in the business.

No sooner had Clark taken up the reins than the atmosphere was suddenly filled with rumours of merger. A quarter century earlier The Gramophone Company had bought out their leading European rival, the Zonophone Company—only to see another rival, Columbia, rise in its place under the direction of Fred Gaisberg's old friend Louis Sterling. During the past few years Columbia had absorbed several smaller firms. Now it seemed that the two largest English companies, Columbia and 'His Master's Voice', might pool their resources to form a gigantic international cartel.

The merger, when it came in 1931, created a new organisation named 'Electric and Musical Industries Ltd'. Alfred Clark was Chairman, and Louis Sterling became Managing Director. Fred Gaisberg found his own responsibilities expanded. His assistant David Bicknell recalled: 'From the date of the merger with Columbia the former Columbia Classical Department was abolished, the HMV International Department took over, and Fred became in effect artistic director of *both* HMV and Columbia. They had some really important artists such as Beecham, Bruno Walter, Weingartner, Szigeti, Huberman, Petri, Gieseking, the Lener Quartet, etc.'[2]

Fred Gaisberg's position in the new giant EMI cartel was later described by David Bicknell (who was ultimately to succeed to the post) in this way:

> Fred was the most important person in the International Artistes Department. But strangely enough he was never

[1] Quoted in *Elgar on Record*, p. 116.
[2] Letter to the writer, 24 October 1974.

manager of it. He didn't have a title at all, but he really was artistic director, and everyone knew what he was. In fact everyone throughout the whole musical world knew what he did.

He was very, very intelligent, and he realised perfectly well where his talents lay. His talents lay as an impresario. He was an impresario of genius—his instincts in regard to artists were very nearly infallible. . . . I do not mean simply that he was able to judge whether a man or woman possessed a good voice or could play an instrument well. His perception went much deeper. He summed up, and very rapidly, whether in addition to their musical talents they possessed the good health and determination to sustain a great career, and furthermore whether they would create by some means a widespread interest in their activities. These gifts are given to a few but not to many, and Fred recognised them instantly even though they were not fully developed. Once he had made up his mind, he acted with great speed—as he had done with Caruso. Yehudi Menuhin is a good example of someone Fred recognised as having all these gifts in our time. At one moment Yehudi was unknown, and a moment later Fred was producing a steady stream of records which matched and sustained Yehudi's rapidly expanding career.

Really I can say that in the years between 1927 (when I first met him) and 1939 (when he retired), there wasn't a single artist who subsequently became of importance, whom Fred didn't contract for the Company, and who didn't live up to the expectations Fred had of him when he was engaged. He didn't expect them all to do as well as Caruso, but he knew perfectly well what their talents were and in what directions they should be developed. And he developed them.

His power within the Company was not at any time autocratic. All his important decisions were approved by a series of interlocking committees, which were then an important element in the administration of the Company. But nevertheless his long experience, proved record of success in past dealings, and far-reaching prestige meant that usually (but not always) his recommendations were accepted. Had this power rested in the hands of a man less scrupulously honest it might have led to irregularities in the form of bribes; but such practices were unthinkable to anyone acquainted with his character, and he would have made short work of anyone who had attempted it.

He hated pomposity in any form and he had none himself. I was amused and astonished soon after joining the Company to hear him say at a Committee Meeting which had turned down a request from Melba for a gift: 'Well, all right, I will tell her. But I must remind you that the last time she saw me she said that if she ever set eyes on me again she would wring my neck, and she is bigger than I am!'

On the other hand, he could be ruthless when confronted with pomposity in others when he considered that it was unmerited. Once I went with him to meet a very grand mezzo-soprano, who said to him in a very hoity-toity sort of voice:

'Oh, Mr. Gaisberg, you *must* tell the Manager at Covent Garden—with whom you have so much influence—to engage me for *Carmen*.'

To which Fred replied: 'Oh, but I thought that you had abandoned opera.'

'*Abandoned* opera?' she said. 'Why, I am the greatest exponent of the part!'

'Oh,' he reiterated, 'I heard that you had given it up—at last.'

She naturally departed in a rage, but he remained quite unrepentant.

He knew from first-hand experience, acquired in contact with so many people in so many lands, a great deal about poverty, dishonesty, rapacity, intolerance and the rough sides of life. And he took this knowledge into account in his dealings with the people whom he met in his work. On looking back after all these years, my lasting impression is that he was one of the best men whom I have ever met—not in the Sunday-school plaster-saint sort of way, but in the straightforwardness of his dealings, his ability to look life straight in the eye, by his kindness, his comprehension and protection of those dependent on him, and the cheerful, productive atmosphere which he generated to the benefit of all those who came intimately into contact with him.

He believed that the classical business could only be maintained by establishing economical standards throughout its administration, and one of his greatest talents was to transmit this feeling not only to his assistants but to the most celebrated and successful musicians. In fact I have seen a world-famous pianist and conductor run from the machine-room where they had heard the latest play-back together, so as to complete a record and avoid the necessity for an extra session. Moreover, they were as pleased as he when they were successful.

But he was not mean so far as artists' payments were concerned, and I heard him fight great battles in committee against less imaginative men to ensure that artists were adequately rewarded. He believed profoundly that the success of the Company could only be maintained if the artists were generally contented. He rubbed into me and everybody else who worked for him that we were—well, I suppose we were first servants of the Company—but above all we were servants of the artists, and it was our job to help them in every sort of way. And he was a living example of how to do it.

At Hayes he worked in a large, quiet room on the top floor near the recording studios, and I worked in the next room (which had a connecting door). Both offices could be entered from the passage by other doors, but when Fred arrived in the morning half an hour after me he usually walked through my office before entering his own so that he could hear what was going on, as I was the first person to read the post.

He sat at a large desk which had numerous drawers on both sides, which should have been preserved as a national monument. At the bottom on the right was his 'self-answering drawer', where he put letters which he did not wish to answer. Months later he would remove them and announce that they had now answered themselves, and consequently they could be filed. But there were not many of these, and on the whole he was a good correspondent with a vivid personal style very closely allied with his personality and mode of speech.

In spite of the fact that he could have possessed the finest collection of autographed photographs in the world, the walls of his office were not plastered with them (as is so often the case in the offices of less gifted Artists Managers who wish to show how important they and not the artistes are). He had a few photos which he had taken of himself in the garden of Chaliapin's villa at St. Jean de Luz. . . .

He sat facing a bookcase filled with musical scores and

reference books. On top of the bookcase was a rather nice bust of Beethoven. One day I was surprised to see that he had propped up the photo of a German baritone next to Beethoven. He was a good baritone but no beauty, and it did not seem to me that he improved the view. So I said:

'Why have you put up that photo there?'

To which he replied immediately: 'To keep the rats away!' I suppose that his real reason was as a reminder that he wanted to write to him.

He had an excellent memory, but to ensure that he did not forget important messages he used to write them on strips of paper which he then placed inside his bowler hat. They remained there when he put his hat on his head, and often floated about when he took it off on arrival at the Savoy or wherever he was going. But the system worked well.

One day when he was about to leave for London, I said to him as he walked through my office:

'Mind that you do not forget to tell Mr.— (something or other).'

To which he replied good-humouredly: 'You be darned. I have forgotten very little of real importance in this business.'

He never made a truer remark.[1]

[1] Typescript talks and communications to the writer.

Chapter Nineteen

AMONGST ALL the recording artists of the 1920s and 1930s, one figure was unique. Sir Edward Elgar was the only composer of great stature who was also an enthusiastic performer for the gramophone. Elgar had already conducted records for more than a decade when the introduction of the electrical microphone transformed the significance of his presence in 'His Master's Voice' studios. Fred Gaisberg wrote: 'Elgar's association with my company before 1925 was chiefly decorative, his name carrying the prestige of England's greatest composer. After that date the introduction of the electrical process made it possible to record with satisfaction his great symphonic works under his own baton, one after the other, until the year of his death. Thus the greatest English composer has, for the first time in history, left to posterity his own interpretations of his works. I took personal charge of the many sessions required to accomplish this task.'

In 1930 Sir Edward was seventy-three. He had written nothing of consequence for more than a decade. The rage to perform his music, so strong in the earlier years of the century, had diminished considerably. But near the end of that year Elgar did produce a new orchestral suite—it was said, at the suggestion of one of the Gramophone Company men. The new music was a *Nursery Suite*, dedicated to 'Their Royal Highnesses The Duchess of York and the Princesses Elizabeth and Margaret Rose'. Naturally The Gramophone Company wished to record it. Writing in January 1931 to advise Gaisberg about when the parts would be available for recording, Elgar in his capacity as Master of the King's Musick suggested some stage-management of his own:

I do not know if

PRIVATE

the Duchess of York has ever attended a *recording session*: if you think well I might propose this;—it might interest her & she might allow a photo: etc.[1]

In the event both the Duke and Duchess came with the elder of the Princesses to Kingsway Hall for the *Nursery Suite* session on 4 June. Bernard Shaw and Sir Landon Ronald were also present. In the recollection of the London Symphony Orchestra leader, W. H. Reed: 'Fred Gaisberg (artistic director of the company) handed them each a copy *de luxe* of the score, and we then proceeded to play it under Sir Edward's own direction. When we had played the number "The Waggon Passes", Their Royal Highnesses' faces were wreathed in smiles and, at their request, Sir Edward repeated it.'[2]

As the new Abbey Road recording studios neared completion in the autumn of 1931, the question arose of a suitable gesture for officially opening them. The obvious gramophone artist for such an occasion was Elgar. Sessions had already been booked with the London Symphony Orchestra on 11 and 12 November for Elgar to record his *Falstaff*, and it was now decided to hold these sessions in the new No. 1 Studio at Abbey Road by way of inauguration. Gaisberg wrote to Sir Edward.

At the termination of the session to be held on the 12th, we have taken the liberty of inviting a few of the Press to see and hear the new recording hall—the first of its kind built specially in England for gramophone recording. This will occur at about 12.30, and we should be glad if you would then repeat the record comprising the Finale of [*Falstaff*], so that the visitors can hear it played and also reproduced directly from the waxes, so as to hear the acoustic result of the new hall.

Half an hour before beginning the session—namely at 9.30 a.m.—we have asked the orchestra to be present, and the Pathé Film Company will make a short talking film of the orchestra in action. This will carry us up to 10 o'clock, when our proper session will begin. Can I ask you also to conduct

[1] Quoted in *Elgar on Record*, p. 127.
[2] *Elgar as I Knew Him* (V. Gollancz Ltd., 1936), p. 104.

during this half-hour the Aubade from your *Nursery Suite*?

Elgar replied immediately:

My dear Gaisberg:

Yours of the 4th. All right—I fall in with your plans—only if I have a *speaking part* in the Pathé I shall look for a Hamlet fee. . . .

Haste
Yrs ever
Edward Elgar.[1]

A great composer, a famous orchestra, a new and untried recording studio, cameras, technicians, Company executives, honoured guests—Fred Gaisberg had really to field-marshal the occasion. In the event the records they made at those sessions turned out splendidly. Gaisberg wrote to Elgar:

They are without doubt the finest orchestral records we have made, and show that the new studio is a great success. Indeed, to obtain a successful series under the excitement of the many visitors present, and with the many distractions, was beyond my greatest hopes.[2]

Falstaff was a late entry in the lengthening list of Elgar's major orchestral works recorded under the direction of their composer: the '*Enigma*' *Variations*, the two Symphonies, the Violoncello Concerto, *In the South* and *Cockaigne Overtures*. There remained the Violin Concerto. Ever since 1925 they had been trying to get Fritz Kreisler, the Concerto's dedicatee, to record it with Sir Edward. Kreisler did not refuse, but time after time he was evasive. At last Gaisberg felt that they could wait no longer: Elgar was then rising seventy-five. So he formulated what was to be recognised as one of his most inspired recording schemes.

As a youthful and pliant performer without prejudice, who would respond best to [Elgar's] instruction, I selected Yehudi Menuhin as the most promising soloist. I posted him the music with a letter asking him to prepare it for recording, and promised him that Sir Edward would coach him and conduct

[1] Quoted in *Elgar on Record*, pp. 144–5.
[2] Ibid., p. 153.

the records in person. Also I suggested that he should include it in an Albert Hall Sunday concert programme with Sir Edward in charge of the orchestra.

Yehudi was enthralled with the work and his father accepted the idea in its entirety, even planning an additional performance of it to follow in Paris at the Salle Pleyel.

The spring of 1932 brought the Menuhin family to London, where frequent meetings between the great composer and his young admirer took place. Yehudi's fresh, agile mind, so quick to grasp the instructions, drew from Sir Edward high praise and encouragement; in fact he became very fond of the lad and his sisters.

The recording, made in the Abbey Road Studio No. 1 in July 1932, was an amazing success. And Menuhin did indeed include the Elgar Concerto in a concert at the Albert Hall in November. Elgar conducted again, and afterwards wrote to Gaisberg:

22nd November 1932
Private
My dear Fred:

I hope you were at the Concert on Sunday—I think you were.

Now I shd. be a very ungrateful person if I did not at once send hearty thanks to you, who are really the cause of it all, for bringing about the wonderful performance. Yehudi was marvellous & I am sure would never have heard of the Concerto if you had not set the thing in motion.

However, although this is the biggest thing you have done, it is only one of the many kindnesses you have done for me.

Kindest regards
Yours sincerely
Edward Elgar.[1]

But when the question arose of the performance in Paris, Elgar was full of doubts, and he turned to Gaisberg for advice.

28th November 1932.
Dear Sir Edward,

. . . I have just had a letter from Menuhin Senior in which he goes at great length into the question of your going to Paris to conduct the Concerto. It is quite evident that the more you

[1] Quoted in *Elgar on Record*, p. 183.

protest against Paris the greater will be his insistence. He is determined that you shall go to Paris, and I think that his judgment is sane on this point and that there will be no embarrassment of any kind to fear. That the Pleyel Hall will be sold out solid is a sure bet; in fact Menuhin's big concert is now the feature of Paris in May and is sold out two or three months ahead, so that you will have an intensely sympathetic audience that is bound to sweep the critics and everybody on ahead no matter what their prejudices may be.

I will certainly come to Paris for this concert as it is going to be unique. I would not be a bit surprised if the President of the French Republic and the British Ambassador and every important Minister and personage were at this concert. I do not think you have anything at all to fear from the Press. They will be simply overwhelmed by public opinion.

Looking forward to seeing you on Wednesday and hoping you are robusto,

Yours sincerely,
Fred Gaisberg.[1]

And so it was decided. The Menuhins arranged that Georges Enesco should do the main work of rehearsing the Concerto with the French orchestra before Elgar's arrival. Elgar himself wanted to go and see the now much enfeebled Delius, who lived forty miles from Paris and with whom he had been in affectionate correspondence for a number of years. Fred Gaisberg responded to Sir Edward's request that they travel together by arranging the journey by air.

On the Sunday before Ascot a crowd saw us off at Croydon Airport, among whom was [Sir Edward's daughter] Carice, who gave me precise and careful instructions for looking after her father. It was a fine day and Elgar enjoyed it, with just a tinge of anxiety when we struck some air-pockets on this first flight of his. He seemed to feel like a hero, and had a daring smile on his face like a pleased boy. I still possess a crossword puzzle he successfully completed on that journey.

We put up at the Royal Monceau Hotel, Avenue Hoche, and celebrated our first night in Paris with a fine dinner in the bright company of Isabella Valli[2]. Exhilarated by the

[1] Quoted in *Elgar on Record*, pp. 184–5.
[2] Isabella was then in Paris to study the piano with Isador Philipp.

journey and a good night's rest, we arrived fresh and bright next morning for a rehearsal of Elgar's Violin Concerto. Yehudi and the members of the Orchestre symphonique de Paris gave him a warm welcome, and as they had previously studied the music with Enesco, they quickly comprehended the points he wished to make.

Happy meetings with the Menuhin family, the visit to Delius, and the concert itself were all unobtrusively overseen by Gaisberg. But the Concerto did not achieve quite the success he had hoped for it: 'One felt that it had not made the impression that was its due. I fear Elgar's music will never receive real appreciation from Frenchmen, at least in our generation.'

Meanwhile Fred Gaisberg had devised a way of giving Elgar encouragement of a different kind. It was in the wind that Landon Ronald had put Bernard Shaw up to asking Elgar for a Third Symphony to be commissioned by the B.B.C. The chances of the old composer's accepting the suggestion were not good. Then Gaisberg either saw or made a chance to help. There was a suggestion that the B.B.C. Symphony Orchestra should record an orchestral version of the Funeral March from Chopin's B flat minor Sonata. Why not encourage the association by asking Elgar to do the orchestration for the B.B.C.?

Gaisberg went to the Company directors and insisted that they commission Elgar's orchestration for the B.B.C. Orchestra's first recording. The idea reached Adrian Boult, the B.B.C.'s Director of Music.

Savoy Hill, London.
3rd March, 1932.
Dear Mr. Gaisberg,

. . . I understand that it was you who had expressed a wish that Sir Edward Elgar should consider the orchestration of the Chopin Funeral March before the B.B.C. recorded it.

I have been in touch with him, and find that he is quite willing to do this if satisfactory fees can be arranged. Perhaps therefore, you will be so kind as to communicate with him direct.

Yours sincerely,
Adrian C. Boult.[1]

[1] Quoted in *Elgar on Record*, p. 162.

All this was splendid, but it did not suit the purpose at all to have the idea appearing as the brainchild of Fred Gaisberg. So when Gaisberg wrote to Elgar the origin of the suggestion had become obscure:

7th March, 1932.
Dear Sir Edward,

I have had a letter from Adrian Boult in which a suggestion is made by a correspondent of his that you should orchestrate the Chopin Funeral Sonata, the idea being that it should be added to the repertoire of the B.B.C. Orchestra's recordings for us.

If you could prepare us a score, we will have it copied out, and I think I can induce our Company to pay £75 for this work, provided you cede us the mechanical rights.

I am very anxious to know how you will meet this proposal.

Hoping you are in the best of health,

Yours sincerely,
THE GRAMOPHONE COMPANY LIMITED,
Fred W. Gaisberg
Artistes Department

And when he replied to Boult's letter, Gaisberg muddled the question of origins still further:

7th March, 1932.
Dear Dr. Boult,

Thank you for your letter suggesting that Sir Edward Elgar should orchestrate the Chopin Funeral Sonata.

We have passed this suggestion to him, and are certain it would prove a big seller with Sir Edward's name attached to it.

Kindest regards,
Yours sincerely,
THE GRAMOPHONE COMPANY LIMITED,
F. W. Gaisberg
Artistes Department.[1]

Thus, by sleight-of-hand, Fred conjured his own idea into the atmosphere. Having done that, he was free to endorse it enthusiastically and so galvanise all sides of the operation. Elgar accepted the idea, The Gramophone Company implemented it,

[1] Quoted in *Elgar on Record*, p. 162.

and by the end of March the new orchestration stood finished in good time for the B.B.C. Orchestra's first recording later in the spring. But the real point was that Elgar's orchestral imagination had been wound up and set going once again on a large scale. That this had happened in connection with the Orchestra of the B.B.C. looked like pure coincidence.

In July came the Violin Concerto recording with Yehudi Menuhin. Then Gaisberg was on holiday until mid-August, and if he was moving anything further behind the scenes, he took care to move silently. It wouldn't even have been clear that Fred Gaisberg was lying low when on 24 September Elgar received a telegram from the new Head of the International Artistes Department, Rex Palmer:

> ANXIOUS REMAKE POMP AND CIRCUMSTANCE MARCHES NUMBERS ONE AND TWO FOR CHRISTMAS ISSUE STOP ONLY POSSIBLE RECORDING DATE WITH BBC ORCHESTRA FRIDAY AFTERNOON OCTOBER SEVENTH AT KINGSWAY HALL STOP CAN YOU PLEASE CONDUCT REGARDS PALMER[1]

A sudden demand for *Pomp and Circumstance*—the B.B.C. Orchestra just happening to be uniquely available on the only possible date. Thus Elgar would meet the B.B.C. Orchestra for the first time in the recording studio. But then, what was there in that? There can have been no general knowledge, at the time those records were made in October, that the B.B.C. were by now completely involved in the plot to extract Elgar's Third Symphony. The première of a B.B.C. commission, however, would naturally go to the B.B.C. Orchestra.

In December 1932 the announcement of the new Symphony's commissioning was made by Sir Landon Ronald. He was of course a close friend of the old composer and also a member of the B.B.C.'s Music Advisory Committee. It seemed only another coincidence that Ronald had also been for many years Musical Advisor to The Gramophone Company and was now in fact a Director of E.M.I.

Fred Gaisberg took care to write immediately to Elgar of his own joyful surprise at the announcement. But he added a very practical encouragement—practical because it came so recently upon Sir Edward's experience of making records with the very Orchestra that would première the new Symphony.

[1] Quoted in *Elgar on Record*, p. 181.

15th December, 1932.
Dear Sir Edward,

No sooner do I wake up this morning than I see the bombshell which Sir Landon Ronald has thrown regarding the completion of the Third Symphony. Of course all the papers are full of it and I have had telephone calls from various people wanting to know if we are going to record it. We would certainly like to record it immediately before or after the inaugural performance by the B.B.C. Orchestra.

. . . Hoping you are in the best of health,

Yours sincerely,
Fred Gaisberg.[1]

In the months that followed, the Symphony began slowly to take shape. At the end of August 1933 Fred Gaisberg spent a week-end with Elgar at his home in Worcester, Marl Bank:

Aug. 26 (Saturday) . . . Sir E. first took me over the house and proudly showed me his study & bedroom etc. and opened a portfolio by his bedside containing his III Sym. upon which he is now working. . . .

Aug. 27 (Sunday) . . . Tea in the Music Room—Elgar in fine humour. Started by playing me bits of his opera—a bass aria, a love duet, and other bits. He then started on his IIIrd. The opening—a great broad burst *animato* gradually resolving into a fine broad Elgaresque melody for strings. This is fine. IInd movement is slow & tender in true Elgar form. The IIIrd mov. is an ingenious Scherzo—well designed. A delicate feathery short section of 32nds contrasted with a moderate sober section. IVth movement is a spirited tempo with full resources, developed at some length. The whole work strikes me as youthful and fresh—100% Elgar without a trace of decay. He makes not the smallest attempt to bring in any modernity. It is built on true classic lines and in a purely Elgar mold, as the IVth Brahms is purely Brahms.

The work is complete as far as structure & design, and scoring is well advanced. In his own mind he is enthusiastically satisfied with it and says it is his best work. He pretends he does not want to complete it and surrender his baby. His secretary Miss Clifford says he has not done much recently

[1] Quoted in *Elgar on Record*, pp. 185–6.

on the Sym. and seems to prefer to work on his opera. I think he misses the inspiration and driving force of Lady Elgar. Some sympathetic person—lady or man—of strong character should take him in hand and drive him on. Some exciter is needed to inflame him. He complains of the drudgery of scoring. . . .

Aug. 28 (Monday) . . . Sir E. & I with Richard (Dick) his valet took 12 o'c train for London. Lunched on train with good appetite in spite of very hot weather. . . . Sir E. pointed out all the beauty spots as the train rolled through Worcestershire. . . . He said he had been travelling on the line for 60 yrs. and everyone knew him. He seemed to have a word & smile for everyone on the line and all responded happily to his sunshine. . . .

Aug. 29 (Tuesday) . . . Elgar in Kingsway Hall in afternoon: Serenade for Strings and Elegy. . . .[1]

It was, alas, Elgar's final appearance in the Gramophone studios. Early in October he was taken ill, and the news grew worse and worse. What Fred Gaisberg could do he did quickly: a fine gramophone was installed in the nursing home, and test pressings of a new recording of Elgar's Piano Quintet were sent down for the old man to listen to. On 13 November Gaisberg himself went down to Worcester, where he was met by Elgar's daughter Carice.

We went to the nursing-home and as we climbed the stairs we heard the strains of the slow movement of the Quintet being played on the gramophone. He repeated the entire slow movement for my benefit and it seemed to act as a balm. I remained about fifteen minutes, telling him what was happening in the musical world. Then he said:

'Now you go, so that I can have my nap, and come back at four and I'll play some more of the Quintet for you.' . .

I returned at four and was with him for five minutes or so but . . . he was in pain from sciatica. He fell asleep. I waited for two hours but he remained in a deep slumber. That night I left by the 6.10 for Paddington.[2]

Nothing had been said about the Third Symphony. Much of it

[1] Quoted in *Elgar on Record*, pp. 211–14.
[2] Ibid., pp. 219–20.

that was in Elgar's mind had not yet been written down before illness had overtaken him. But the old man rallied several times, and Fred Gaisberg was repeatedly able to invent diversions, whose very quickness of imaginative sympathy ensured their success.

> He had a whim in December to have himself photographed, and to the nursing home one day I brought a photographer. . . .
> In January Carice and I carried out the idea of holding a gramophone recording session by telephone circuit. With the energetic assistance of my friend Rex Palmer, who interested the Post Office and obtained their sympathetic co-operation, the work was successfully accomplished. Ignorant, biased prudes tried to knock out the idea as being morbid and scandalous. I only know it gave Elgar two full weeks of diversion and anticipation. . . .

Altogether, with the equipment and facilities of 1934, it was a business of both complexity and chance. Gaisberg realised this fully only when he arrived at Worcester to direct operations there on 22 January. But the long years of studio experience told in making a success of this most fragile moment.

> I went in to see Sir Edward when I arrived at one o'clock. He began many conversations, but his voice seemed to fade and he dozed off. I was much concerned for fear he would not rouse himself in time for our recording. He recognised me, but could not concentrate. I was told by [Carice] that he had had frequent injections of morphia, but it was principally the toxic poisoning from the wound that was making him so drowsy. However, he had lunch and a long nap, and already at 3.30 when I entered the room he was impatient to begin. . . .
> In fact we had a good reception from London Studio No.1, and tests were most satisfactory until a little after three o'clock when suddenly there was a fading out, and it was not until after desperate telephoning through and urging the telephone people to find out where the disturbance was, that at 4.15 . . . suddenly without warning Rex Palmer's voice came through with the introduction—full, rich, and round, and everyone was amazed at its clearness. It was almost as though we were actually present in the studio. Then the conductor Lawrance Collingwood's voice came through and

Willy Reed with greetings and good wishes. Rex Palmer called for three cheers from the orchestra, and it was most stirring.

Then Sir Edward was eager and alive and quickly took up his cue. He made a most marvellous speech of thanks, telling them of his great pleasure in being able to speak to his old friends from his sick bed, and how he was thrilled with the idea of being useful again. . . . Later on he told the violins to draw out a certain *andante* passage—'ten feet long', he insisted. . . .

Then . . . the orchestra played entirely through the 'Triumphal March' from *Caractacus*. . . . After that Rex Palmer, in the studio, switched on and asked if there were any remarks or comments to make. Almost before he had finished speaking, Elgar immediately commenced to criticise the tempi and make suggestions for bringing out the melody more strongly in certain passages.

No. 1 record was then made twice. Then they started on the second part of the 'Triumphal March'. This begins with a long, sweeping melody. Elgar bent over to me and said:

'I say, Fred, isn't that a gorgeous melody? Who could have written such a beautiful melody?'

During the entire period of this recording Sir Edward was literally on the *qui vive*—much to the amazement of everybody including Dr. Moore Ede, who from time to time gave him a little water.

At the end he specially asked for the 'Woodland Interlude' from *Caractacus* to be played, and this was done. He made comments and insisted on its being done again; and then after this, even once more because he was not quite satisfied. Certainly each time there was a great improvement on the previous performance.

This finished with farewell greetings from everybody, and at 5.15 we all bade Sir Edward good-bye.

On the following Sunday, 28 January, Gaisberg returned to Worcester, taking with him the test pressings of the *Caractacus* records. Everyone realised it would be the last visit. (In fact Elgar had less than a month to live.)

On his own initiative, Sir Edward dedicated to me a small work entitled *Mina*, the name of his favourite Cairn. . . . He asked for a pen and, producing the manuscript from under his pillow, wrote across it a dedication to me. I could not restrain tears of emotion as I thanked him. . . .

Grove's Dictionary . . . mentions *Mina* as his last work. It also mentions, as a work without opus number, the scoring of the slow movement of Chopin's Sonata op. 35, popularly known as the 'Funeral March', which I on behalf of my Company commissioned him to orchestrate.

Thus Fred Gaisberg's influence in the life of a great man found its acknowledgment. Did the inscription on *Mina*, placed over Elgar's last completed work only when the Third Symphony was clearly lost, signify more than simple affection for a devoted friend? For the rest of his own life Gaisberg was to remain silent about his role in persuading Sir Edward to return to big composition in his old age. But he quite obviously attached a separate and special value, amongst all the associations of a lengthening career, to his friendship with Elgar. That a gramophone man might so touch the creative life of a great composer was something that perhaps even old Emile Berliner himself would scarcely have dreamt possible.

Chapter Twenty

FRED GAISBERG had passed his sixtieth birthday at the beginning of 1933. His professional life continued at full vigour, despite occasional heart trouble. Age had laid heavier hands on more than one of his contemporaries and lifelong friends. In October 1933 Tetrazzini arrived in London for what was to prove a final British tour. Alas, there was at this date no question of gramophone records. Writing about this even in his private diary Gaisberg was circumspect:

> The voice at this time was never equal in purity and timbre to her pre-war voice, but she had the *practique* of long experience on the concert platform that enabled her to give entire satisfaction to her public, who were faithful to her and thronged to her concerts. I say this to excuse the absence of modern recording in the long list of records on the Gramo. Cat.

Nonetheless Fred himself did everything he could for his old friend. There was the usual press conference at the Savoy:

> Many times had I assisted her in these receptions, but this time it was heavy going. Her private affairs had been noised in the Press—everyone knew she had instituted divorce proceedings in Italy. One had difficulty in keeping this topic out of the news.
>
> I remember at her request I went to Reading for the first concert, with her accompanist. It was an afternoon affair. The 'Theatre' was drab & depressing. We sought the dressing room assigned to her. It was also drab, and without proper convenience. Things seemed suspiciously quiet, & I peeped out

into the house. It was only half filled. Tet. was not feeling too well, and to cap the situation only a narrow ladder-like stairs led to the stage, up which we all had to lend a hand to assist the somewhat portly singer up & down. But to crown all, this time there was no Tato or Bizelli to kiss her behind each ear before her audience. This time all she had was her rosary, which she kissed devotedly, & I could see a tear trickling down her cheek.

Sunday 12th Nov. Tetrazzini concert. . . . We all went to Albert Hall—Carrie, [William] Manson, Louise, Camillo [Valli]. I was in the Artists Room with Tetrazzini. She was in a terrible emotional state, and although she pulled through the concert it was pathetic.

Tet. attempted to play her old role of Prima Donna, but the going was heavy. The tour was begun, but ended in a collapse when Tet. contracted a cold. This involved the impresario in heavy losses. . . .

One bright spot emerged out of Gaisberg's devising entertainment for her last few days in England.

As a relaxation on her last visit, I took Tetrazzini to hear Gracie Fields in a revue at the London Coliseum. Tetrazzini's is one of the celebrity heads painted on the striking curtain of that theatre, and this pleased her immensely.

Gracie played in a sketch where, as a charwoman on her knees, she is supposed to be scrubbing the opera house stage. She says, 'I want to be an opera singer and sing like Tetrazzini,' and proceeds to burlesque a prima donna with those comic cadenzas of hers.

Tetrazzini laughed so loud that she could be heard all over the house. The audience, who had recognised her, proceeded to give her a warm reception.

After the show we went on the stage, and Gracie and Luisa met for the first time. They were two congenial souls in complete sympathy.

Thus at last Fred Gaisberg had been able to find a happy note on which to bid farewell to one of the supreme artists of his own generation—and another of his greatest friends.

By now, however, there was more need than ever to balance

the past with the future. It had begun in America, with events that seemed at the time only remotely connected with gramophone affairs in Europe. 'When I revisited Camden, N.J., in 1928, my friend B. G. Royal, one-time Treasurer of the Victor Talking Machine Company, mentioned that [Eldridge] Johnson had sold out to a group of bankers for £6,000,000 the previous year. . . . The bankers, in their turn, sold out at a substantial profit to that colossus, the Radio Corporation of America, during the frenzied flood of mergers that preceded the financial crisis of 1929.

When the crash came, all the confidence seemed to evaporate from the American record industry. By 1932, Gaisberg's young colleague David Bicknell recalled, there seemed to be nothing left of record making there.

> Up to that year the artists had been divided equally, approximately in numbers and importance, between the American and English Companies. But in 1932 the Americans lost their nerve—I do not think that is too strong a word—and believed that the record business was finished. Victor started to unload their artists and Fred, who had lost none of his faith in the record business, bound them to HMV one by one. . . .
>
> I remember one day coming back to my office after lunch to find a cable reading: 'DROPPING DE LUCA AND HOROWITZ STOP ANY INTEREST VICTOR'. It seems unbelievable today that such cables were arriving daily. And not only cables—the artists themselves started to arrive in person.
>
> Heifetz was one of the first. Fred invited him to lunch and the three of us met at the Berkeley, where Heifetz started the conversation by saying:
>
> 'Well, Fred, in this fearful slump there were some fortunate people who got out and some who were cleared out, and I belong to the latter category. I must get going again, and what can you do to help?'
>
> By the end of that luncheon we had him signed up too.

But then the economic reverses began to affect the lives of the Gramophone people at home. David Bicknell remembered:

> When the Wall Street Slump hit us, it was with the force of a tornado, and very soon members of the ship's company

started to disappear over the side—first singly and then in droves. Even men and women who had served the Company for many years were not immune.

One morning on arriving at the office I heard that a man who had worked in the early days with Fred, and who had over thirty years' service behind him, had been dismissed the night before. I knew that Fred would be much distressed by this treatment of an old colleague, and as soon as he arrived one glance at his face told me that he had heard the bad news. But he did not say a word; he went into his office as usual and quietly closed the door. When I had disposed of the work which I had in hand I went in to see him. He was writing a letter. Trying to put the best face on the matter I said:

'But George is a very popular person—he has got lots of friends. Surely *someone* will come to his rescue now.'

He looked up and paused as though to ask himself how anyone could be so ingenuous. Then he replied angrily:

'He *had* lots of friends up to last night. I don't know whether he has got any left this morning.'

. . . But this man was not to be without friends, because I was not surprised to hear that Fred had helped him privately but surreptitiously.[1]

Gaisberg himself continued to work hard, and once again his insight and quick reaction to an entirely new situation was to be of invaluable help to his firm—and beyond it. David Bicknell recalled especially one aspect of Gaisberg's initiative at this time:

He had wonderful instincts regarding the direction in which the whole gramophone industry was moving. And one of the decisions he took was to switch from recording small pieces—which had been the life-blood of the record business since it was started: that is, operatic arias, single piano pieces, and so on—to building a library, which he did through the medium of the HMV Societies and Connoisseurs' Catalogue, and many other ways of that kind. And he looked for the artists—and found them—those who were capable of not just playing one or two Chopin Nocturnes but all the works of Chopin; the best example of course being Schnabel's recording of the thirty-two Piano Sonatas [of Beethoven].

[1] Lecture at the British Institute of Recorded Sound.

The Beethoven project was to bring into play several of Gaisberg's special talents: his vision, his tenacity—and in the end his ruthless and utterly practical wit. He told the story himself.

> One of the wisest and most remarkable artistic enterprises of the 'thirties was the engagement of Artur Schnabel in England as the executant of Beethoven's piano works complete. When in 1930 Malcolm Sargent, on Bruno Walter's recommendation, placed him under contract for the famous Courtauld–Sargent Concerts, outside of Germany he was only known as a professor at the Berlin Hochschule. His success in London was immediate, and gradually he collected a big following of enthusiasts who regarded him as the greatest living exponent of Beethoven. I was agreeably surprised at the serious-minded crowds that filled the Queen's Hall to capacity and would follow his playing with weighty tomes of the Sonatas propped on their knees.
>
> It was given out that Schnabel would never stoop to recording as he considered it impossible for a mere machine to reproduce the dynamics of his playing faithfully. Therefore when I interviewed him he was coy, but all the same prepared to put his theory to the test—though he would need a lot of convincing. At long last I was able to overcome all his prejudice. Tempted by a nice fat guarantee, he eventually agreed that it was possible to reconcile his ideals with machinery.
>
> I can still see the dubious looks on the faces of our directors when I joyfully told them that we would get him, on the sole condition that we must record all the Piano Sonatas and the five Concertos of Beethoven complete. . . .
>
> I supervised every one of our twenty sessions per annum during the next ten years, and rate the experience of hearing his performances and listening to his inevitable impromptu lectures as a most liberal allowance of instruction combined with entertainment.

Fred asked his niece Isabella (who was studying the piano professionally) to turn pages for the Beethoven Sonata sessions.

> Schnabel loved an audience, and I was useful to my uncle in this way. But turning pages for him was a very nerve-wracking

experience. Schnabel was not essentially a virtuoso and he approached recording with real trepidation.

Uncle responded in his usual charming way—very relaxed. He would come out of the Recorder's Box after a 'take', talk and joke with Schnabel. He used to lead him on a bit—get him on to his philosophy and then tease him about it. He always tried to keep the atmosphere light, and to placate the man when he was getting nervy and touchy. He handled him magnificently.

When things got rather tense in the studio, I've seen my uncle do a funny little dance. He would put his legs together, turn his feet out, and do a sort of Charlie Chaplin routine—you just couldn't help laughing, it was so ridiculous—to break the tension. Or he would sit down at the piano and play something funny. And the artist would be in fits of laughter and refreshed.[1]

By such means the library was gradually built: the Violin Sonatas of Beethoven played by Kreisler, the Sibelius Symphonies and Tone Poems, the Mazurkas of Chopin with Artur Rubinstein, much of the rest of Chopin played by Alfred Cortot, the songs of Hugo Wolf, harpsichord music of Handel, Couperin, and Domenico Scarlatti in the performances of Wanda Landowska.

Orchestral music and opera were also—in spite of worsening international conditions—being vigorously pursued. Great conductors from many countries were one by one secured for the gramophone. Weingartner had come to EMI with the Columbia merger. So had Bruno Walter. Franz Schalk had recorded some of his Beethoven interpretations shortly before his death in 1931. Koussevitzky came to London for the B.B.C. Festivals, and some notable performances were preserved on disc. After eight years of elusive negotiations, Fred Gaisberg finally captured Fürtwängler and began a series of recordings with him in Berlin.

Not quite all of the orchestral recordings done in those years were so happily accomplished. David Bicknell was later to write:

Fred, in my recollection, got on well with the hundreds of artists with whom he dealt, except two, and those two most important—Toscanini and Beecham.

[1] Conversation with the writer, 1973.

Beecham, Fred did not understand. He was unable to appreciate or take part in the witty, polished conversation of which Beecham was a master. He thought that he was extravagant in terms of money (correct), disorganised, and a charge on our budget which we could not afford—although he knew of course that he was a man of genius. Beecham thought that Fred preferred German conductors. Fred's support of Chaliapin in various rows made Beecham hostile, and there was little common ground between them.

The acquisition of [Toscanini] was really achieved by Louis Sterling. [With Fred there had been] a row years before when Toscanini was at La Scala. . . . The ill-feeling between them was such that Sterling instructed Rex Palmer that if possible Fred should be kept away from the recording sessions, although he added that if this could not be done without hurting Fred's feelings then he (Sterling) would prefer to lose Toscanini.[1]

Nevertheless, Fred Gaisberg was to play his part in the Toscanini negotiations. When the B.B.C. wanted to secure Toscanini for a series of concerts with their orchestra, it was to Gaisberg that they turned for help. It took a year, but at the beginning of June 1935 Toscanini conducted his first concert for the B.B.C. Three days later Fred wrote in his diary:

June 5th (Wednesday). Today gave a lunch at the Savoy—present Mr. & Mrs. Toscanini, Vladimir Horowitz & his wife Wanda (formerly Miss Toscanini), John Barbirolli, young Clausetti (manager of Casa Ricordi, London) & Rex Palmer. . . .

T. was very interested in Barbirolli and easily recalled 40 years ago when as a young man B's father as viola and T. as cellist played in the same orch. of a provincial touring opera co. & were chums. . . .

Mme. T., whom I am vamping and enlisting as an ally to induce T. to make gramo. records: she looks well after the Maestro's interest and is very artful. . . . She, as well as Horowitz & Wanda, seems in his presence very diffident & repressed. . . . T. himself makes all important decisions, but perhaps they influence him by suggestion. After all, he leans

[1] Letter to the writer, 24 October 1974.

on them now for his diversion, and the baby (Sonia) must hold him.

When I asked T. for permission to record by land wires during the actual concert, he objected that for years he had been receiving a retainer of $20,000 a year from the N.Y. Phil. O. & he has steadily refused to record because he loathed all records. He therefore could not break faith with them and allow us to record. I then begged permission just to make a test for comparison to similar records he had made in America & he grudgingly gave consent. I then said he should record a piano concerto with his son-in-law for the baby, and he agreed next season to put a piano concerto in the programme for this purpose.

It was a beginning, and some of the Toscanini B.B.C. concerts were recorded. But the discs were largely unsatisfactory. Gaisberg recalled 'how every time the timpanist made a thunderous attack on his drums the controller would have a heart attack or when, in some soft 'cello passage, Toscanini's voice singing the melody would drown the solo instrument; pianissimos inaudible above the surface of the disc or fortissimos that sent stabs across into the next groove.'[1]

The results of these performance recordings were hardly good enough to publish: their main use was as a means of wearing down Toscanini's objections to recording. After a time he did in some degree relent. But in the end Gaisberg himself admitted that the Maestro's association with the gramophone was not an unqualified success.

Our recording experience with Toscanini showed that he was, quite honestly, bored by it. . . . I remember one session which we arranged in our own studio. We assembled the full B.B.C. Symphony Orchestra and anxiously awaited Toscanini. When he arrived we detected dark clouds on his brow. We escorted him to the podium, but he would not ascend it. He just stood there, obviously unhappy. At length he took his place and signalled the orchestra to begin, but halted the musicians after twenty bars or so and said:

'I do not like the placing of the instruments and the acoustics. . . . If I conduct records to-day I shall not be able to conduct your concert to-morrow. . . .'

[1] Typescript, 'Notes from my diary on Toscanini'.

And in a flash he had got down from the podium and was motoring away before we could recover ourselves and think the matter over. We then reasoned that he was right about the acoustics and the placing of the instruments. Perhaps his motive was to administer a salutary medicinal draught. For my part I am certain it was beneficial although at the time it seemed drastic.

It was more frustrating still trying to record opera. For that purpose Gaisberg repeatedly pursued Toscanini to the summer festivals in Salzburg.

Toscanini worked like a slave, enjoyed every minute of it and called it a holiday. He was surrounded by congenial spirits like Stabile, Baccaloni, Dusolina Giannini and a relay of Italian friends from Milan who invaded Salzburg through the Brenner Pass in cars and trains, in spite of the bristling guns and frontier friction.

I hovered around during those three seasons 1935, 1936, and 1937, enjoying it immensely, but always with the hope of recording gems of production. I had consolation in plenty of lounging in the Bazar Cafe, where one met the great and near-great in this oasis of bliss in a world of storms. I had long decided that recording the Festival was hopelessly impossible, where singers, musicians, and the theatre were employed twenty-four hours a day between rehearsals and performances.

When I read of John Christie's project to found a Mozart Festival theatre at Glyndebourne I thought it a pipe dream, but when I learned that Fritz Busch and Carl Ebert were to have full artistic control I realised it was a serious effort. Their standing and names were a guarantee that it would not be tarred with the brush of the amateur. . . . I saw enough of [Christie's] careful groundwork and personal attention to detail to convince me that his success would be beyond dispute. . . .

With enthusiasm I signed with Christie an agreement for the exclusive right of making discs. We did our recording with a mobile van at the end of the season, when the company were well soaked in their parts and their teamwork perfect.

In the 1935 season Gaisberg noted with rare satisfaction some impressions of the records they made:

During the week H.M.V. recorded on 5 mornings records of the complete *Cosi fan tutte* with Busch conducting—Ina Souez, Helletsgruber, Irene Eisinger, Willi Domgraf-Fassbender, Heddle Nash, & John Brownlee. A wonderful cast—perhaps the best ever assembled. Of course the Fiordiligi is unique—Ina Souez; there never was such a wonderful voice. The records have resulted most successfully, and are perhaps a monument of all time for this opera. . . .

An average of 13 titles were recorded twice each morning, during a session of 3 hrs from 9.30 to 12.30 (a.m.) 3 days completed *Cosi fan tutte* & 2 days to complete *Figaro*. In *Figaro* Audrey Mildmay (Mrs. John Christie) plays Susanna, and very well too.

But they never did record Toscanini conducting opera, at Salzburg or anywhere else.

Chapter Twenty-one

THE LATER 1930s brought further experiences of recording opera and other large works throughout Europe. Looking back on this time, Fred Gaisberg wrote: 'Happy is the man who has congenial associates. His path is made easy and his work a pleasure. After the merger with the Columbia Company I made many trips to record complete operas with Charlie Gregory, a colleague who had joined the Columbia Company as a boy in Washington, when I was with that company briefly in the early nineties. . . . Gregory and I, in the autumn of our careers, recorded in association . . . widely diverse subjects . . . solid achievements that Gregory and I skimmed off those boiling cauldrons of unrest during the five years preceding the outbreak of . . . war.'

One of the recordings they made was Puccini's *Tosca* in Rome. There was already a *Tosca* in the catalogue, a relatively modern recording of 1930. But as Gaisberg wrote:

> With such a tenor as Gigli under contract—whose voice and acting were so ideally suitable for the role of Cavaradossi, it would be the height of folly not to re-make the whole opera with Gigli and a cast equally important, and to issue them in the highest category of records.
>
> This programme was then decided upon for the spring of 1938. It would probably cost £2,000 and because of the political unrest it was a risky undertaking. However, with the great success of *Pagliacci* and *La Bohème* (both recorded complete with Gigli) we were encouraged to take the risk.
>
> The great difficulty was to find the time and place in the tenor's timetable to fit in the seven sessions required to record the 28 sides comprising the complete work. Gigli was then in

his forty-eighth year—the age at which Caruso died—and he was crowding in as many profitable concerts, operas, and films as he could, to make hay while the sun shone and to pile up his banking account. He had a contract with the impresario Max Weber for one hundred engagements at £400 each during a period of twelve months, and such odd jobs as making gramophone records and films had to be squeezed in when and where it could be managed. His diary called for eight performances of *Aida* in the open air theatre of the Terme di Caracalla. . . . Between these performances Gigli fitted in the recording of our *Tosca*.

Iva Paceti (who had that spring sung Tosca at Covent Garden) and Armando Borgioli (the Scarpia), as well as all the other singers, were engaged before Charlie Gregory . . . and I left Victoria Station for Rome. . . . We put up at the excellent Hotel Flora, adjoining the Giardini Borghese, and found it still good but deserted by the usual hosts of American and British tourists, whose absence indicated the increasing tension and unrest settling over Europe.

I now had to prepare the timetable of sessions to fit in with the performances at the Terme di Caracalla (since orchestra, chorus, and principals were all employed there). Then Gregory checked up on the placing of the microphones in relation to the orchestra and chorus, and after that we were ready.

Our *chef d'orchestre* was the youthful de Fabritis, whom I engaged not only because he was good and practical but because he had a pull with the Mayor of Rome—who alone could grant us permission to use the Teatro Reale and its staff for a recording studio. The Reale was noted for its good acoustics, and luckily for us it was closed for the summer. A condition was a time-limit of seven days to complete the opera.

The stage is nearly as vast as the Scala or the Carlo Fenice in Genoa, and in a large dressing room we set up our recording machine and began tests for improving the acoustics by letting down the various drops. While we were working, my old friends Vincenzo Bellezza and Tullio Serafin—both conductors attached to the Reale—looked in on us, curious to learn how The Gramophone Company could be recording in *their* opera house without making use of them. I could not tell them that their young colleague was able to bring about the use of the house which alone made the recording possible.

Although the heat in Rome during this month is very great, we found working in the vast space of that stage quite comfortable. The recording went along smoothly until the beginning of the third session, when Paceti collapsed. The theatre doctor was called and said she needed at least three days complete rest. With the time-limit half gone, we were forced to call in another soprano.

We knew that Maria Caniglia had the previous evening finished her contract at the Terme, and would leave that evening for her next engagement in Palermo. Would she help us out and save the situation? Gigli and I left the chorus and orchestra sitting there waiting and hurried round the corner to Maria's hotel.

The porter phoned her room. Yes, she was there. Gigli said: 'Let me speak to her *per favore*.'

'Is that you, Maria? Come down quickly: there is an urgent matter I want to discuss with you.'

After a few minutes she appeared. 'Is the house on fire? I was just sleeping—dreaming of something pleasant.'

'Well,' said Gigli, 'this is your dream come true. Gaisberg here is in trouble and wants you to help him out. We are in the middle of recording *Tosca*, and Paceti has collapsed. The chorus and orchestra are waiting, and I want you to come right now and sing the role.'

'What, right now? I am still half asleep, and haven't sung the part for months.'

By that time we had her in a taxi, and before she could say 'Well after all this is my dream come true to sing a complete opera with you, Beniamino', she was in front of the microphone. Less than an hour from the collapse of Paceti, Charlie Gregory gave the signal to start the recording from the entrance of Tosca in the First Act.

Maria's fresh, young voice was equal to every demand she made upon it, and continued so for four sessions crowded into two days; she arrived by plane at Palermo in time for her engagement there.[1]

Gigli showed his magnanimity, since owing to the change

[1] 'Notes from my diary: Gigli and Tosca'.

of sopranos he would have to re-make a number of titles already sung with the other Tosca—and this just when he was already singing trying roles at the open-air festival at the Terme di Caracalla. During that season he was at the height of his form, for in spite of the summer heat and the heavy calls on him he sang so easily and with such purity and volume as to amaze everyone. During the pauses in recording he would joke with the men and the *comprimarii*, who exchanged stories with him. His good nature and patience communicated themselves to all, and helped to ease the many awkward moments. . . .

I marvel sometimes that we ever obtained a perfect master-record. On one occasion we made ten attempts at one title in the first act of *Tosca*, and then gave it up and tried again the following day, when ten more attempts were made before we obtained a master. No wonder our recorder—not to be out-done by Maestro de Fabritiis, who threw the score on the floor—smashed a wax and swore that no one gave *him* a chance to make a mistake. . . .

Once somewhere in that vast theatre an artisan—perhaps a little tinsmith—was hammering merrily on the roof like the cobbler Hans Sachs interrupting Beckmesser's serenade. In the middle of the *Te Deum* he would suddenly begin. Precious moments were wasted and two hundred people suspended their animation until the little 'Hans' could be tracked down and stopped. In the great Teatro Reale it was like finding a needle in a haystack. . . .

Yet eventually a perfect set of master-recordings was obtained. When we listened to them we forgot their cost, and that at one point the maestro had let out a terrific yell and broken his baton, or that at another the soprano had forgotten her entrance, or that the solo 'cellist had played E flat in the eleventh position of his obbligato. . . .

In the final analysis, of course, making successful records in such conditions and with so many factors to control depended squarely on the initiative, patience, and solid ability of the gramophone men themselves.

Fred Gaisberg and Charles Gregory also recorded some notable orchestral and instrumental performances during those last years before the war. Two that stood out in Gaisberg's memory were in a special way products of the time which gave them birth.

Looking back on that April of 1937 when in Prague Casals made those fine records of Dvorak's 'Cello Concerto, I feel it to be something precious and rare snatched from that seething cauldron of Europe before the storm broke. I had always wanted to record this great work, and then one day Georg Szell mentioned that he was to conduct it in Prague with the Czech Philharmonic Orchestra and that Casals would be the soloist. . . . Revolution in Spain and unrest in Europe should have discouraged my hopes, especially knowing how involved Casals was in political issues.

In response to my wire he replied that he would remain in Prague for one day after the concert and would devote it to recording the work. Promptly we despatched recording equipment and engineers to make preparations. The Deutsche Saal was engaged and turned into a studio. I remember Starkmann (our local assistant) remarking, 'We must expect this hall to be smashed up if trouble breaks out.'

I travelled there via Berlin to be present at the session. On a rainy Sunday night I left the dismal Anhalter Station for Prague. I was the only passenger in the sleeping car, and in fact it seemed an empty train. The railway personnel were sullen and discourteous. At the frontier frequent and deliberate examinations of my baggage and papers were made. It was a most unpleasant journey and brought sharply home to me the tension in the air. I put up at the excellent Golden Crown Hotel, where I was joined by Georg Szell and a very tired Casals, who had come directly by plane from Barcelona.

The great hall in the heart of the town where the concert took place was unique in that it was completely underground and the gallery was on the street level. Casals played magnificently and received an enthusiastic ovation from an audience that included all the important State officials, headed by Dr. Benes himself.

The next day, still exhilarated by his success, he smartly rehearsed and recorded one after another the ten sides forming the complete work, while during the pauses journalists and reporters would try to extract interviews from him. As the last record was made he collapsed completely and allowed us to take him to his hotel, where we saw that he was carefully looked after. We waited until he lit up his pipe and got it going well and then left, knowing the little man was all right.

The records turned out to be an unqualified success, and as soon as they were published I sold the first set to a most appreciative music-lover and record collector, Jan Masaryk.

As 1937 neared its end, despite ever-increasing political tension, it appeared that some further European recording might still be managed.

> . . . I put forward the suggestion that The Gramophone Company should record the complete [Mahler Ninth] Symphony at a performance in the old Musikverein [in Vienna] to be held on Sunday morning, January 16th 1938. Of course that Bruno Walter (the direct link with Mahler) would be the conductor and that there would be five rehearsals during which our engineers could make their tests and experiments in 'mike' positions and give our switch-board controller an opportunity to follow with the score, were all arguments that clinched the decision. Another argument was that the work was difficult and could never be economically recorded in a studio, as it required many rehearsals and a big orchestra. For the same reason it rarely made its appearance in a concert programme, so this opportunity of using Mahler's own orchestra and his pupil as conductor was historic and must not be missed.
>
> So on that cold, grey morning of January 16th 1938 we set out to record what amounted to the swan-song of the Vienna Philharmonic Orchestra under their old conductor Bruno Walter—because from then on until the Germans overran Austria two months later political upheavals absorbed all social life and made music-making impossible. (In fact all the orchestra leaders like Dr. Arnold Rosé, Professor Buxbaum, Berghauser, Starkmann, and Anton Weiss disappeared from the scene shortly after this concert, and the next time I saw them was in Paris or London.)
>
> As I watched the crowd of Mahler music-lovers filing into the hall—over two thousand of them—I thought what a contrast there was between shabby respectability and the elegant and rich audiences of the Franz Josef days. Present

also were the high officers of the State, including Chancellor Schuschnigg. . . .

In the Green Room I made [a] photograph of Bruno Walter just before he stepped onto the platform. He is leaning against an old Bösendorfer piano, and on the walls are signed photographs of many great artists—including one of Pablo Casals, one of the patrons of the old Vienna Philharmonic Orchestra and responsible for raising big funds that [had] carried them over trying periods of post-war depression.[1]

Over one hundred players filled the tiers of the stage and I took my place in the top corner amongst the timpanis facing the conductor. Through me passed the conductor's signal to the engineers for the start of each movement of the work. That was the cue to drop the cutting stylus on the revolving wax disc. Two recording machines each in charge of an engineer were used alternately: while one was recording, the other was being loaded with wax and was ready to take up the thread after number-one record was finishing. A switchboard control box was in the charge of the senior engineer, Charlie Gregory, who was advised by a musician who followed the performance with a full score and indicated the 'hurdles' that had to be avoided—such as sudden *forte* timpani blows, or extreme pianissimos or fortissimos; also when at the end of a Movement the current had to be closed off before the applause began. The well-filled hall toned down the resonance of this great orchestra to a rounded-out sound of rich mass and depth, yet without dissipating the higher frequencies of the instruments.[2]

All the waxes recorded that morning were got safely back to England and processed. But before they were approved for publication the entire musical world of which they made so poignant a souvenir had been destroyed by the Anschluss.

A few weeks after this Walter turned up a bewildered refugee in Paris, where I met him to play over and obtain his approval of the twenty records recorded that Sunday. So delighted was he with the results that his usually sober face brightened up considerably.[3]

[1] Typescript, 'Casals'.
[2] 'Notes on Actual Performance Recording'.
[3] Ibid.

Neither Bruno Walter nor I enjoyed the prospect of commencing relations with a new orchestra and in a strange environment. We need not have felt so preoccupied by these considerations, for in selecting the Orchestra of the Paris Conservatoire we found an instrument of fine possibilities. . . . [A] recording took place in the very modern Salle de la Chimie. At first only slow progress was made, and after the session Bruno Walter apologised saying, 'You know, it is like a honeymoon: oftentimes things do not go so well. Anyhow, the material is good. We'll make up for it tomorrow.'

Everywhere in Europe similar situations were being acted out:

In 1938 I spoke to Fürtwängler about the deep impression his recordings with the Berlin Philharmonic Orchestra had made, and I said that I was doubtful whether he could obtain such response with any other orchestra. He thought that he could do so with the London Philharmonic Orchestra, and said that his experience in working with that combination during the past season had convinced him that he could.

If every achievement now seemed a precarious victory snatched from an all-devouring time, there was more than political cause for that. One by one the musicians whose friendships had lighted Fred Gaisberg's career seemed to be fading away almost before his eyes. On his way to Vienna for the Mahler Ninth recording in January 1938, Gaisberg had stopped briefly in Paris to see Chaliapin once more. Feodor Ivanovich's health had been causing some anxiety. During his visit to London the previous year he had been visibly ailing. Since then he had consulted a Viennese specialist who had ordered him to cancel all concerts and live virtually in bed. In his sickroom now, the great man seemed 'rather poorly'. But in Fred's presence the old enthusiasm seemed for a moment to rekindle:

He talked about repeating his favourite arias on records, and sang for me several scales to show how fresh and supple was his voice. He said his great hope was a jubilee *tournée* and then an Academy of Acting. . . .

But it was not to be. Three months later Chaliapin was dead.

To Paris I journeyed in April 1938 to pay my last respects to the great artist, and there mingled with the thousands of

Russians of every degree who filled the small Russian Cathedral in Rue Daru and overflowed into the streets.

For six days Chaliapin lay in state in his home in the Avenue d'Eylau while a constant stream of friends and fellow countrymen as well as fellow artists looked their last on him. On the day when he was buried the funeral cortège stopped at the Cathedral, where as Mass for the Dead was read, with unaccompanied chorus consisting of the famous Afonsky Choir and the Aristoff Russian Opera Chorus . . . many of his old colleagues sang as choristers—among them Pozemkovsky, Alexander Mozjoukin, Maidanov, Zaporozhets, Borovsky, Madame Davidov, Smirnova, and others. It was the most wonderful choral singing I have ever heard, and everyone was profoundly moved.

After the custom in France, about mid-day the long funeral cortège, with many vehicles of floral tributes, began its journey to the cemetery. Members of the Paris Opéra, headed by Serge Lifar, had arranged to honour their colleague. The procession paused in the courtyard of the Opéra, where in the open air, amid the hum of Paris traffic, a prayer for the dead was read and the choir intoned a chorale. I had not expected such a display of emotion by these choristers and former colleagues, and turned to my neighbour, Prince Zeretelli, for an explanation.

'Chaliapin is dead,' he said; 'all is forgiven. They realise now that there will be no other like him. Whatever his faults, for them he was Russia.'

In August a friend of even longer standing died, Landon Ronald. Writing a eulogy for *The Gramophone* magazine, Fred Gaisberg was moved to draw a silent contrast between Ronald's career and his own: 'Over the thirty-eight years that I was associated with him I have learned to admire his genius and wisdom —and when I say "wisdom" I mean that he knew how to enjoy himself, at the same time limiting his activities in such a way as to result in a well-balanced life of human contentment. I often feel that the genius of Sir Landon Ronald should have made him one of the greatest international conductors, but he knew that this would make too great a demand on his personal liberty and health. He was unwilling to become a slave to a career.'[1]

[1] *The Gramophone*, September 1938, p. 148.

Both Chaliapin and Landon Ronald had been children of Fred's own year, 1873. Still, some older artists yet lingered on the scene. How long they could linger was clearly a question in Fred Gaisberg's mind as he journeyed once more to the Swiss home of the septuagenarian Paderewski, carrying test pressings of the old pianist's latest efforts in the recording studio.

The household assembled at noon in the large hall to await his appearance. There was his sister, a lady of eighty, very alert and carrying her years well, his secretary and nephew Mr. Strakacz, with his wife, besides six or more friends from the neighbourhood invited for luncheon and to hear the records. At one o'clock the Master descended the staircase smiling, and greeted each person present with a few apt enquiries about their health and activities.

Twenty-five momentous years had passed, during which many of his dreams had been realised. But the toll on his vitality had been heavy, and showed plainly in his great frame—now shrunken, almost transparent. Helena, his wife and companion had just died, and his beloved Poland was menaced. As he grasped my hand warmly and looked searchingly into my eyes he said:

'My dear Mr. Gaisberg, how are you and your sister Carrie? How is my friend Mr. Clark and his dear wife?' His fine voice still carried its well-known charm and sincerity.

He then led the way into the dining room where, seated at the head of the table, he saw that everyone was cared for. Recalling that the day was Washington's Birthday, he courteously toasted America in my honour. At lunch he took command of his twelve or more guests, and to everyone's delight told story after story as only he could tell them. I remember he subtly reproved my neighbour who, on being served soup, without testing it started to salt and pepper it. Paderewski began:

'Did you ever hear of the Russian Grand Duke Dimitrov, noted for his wonderful chef and the table he set?' He paused, we were all attentively listening. 'At a dinner party the butler had just served soup, when a certain gentleman began freely to add salt and pepper. The butler whipped out a revolver and shot him dead. The body was removed and the feast continued. Everyone approved.'

We all relished this story, and Paderewski's eyes twinkled with merriment at the discomfort of my neighbour.[1]

The records I brought with me were heard in the music room later and proved a great success, as they were exceptionally fine and provided a fitting climax to a delightful occasion. It was in the same room, in 1911, that I first recorded him. On the piano were large photographs of Queen Victoria and Queen Alexandra, both autographed and with cordial dedications. There were also many portraits of other royalties and of the American President. Conspicuously absent were members of the house of Hohenzollern. . . .

The salon was fragrant with the atmosphere of a past age and made one feel a bit sad. I missed the warm welcome of Madame Paderewski. . . . Gone was the parrot which accompanied them on all their travels and whose elaborate cage always distinguished the Paderewski luggage. This was the bird that always hovered on his master's shoulders or perched on his foot while he practised, and seemed to enjoy the music. It was thoroughly spoiled, but they regarded it as a mascot and so tolerated its impertinences. I missed too the all-pervading presence of Paderewski's faithful Marcel, now dead, who accompanied him for forty years as valet and baggage man wherever he went. If one saw the thirty or forty pieces of luggage that the Paderewskis carried, one could realise the magnitude of Marcel's task. On the long and arduous tours in America, when a private [railway] car became their home for months on end, Marcel would be called upon to act as a fourth at bridge.

But Gaisberg was to see the old lion yet once more:

In fulfilment of a promise to complete some titles begun in the previous year, Paderewski paid his last visit to our studios on November 16, 1938. It was a typical London November day, foggy and cold, when we waited at the Abbey Road studios for his arrival. His old friend and agent for many years L. G. Sharpe was to bring him. His special Steinway was in place in Studio No. 3, where the lights were turned low and his favourite tuner hovered in the background.

[1] 'Paderewski as I Knew Him'.

We were growing very doubtful, when a taxi rolled out of the gloom and I rushed to help a wispy, frail old gentleman out of the car and up the stairs. Reaching the studio with slow steps, I removed his heavy fur-lined coat. Like the *grand seigneur* of old he then warmly grasped my hand, and with that voice of deep sincerity he said, 'How are you, my dear Gaisberg, and your dear sister?' . . .

The recording proceeded smartly and one after the other the five sides were made. Now and again while waiting for the red light to go up he seemed to relapse into a coma, from which he would arouse himself with a jerk and offer apologies. Once in the middle of a passage he went off silently, and we had to begin the record again. Generally the playing lacked virility and only in places were there flashes of his old brilliance. I took [a] photograph at the conclusion of the session, which had hardly lasted an hour and a half.

I was filled with sadness to see how in a few months the great man had aged. As I helped him into the waiting taxi and grasped his warm, soft hands to say good-bye, I had a feeling that this would be the last time. The taxi quickly passed out in the fog.[1]

It was the Götterdämmerung. New personalities, challenging events were no longer powerful to dispel it, hard as Fred Gaisberg might still try: 'Memorable was the debut that Brailowsky made as an H.M.V. artist at our Abbey Road studios. . . . He boasts of being the last pupil of that great Polish professor [Leschetizky], long resident in Vienna, who leaped to fame through the success of his first pupil, Paderewski. While Brailowsky was talking to me, I reminded him that Paderewski had played [in] the studio . . . just a month before. . . .'

Old faces vanished, new ones appeared in their places. It was forty years since Fred Gaisberg had arrived in London to make the first records for the new Company—fifty years since he had played piano accompaniments for John York Atlee and the other phonograph performers in the summer holidays of his Washington school days. He had influenced perhaps more than anyone the development of the gramophone as a recorder of serious music. But he himself was now closer to seventy than to sixty. It was time to retire.

[1] 'Paderewski as I Knew Him'.

Chapter Twenty-two

WHEN FRED GAISBERG'S retirement was announced, the entire gramophone industry stood to attention. To do him honour—though he deplored it —a banquet was planned at the Savoy Hotel for 21 April, 1939. Those who lent their names to form an Honorary Committee for the event made a virtual encyclopedia of the world of music that Fred Gaisberg had helped to create:

Sir Hugh Allen
Wilhelm Backhaus
John Barbirolli
Sir Thomas Beecham
Sir Adrian Boult
Adolf Busch
Fritz Busch
Pau Casals
John Christie
Albert Coates
Alfred Cortot
Richard Crooks
Ben Davies
Peter Dawson
Ania Dorfmann
Edwin Fischer
Kirsten Flagstad
Sir George Franckenstein
Elena Gerhardt
Walter Gieseking
Beniamino Gigli
Eugene Goossens
James Gray
Sacha Guitry
Richard Haigh
Mark Hambourg
Jascha Heifetz
Myra Hess
Harold Holt
Edward Johnson
Serge Koussevitzky
Fritz Kreisler
A. T. Lack
Wanda Landowska
Sir Harry Lauder
Lotte Lehmann
Frida Leider
Compton Mackenzie
Sir Robert Mayer
Giovanni Martinelli
Jan Masaryk
Lauritz Melchior
Count John McCormack
Yehudi Menuhin
Ivor Novello
Ignaz Paderewski
Egon Petri
Yvonne Printemps
Sergei Rachmaninoff
Elisabeth Rethberg
Artur Rubinstein
Tito Schipa
Elisabeth Schumann
Rudolf Serkin
L. G. Sharpe
Artur Schnabel
Malcolm Sargent
Herbert Sinclair
Christopher Stone
Leopold Stokowski
Georg Szell
Luisa Tetrazzini
Lawrence Tibbett
John Tillett
Bruno Walter
Felix Weingartner
Vaughan Williams
Sir Henry J. Wood

The Executive Committee included both the Chairman of E.M.I., Alfred Clark, and the Managing Director, Louis

Sterling—now Sir Louis—as well as David Bicknell and Rex Palmer.

Letters arrived from all over the world. One of the first was from the old Chairman Trevor Williams, now almost eighty:

My Dear Fred,

During your many years of industry, you have by your natural charm and instinctive courtesy gathered around you a very large coterie of friends with that true friendship which is based on affection and admiration.

To show appreciation of your many qualities after your 50 years' connection with the musical world, a banquet is to be given in your honour, at which very many of those friends will gather together. Mrs. Williams and I are distressed to contemplate our absence from such a function but our days of banquets are over and we must content ourselves with kindly thoughts and good wishes for your continuing activities for many years to come.

I have acquired 6 tickets for this banquet and venture to ask you to accept them as some tribute to the honour which is to be yours. You may be able to use them so as to have with you some of those near and dear to you who would not otherwise have been present.

Of that coterie of true friends, to which I have referred, I think I must be the oldest survivor in this country and as such I do most sincerely congratulate you upon this signal evidence of appreciation of your life's work. And may I at the same time thank you for your active participation in the great industry which we have helped to build up and has given me the ease and comfort which I enjoy in my old age.

Yours very sincerely

Trevor Williams.

An even older light in Fred Gaisberg's life was re-lit by a letter from the piano teacher of his youth, Henry Xander, still alive in Washington at what must have been an incredible age. William Michelis wrote from Baden-Baden to recall the recording of Caruso. And John McCormack wrote this letter to Rex Palmer:

My dear Rex

I wish it had been possible for Countess McCormack and me to be with you tomorrow to pay tribute to—and incidentally rag just a little—our old friend Fred Gaisberg. But alas and alack! ! ! ! Perhaps Fred will be just as glad! ! ! ! Someone called 'Grimes' writing in the Daily Express this morning said that Fred had '*discovered*' all the great people who ever made Gramophone records, from Melba to Gracie Fields (I almost prefer it the other way) and from Caruso to Chaliapin, not to mention Kreisler, Rachmaninoff, and Toscanini! ! ! ! Two names were conspicuous by their absence, as far as I was personally concerned, 'Patti and McCormack', but I am sure Freddie is too young to remember such 'antiquities' as those! Perhaps Louis Sterling will remember the 'McCormack guy' who sang for his Company *thirty-five years ago*! ! ! ! I think I'd better stop! My grey beard is getting in the ink! ! ! !

My love to Fred. God love him and spare him long!

Ct John McCormack.

On the great evening Carrie bundled a reluctant Fred into the Valli family car and got him safely to the Savoy. There was an elaborate printed programme containing Fred's portrait, a summary of his career, the names of the Honorary and Executive Committees, and a list of the scheduled speakers and entertainers headed by the Chairman for the occasion, Sir Adrian Boult. E.M.I.'s magazine *The Voice* reported as follows:

Speeches were of course a feature of the evening, and they were of a very high order. The disappointment that Mr. Alfred Clark's medical advisers had forbidden him to use his voice was compensated for by the sight of him and Mrs. Clark, both looking very happy.

Sir Louis Sterling said: 'It was almost the beginning of this century when I first met Fred Gaisberg and his late brother Will. With these two there was always associated a great character of the gramophone industry, Russell Hunting, who is still alive in America and who was known for his originality in creating such masterpieces as "Departure of a Troopship" and the series of Michael Casey records amongst many others. We four almost immediately became very intimate, and were known in the City Road days of the industry as the American Quartet. We had very many happy times together, and the three of us who still remain have the same friendship and affection for each other that was started in those far-off days.

'From the beginning of the invention of the gramophone,

in fact from its infancy, Fred Gaisberg had faith and believed it was destined to become the greatest musical instrument, which it eventually did become, and even as far back as forty or fifty years ago when the gramophone was looked upon as a toy, he cherished the ideal that this instrument would become one of the greatest benefactors to humanity for the development of music in the homes of the people.

'I and all his associates here wish him a long continuance of health and happiness and, although he has completed fifty years' service in the musical world, we are happy that he will in the future as in the past continue his great work with us.'

By Fred's own request, the entertainment was of a light character, and the artists were Richard Tauber, Gracie Fields (who had interrupted the making of her latest film in order to be present), Peter Dawson (one of Fred's oldest friends), Mr. Flotsam and Mr. Jetsam, Zomah the Unsolved Mystery (who came out of retirement to perform wonders of telepathy), Oliver Wakefield and Ronald Frankau. Accompanists included Mr. Ivor Newton and Mr. Percy Kahn.

Yet at the end of the day Fred Gaisberg typically saw the whole affair more in the light of a tribute to the industry itself:

> I could not help feeling pleased that the occasion provided a neutral ground for all the elements composing this great industry to get together, and that it was eagerly awaited and taken advantage of. In a way the evening marked the close of an epoch. It was one of the last gatherings of musicians in London before the war set in. It almost seemed as though some premonition had brought about a rally of the clans before the storm burst.

In the weeks before the Savoy banquet Fred Gaisberg had given much thought to his own future plans. Two ideas had emerged. The first was to visit the States again while still he might—to go and see the old things, the home people again. The second was that total retirement seemed unthinkable. Alfred Clark had offered to retain him on a consulting basis for recording sessions and record-testing committees. So the plan emerged to pay the American visit immediately, hoping to get back safely before the outbreak of the war which by now appeared inevitable.

A week after the Savoy banquet Fred sailed for America. His arrival in New York seemed like the old days, for there was Sinkler Darby to meet him, together with his sister Emma's son Warren Forster. But Emma herself had died a few months earlier, and Washington turned out to hold as many ghosts as there were familiar faces. Still there was Fred's brother Charlie and his large family near Baltimore. Further north, not far from Philadelphia and Camden, lived the daughters of his friend B. G. Royal. And one evening he went to see old Henry Xander. In New York he looked up one of the other laboratory assistants from his earliest days with Berliner, and then called on the aged and frail Russell Hunting.

A touching tribute of friendship was paid by the Polish violinist Marek Weber, with whom Fred had made hundreds of records in Germany. Weber had fled in 1933, and had established himself in Chicago. Now he made a special trip east just to see Fred. They spent the day together at the New York World's Fair. Gaisberg found his old friend 'proud of his newly acquired United States citizenship, although his vocabulary now consisted of equal proportions of Polish and German, spiced with Chicago slang which he had picked up from his bandsmen.'

When Fred Gaisberg returned to London early in July, however, who should be there to greet him again but just Marek Weber:

> To my surprise he explained that the European situation was developing so fast that he had shipped his bank balance of £20,000 to America only the previous day. Later that same week I noticed that the Bank of England had placed an embargo on shipping gold abroad. By that time Weber was on his way back to New York rejoicing.

For a few moments the threads of the old life seemed to be coming into Gaisberg's hands once more. There were recording sessions with Weingartner in Paris to supervise, and then on to Lucerne for Toscanini performances at the Summer Festival there. But the political situation was so bad that Fred was thankful to return to London at the beginning of August.

A month later war was declared. Fred decided that his sister Carrie must go back to safety in America. Carrie protested that after all these years her place was in London with him. But she was now nearly seventy, and Fred insisted she go. At the end of

September he went down to Southampton with Carrie to see her aboard the S.S.*George Washington*. Amongst the throngs of other passengers there Fred suddenly caught sight of Vladimir Rosing.

> He was one of a thousand or more to board the *George Washington* for New York. Others I saw in that great mass were Albert Coates, Count de Basil and his Russian Ballet troupe, and Betty Lawson-Johnson. At Bordeaux the ship also picked up Toscanini and his entire family.[1]

For a few months longer recording in London maintained some resemblance to former times, and in the absence of younger men Fred Gaisberg was much to the fore. But gradually the war ate deeper and deeper into everyday life, and after the air raids began it was more and more difficult to assemble musicians and engineers for any planned sessions. Supplies of shellac—an imported material in demand for war purposes—dried up, and much of the record factory was given over to making war equipment.

Living on alone at Crediton Hill, the time seemed to have come to write the book of reminiscences that Fred had often promised himself and his friends. He looked out boxes containing his old diaries and such papers as he had at home. Reading them over recalled vividly the scenes they described and many others. But for the great number of years when no connected diaries had been kept there were only scraps of notes and sometimes nothing at all. Concentrated research at Hayes in the existing conditions was impossible: much of the Company's archive had been consigned to temporary shelters for the duration and was not available. With the severe staff shortages at Hayes it was out of the question to ask for help in research. And there was now both difficulty and danger attached even to the journey between Crediton Hill and Hayes.

He wrote to such of his old recording colleagues as survived, asking them to send him their memories. Several replied with interesting recollections, but over questions of name and date their powers of memory were mostly less good than his own. Fred's former secretary Gwen Mathias lived not too far off, and she was willing to type such manuscript notes as he could send her. That was all the help that looked like being available.

[1] *The Gramophone*, February 1944, p. 133.

XIIIa John McCormack outside the Abbey Road Studios, with Rex Palmer and Fred Gaisberg

XIIIb Fred Gaisberg and Artur Schnabel share a coffee interval between recordings

XIVa Bruno Walter and the Vienna Philharmonic Orchestra rehearsing Mahler's Ninth Symphony, January 1938

XIVb Paderewski at Abbey Road, November 1938: a photograph by Fred Gaisberg

:Va Fred Gaisberg's
etirement, 1939. A
oast at the Savoy
anquet: Mrs. Alfred
'lark, Fred, Sir
.drian Boult

XVb Fred Gaisberg
and Alfred Clark
in the EMI Board-
room examining
the gramophone
of 1899

XVIa Gigli presents Fred with a walking stick, 1946

XVIb Arturo Benedetti Michelangeli, one of the last artists signed by Fred Gaisberg

Some topics yielded fairly easy chapters—his boyhood days in Washington in the infant talking machine industry, the Far Eastern trip of 1902–3 for which he had kept a full diary, his memories of Elgar (from whom he had some letters), Chaliapin. For the rest, the only solution was to abandon chronology and marshal his memories by categories—conductors, pianists, violinists, the Prima Donna, Wagner recordings. Other chapters could be devised to catch the bits that did not fall easily into the categories that suggested themselves.

When it came to the actual writing, many individual anecdotes came off well, but organisation remained a problem. Notes in pencil, drafts in ink, manuscript corrections and additions—every change of order or emphasis suggested some new story that might provide a link or a transition. And then there were the stories that could only be half told, be told by cloaking the participants in anonymity, or not be told at all. It was very worrying. When the chapters came back from Gwen Mathias's typewriter, many of them seemed incomplete or inadequate in places: out would come the pencil again.

Then one night during an air raid a bomb fell at the bottom of the garden at Crediton Hill, and the blast knocked out most of Fred's windows. Replacement just then was hopeless, so the house was more or less uninhabitable and looked like remaining so for the duration. Alternative accommodation in London was problematic. The only thing for it was to go and live somewhere in the country—hopefully not too far from London. He found quarters for a few months at King's Langley in Hertfordshire, and there he settled with his piles of papers and diaries, notes and manuscripts. By now he had enough material for the book in typescript, but still he had doubts.

In King's Langley he made the acquaintance of a professional writer, Percival Graves, who offered to help him with the book. Graves made suggestions for arranging the chapters and he polished Fred's prose in places, but the content and the principles of arrangement remained necessarily much as the author himself had devised them. Together they hired an agent who placed the book with Macmillan's in New York early in 1942. The title chosen was *The Music Goes Round*, and it appeared in the United States later in the year. Because of the scarcity of paper in Britain, the question of English publication had to be suspended until after the war. The American notices were favourable, but of course the book was denied for the moment to its greatest potential audience.

Meanwhile as the bombing around London increased, it was thought better that Fred should go farther away. So he took up residence with his sister Louise and her husband Camillo Valli, now living in Leighton Buzzard. There, in addition to gardening and reading, he kept up as best he could with the artists he had befriended. In August 1942 Bruno Walter wrote from California:

My dear Mr. Gaisberg:

Your letter of July 6th gave me really the greatest pleasure. Anything coming from good old England where my thoughts and wishes center touches me deeply, and if it is such a cordial and friendly message as yours it is particularly welcome.

I am happy to hear that you are well and in good spirits, and that the in some ways unidyllic conditions of our world have induced you to turn to the most peaceful of all human activities since ancient times, to cultivating your soil, seems indeed a very interesting thought. Scarcely less peaceful appears your entrance in the literary world. I shall certainly belong to the first who will buy the product of your introvert leanings and I shall read it with the keen interest that the vast experiences and sincere utterances of such a kind character as yours deserve. . . .

Let me tell you that no reverses and none of the misfortunes experienced so far could impress me so as to interfere with my optimism. I believe in the final victory with a really unshakable faith and believe that it will make me terribly happy to come back to England, see all of you good old friends and renew the ties of affection which connect me forever with the English public.

All good wishes and kind greetings

always sincerely yours,
Bruno Walter.

In March 1943 Yehudi Menuhin arrived in London briefly to give concerts for the Free French Charities Fund. Fred was able to meet him for a meal on the day of an orchestral rehearsal. Arriving in Yehudi's rooms at Claridge's, he found the young man practising:

Promptly at one o'clock Yehudi laid down his violin and attacked with gusto a lunch of river trout that the waiter had quietly rolled in the room. . . .

'Tell me about your trip over in the bomber.'

'Well, they supplied sheep wool lined overcoats, shoes, and gloves and an oxygen helmet: and there you sat $9\frac{1}{2}$ hrs sleeping, thinking, and dreaming—nothing else to do. Going back, the hop from Scotland to N[ew] F[oundland] is 13 hrs.'

Of Fritz Kreisler he spoke a lot—he is a Kreisler worshipper. K's accident laid him up for a year, and this was his salvation. But of course he has returned to his concerts—hale, hearty, and playing as divinely as ever.

We spoke of the William Walton V[iolin] Concerto, but Yehudi thought Heifetz had made it his own, so it would be difficult for him to take it up. His favourite new work was the Bela Bartok V. Concerto, and he would like to introduce it at a favourable moment.

But now Mrs. Millas (his aunt) arrived to accompany him to the rehearsal.

Then came Menuhin's performance of the Elgar Concerto, which Fred attended:

I wonder what was the general emotional reaction to his performance of the Elgar Concerto. I had long looked forward to this, and my impression was that it was one of the best balanced and clearest readings I have ever heard. For hours afterward I was haunted by the vision of the same scene enacted ten years past by the radiant boy of 16 and the proud, happy Elgar. Yehudi confessed to me that the memory had been indelibly impressed on his youthful mind. . . .

All told, I think Menuhin in successfully carrying out this war-time tour has accomplished a heroic and courageous feat which he alone—because of his youth—among all the top-liners of instrumentalists could have done. The young man is so amazingly, intellectually absorbing that it cannot but have a telling effect on his artistic development. I think his real record-making and 'legacy to posterity' will start from now on. For the same reason he symbolises for me the young America to whose safe-keeping the guiding of her artistic direction can be confidently entrusted.

Gaisberg's old colleague David Bicknell was to recall:

[Fred] remained, but not flagrantly, sincerely American and retained his nationality to his dying day. He told me how much he was hurt by the jeering references made of his country by their delay in entering the First World War. Moreover he toyed for many years with the dream of going back to Washington and dying there. . . . But his love and admiration for England went very deep, and in the end he recognised that he had put down roots in this country which were too strong to be pulled up in old age, so he stayed here.

He often said to me that to be thrown on the street in America was a more brutal experience than in England (this was before the Roosevelt New Deal). Nevertheless he regarded the Welfare State with great suspicion because he believed that men should be forced to make their own way in the world and it brought out the best in them to do so. This of course was the philosophy of his age and country.

He embodied many of the greatest American virtues, namely: First, his fearless interest in dealing with difficult, celebrated, and formidable people, never hesitating to tell the truth whenever it was necessary, however unwelcome it might be. Second, his approachability. He was extremely kind to young people and to anyone whom he felt was made nervous by being in an inferior position. He did everything possible to put them at their ease, and he listened to what they had to say. In short, he had sympathy with people who were trying to make their way in the world. Finally, his youthful outlook which he retained right into old age. In the Old World there is a widespread feeling that the best has been in the past and the most that could be expected now is that the standards of life, ethereal and spiritual, will not deteriorate in the future. Fred, for most of his life, lived in the belief that the best is still to come.

In the very month of his meeting with Yehudi Menuhin, March 1943, Fred Gaisberg paid tribute to another American, Louis Sterling. Long a British subject and now knighted, Sir Louis had never been more intensely the embodiment of American imagination and drive than when he appeared as guest-of-honour amongst a circle of friends gathered at a luncheon to celebrate the fortieth anniversary of his arrival as a penniless young man from Brooklyn come to seek his fortune in London—the price of his boat fare advanced by a slightly older American already established there, Fred Gaisberg. But Fred did not include that fact in the tribute he wrote for *The Gramophone* to Louis Sterling's achievement. Alfred Clark's seventieth birthday in December of the same year elicited another *Gramophone* tribute of reminiscence. But there once again Fred had preceded his subject, for he himself had entered the seventies in the previous January.

He filled in the hours and days at Leighton Buzzard by interesting himself in church affairs, attending vestry meetings and playing the organ at services. Occasional lunches in London with Alfred Clark and other old friends helped to keep him in touch, and after the tide of the war had turned recording sessions and record-testing conferences once again began to claim attention. An English publisher, Robert Hale Ltd., expressed interest in *The Music Goes Round*, and during the spring of 1945 there were several meetings on the question at the firm's offices in Bedford Square. Coming up for one of them on 8 May, Fred learned with the rest of the world that it was VE Day.

Chapter Twenty-three

WITH THE end of the war in Europe, gramophone recording could begin to find its way back toward full activity. Yet for the moment many of the younger men were still unavailable. In June 1945 Fred Gaisberg was arranging further recording with Casals, and in September he met Elisabeth Schumann for the same purpose. There was talk of John McCormack's re-appearance in the studios, and Gaisberg's colleague Leonard Smith went to Dublin to interview him. Fred wrote:

> He seemed in good health & spirits—a bit breathy and husky voiced. He imitated Chaliapin singing Volga Boat Song. Weather had been good; he had come in from a walk. The following Tuesday he was taken ill and the following Sunday he died of pneumonia.

It made another in the series of blanks that had come into life during the past few years, and McCormack was ten years younger than Fred himself. Nonetheless, amongst the young recording prospects whose names were jotted in Gaisberg's diaries during late 1945 and early 1946 were no fewer than three in the category of 'Irish tenor': Christopher Lynch, James Johnston, and Michael Duffy.

By the beginning of 1946 Fred's thoughts were turning again toward America, where Carrie had been since the beginning of the war. When his plans for a visit there became known at Hayes, it was decided to ask him to act as a sort of ambassador-extraordinary to the executives of American Columbia and Victor for the making of joint future plans:

> March 21 (Thursday). B. Mittell phoned me. The Company

will finance my trip to A. @ £10 per day. I am to contact Wallerstein & Murray, tell them what we are doing over here for them.

Early in April Fred sailed. Arriving in Canada, he took the opportunity for a day's visit with Emile Berliner's son Herbert, who owned a record pressing factory in Montreal. A few days in Washington, for a joyous reunion with Carrie and the family, were followed by three visits to New York of several days each. Repeated meetings with the executives and recording managers of both Victor and Columbia, with discussions of artists and repertoire on both sides of the Atlantic, alternated with visits to New York recording sessions. Fred made notes on personalities and processes, and he drew several diagrams in his notebook showing how American engineers were now placing musicians and microphones in their studios.

The old Gaisberg observation and judgment were as sharp as ever, but it was all a considerable drain on seventy-three-year-old energies. It was a joy and a relief to be met once again, just as in pre-war days, by Marek Weber. Weber flew Fred out to his huge farm in the mid-western American countryside for a week's visit and rest. Then in mid-June Fred sailed back to England with Carrie beside him. Their house in Crediton Hill had been repaired, and they looked forward to taking up together as many of the pre-war threads as possible.

A good deal of new recording was now going forward, and Fred Gaisberg saw action in and out of the studios, especially when old friends were involved:

Nov. '46—Gigli (at the age of 56 yrs.) returned to London after being cleared as a 'collaborator' . . . G's voice retained remarkably youthful freshness and had even greatly improved in vocal command. All this was borne out when Gigli sang 20 times in 5 weeks in Nov. & Dec. '46 in England, in spite of travelling and poor food in the provinces. And in the chill and fog of a particularly bad November he gave faultless performances, generous of encores and voice.

Following Gigli's tour there was the great pleasure of supervising several recording sessions with him at Abbey Road in December.

But Fred Gaisberg had never been one to live his life on memories. Fitted into his diary amongst the Gigli sessions are other notes:

December 7th 1946 (Saturday). DeJongh asked me to go . . . to hear Michelangeli Sunday.

December 8th (Sunday). Michelangeli concert. Saw him in Artists' Room. Was very much impressed by playing.

December 10th (Tuesday). 31, Portland Pl.—Jan Hambourg: appt. w/ Michelangeli.

December 16th (Monday). 3 o'c at Jan Hambourg to sign Michelangeli contract.

And so it went on through 1947. An idea of Fred Gaisberg's activities can be gleaned from some of the entries in his diary during the late summer and autumn:

30th August. Recording Peter Pears & B. Britten 2 o'c.
9th September. 6 o'c: Michelangeli tests.
15th September. Peter Dawson 6 o'c.
20th September. 11 o'c: A. Rubinstein.
22nd September. Maggie Teyte 5.30—4 titles.
14th October. Cortot.
15th October. Cortot.
24th October. 10 o'c Testing. 3 o'c—tel. Alfred Cortot at Picc. Hotel to hear records.
14th November. Gigli recording 6.30. Call at Savoy 6 o'c.
29th November. Medtner lunch.

He acquired a pupil in his niece Isabella, who decided to give up her career as a musician for the chance of following in her uncle's footsteps as a gramophone recorder.

Uncle had an astounding flair for repertoire. He gave me principles which he used for repertoire, and they are the same ones which record companies use now. The basic sellers. Such popular favourites as the 'Dance of the Hours'. A fine performance of Haydn Symphonies. He had a great love of the music of the seventeenth and eighteenth centuries—Purcell and the early English composers, and also early Italian and German music. He used to say that the basic record catalogue ought to have a fair share of music from this period: you can't go wrong because it's not expensive to make, and provided it's good it's always saleable.

He helped me, encouraged me, and he taught me endlessly. One of the things he taught me was not to care where a person came from or who he was socially. He was passionately interested in people whenever they had something in them which interested him. And he made people interesting by his own interest in them.[1]

On New Year's Day 1948 Fred passed the three-quarter century mark. For the past fifteen years he had carried on all his activities under the shadow of heart disease. He had not much allowed it to hinder him. With the coming of old age and its reduced energies, the illness could no longer be ignored. Still he kept up with each new gramophone development, urging the Company to adopt the long-playing record and even looking ahead to stereophonic reproduction.

Old and new came together in the drawing-room at Crediton Hill in October 1949. A young staff member of the B.B.C. Gramophone Library, Brian Rust, telephoned to say that he had seen an old seven-inch Berliner disc of a singer called 'Miss Lamonte' with the date 2 August 1898. Wouldn't that make it one of the very first discs Mr. Gaisberg had ever made in England? Would it be possible to come and talk with the man whose memory of gramophone recording actually went back to before the turn of the century?

When the day arrived for Brian Rust's visit, Fred took care that he shouldn't appear to this young man of 1949 as just another antediluvian survivor. Rust remembered:

> He greeted me warmly and showed me into his lounge, where I saw on top of the grand piano the first RCA machine for playing the new 45-rpm discs that I had ever set eyes on. It was playing . . . a gutty example of rhythm-and-blues in which the performer hoarsely shouted something about 'Oh, baby! baby!' Fred Gaisberg was all excited about this new acquisition; I had called to see the man who had made the first seven-inch discs in this country, and was greeted by his playing the first plastic 45-rpm seven-inch disc I had ever seen.
>
> 'Oh, baby, baby,' he said as the record finished. 'How d'you like that! Now . . . er—what was it you wanted to see me about? One of those old Berliners, wasn't it?'
>
> I explained exactly what I had seen.
>
> He smiled. 'I remember Syria Lamonte,' he said. 'She was an entertainer: I suppose she must have served drinks—in

[1] Conversation with the writer, 1973.

Rule's, the pub next door to the first recording studio in Maiden Lane. She was the first artist I recorded, I'm sure of that . . . of course, I don't know if the one you saw was *the* first, but it was made at that first session.'

I reminded him that . . . he had arrived in London on July 9, 1898, and the date on the disc was only four weeks later.

He smiled. 'Yes, we really hustled to get things started,' he said. 'I didn't know it was August 2 when we made the first one but I remember Syria Lamonte; she had a big voice, and that was what we wanted.'

I suggested that she had a big voice from having to make it heard above the noise of a public bar.

He laughed. 'Yes, that's probably right; I know she used to sing for the customers there—that's how I found her. Could you bring me the record?'

I said I would try.

After some negotiating, the owner made me a present of it. On Wednesday, November 23, I took it to Fred Gaisberg.

I found him just finishing the packing up of a parcel of food for his old colleague Max Hampe, who was living a miserable existence in Berlin (then still very much the worse from having been sustained by the air-lift that had lasted over a year and had only just been ended.)

'Poor Max', mused Fred Gaisberg, 'he has had a bad deal; I like to send him these parcels as often as I can. Now—is that the Syria Lamonte record? Ah yes . . . that's my secretary's writing. . . . That's mine. . . . Ah, there's the date. Yes, that's about as early as they come. Let's hear it, shall we?'

He put it on his radiogram.

'Well, that must be me at the piano. . . . Oh, yes, I remember that now. . . . Not a bad singer, really. . . .'[1]

Fred Gaisberg had had the immeasurable good fortune to carry on his work into an active old age. But good health he had no longer, and by the late summer of 1951 it was clear that all question of further work was at an end. One day toward the end of August David Bicknell brought his wife to lunch with Fred and Carrie at Crediton Hill.

We had an excellent lunch as Carrie was a good house-

[1] Letter to the writer, 4.vi.73.

keeper, and a very merry one because Fred was in excellent form. He was then in his late seventies but to all appearances very little changed. Nevertheless when lunch was over and we were seated in his garden at the back of the house looking down on the cricket ground, when the others were out of earshot he said to me:

'My doctor was here yesterday, and he says that my heart is much worse and that I must lead a very inactive life. You will understand, David, better than most people that that is not the life for me.'

I did, because he had been one of the most energetic people, both mentally and physically, whom I had ever met. So when one week later his sister telephoned to say that he was dead—he had died in his sleep [on 2 September 1951]—I felt that this was the perfect moment to bring to an end a life which had enriched the lives of other people to an almost immeasurable extent.[1]

[1] Lecture at the British Institute of Recorded Sound.

Index

This index does not include references to Fred Gaisberg or to the names which represent The Gramophone Company—'His Master's Voice' and E.M.I.—for these references are virtually continuous throughout the book. Roman numerals refer to illustrations.